MW00571520

Series: *Language, Media & Education Studies*

Edited by: Marcel Danesi & Leonard G. Sbrocchi

Cover: « *Théâtre du Cap d'Ail* », © *Jean Cocteau/SODRAC (Montréal) 1998.*

THE CINEMA OF
JEAN COCTEAU

Essays on his Films
and their Coctelian Sources

edited by

C.D.E. Tolton

New York   Ottawa   Toronto

Canadian Cataloguing in Publication Data

Main entry under title:

> The Cinema of Jean Cocteau:
> Essays on his Films and their Coctelian Sources

(Series: Language, Media & Education Studies; 5)
Includes bibliographical references
ISBN 0-921252-82-X

1. Cocteau, Jean, 1889-1963—Criticism and interpretation
I. Tolton, C.D.E. II. Series.

PN1998.3.C663C55 1998   791.43'0233'092 C98-901142-9

For further information and for orders:

LEGAS

P. O. Box 040328	68 Kamloops Ave.	2908 Dufferin Street
Brooklyn, New York	Ottawa, Ontario	Toronto, Ontario
USA 11204	K1V 7C9	M6B 3S8

Printed and bound in Canada

CONTENTS

Introduction: The Cinema of Jean Cocteau

C.D.E. Tolton

Jean Cocteau has participated in almost every conceivable aspect of Twentieth Century French culture: theatre, poetry, fiction, criticism, autobiography, diaries, ballet, music, painting, set-design and sketching, for instance. But more than thirty years after his death, it is arguably his reputation in filmmaking that is enduring the most solidly. Intensely literary in his conception and direction of films, Cocteau added this necessarily collaborative medium relatively late in his career to his ever-personal corpus of 'poetic' creations.

From *Le Sang d'un poète* (1932) to *Le Testament d'Orphée* (1960), Cocteau independently directed six feature films in addition to contributing a 'Cocteau touch' to the films of other directors (such as Jean-Pierre Melville's 1950 adaptation of the Cocteau novel, *Les Enfants terribles*). Though at the time, Cocteau's filmic work often had as many detractors as supporters, members of the notoriously anti-literary-film *Nouvelle Vague* paid homage to him as they embarked on their filmmaking careers. Jean-Luc Godard made his short, *Charlotte et son Jules*, from a text written by Cocteau originally for Edith Piaf, and *Le Testament d'Orphée* was made thanks to funds arranged for by none other than François Truffaut.

Such began a description of the graduate seminar on 'The Cinema of Jean Cocteau' that gave rise to the present collection of essays. Over a period of thirteen weeks in the Winter Term of 1996–97 at the University of Toronto, sixteen enrolled students and one auditor studied four printed texts (three plays and a novel)[1] and eight films[2] that seemed to represent the core of Cocteau's adventures in the world of cinema. Ten

---

[1] The plays *L'Aigle à deux têtes* (1944), *Les Parents terribles* (1938), *Orphée* (1926) and the novel, *Les Enfants terribles* (1929).

[2] *Le Sang d'un poète* (Cocteau, 1932), *L'Éternel Retour* (Jean Delannoy, 1943), *La Belle et la bête* (Cocteau, 1946), *L'Aigle à deux têtes* (Cocteau, 1947), *Les Parents terribles* (Cocteau, 1948), *Orphée* (Cocteau, 1950), *Les Enfants terribles* (Jean-Pierre Melville, 1950), and *Le Testament d'Orphée* (Cocteau, 1960). For a full Cocteau filmography, see Claude-Jean Philippe, *Jean Cocteau* (Paris: Seghers, 1989), 147–84.

of the collected essays were among the best submitted in May 1997 by the enrolled students, and an eleventh (on *Le Sang d'un poète*) was subsequently solicited from the auditor. Together, the essays offer a coherent overview of Cocteau's filmic career at the same time as they demonstrate a variety of critical means for approaching the material. From the purely dramaturgical approach to Cocteau's play, *L'Aigle à deux têtes*, to the phenomenological reading of *La Belle et la bête* or the Lacanian reading of the film version of *Les Parents terribles*, the essays' wide selection of methodologies is best collectively described as 'eclectically modern.' The impact of the collection cannot help but result in a clearer understanding of the filmic work of an important original artist who is too often dismissed as personally and creatively superficial. The essays are arranged in keeping with the chronological order of the relevant films. Thus, although the play *Orphée* was written before Cocteau ever thought of filmmaking, its essay is placed well into the volume, immediately before the essay on the film version of *Orphée*. In the following survey of the relevant parts of Cocteau's career, the titles of the films, plays and novels are referred to in French. Quotes from the dialogue are usually translated into English.

*   *   *

From an early age, Jean Cocteau (1889–1963) believed completely in his calling to become a poet. Like the Romantics of the century before him, he believed that the poet was a chosen individual blessed with special gifts of insight, interpretation and even prophecy, obliged by this privilege to express his thoughts and emotions through poetry. Moreover, every possible means of expression became in his hands poetic. For him, the æsthetic principles that governed creative activity were delicacy, finesse, subtlety and elegance, factors that —with varying degrees of success— ruled the style of his own life. (The world of opium notoriously lent other shading to his life-style from time to time — culminating in his appearance in a round-up of alleged opium-users in an unwelcome press photograph of 1947 ...)[1] Most often, Cocteau's friends were drawn from the Parisian worlds of the aristocracy and the artists, worlds that he frequented with respect and pleasure.

It was from this blend of high society and creative artistry that Cocteau came to make his first film. His friends, the Vicomte and Vicomtesse de Noailles, in a fit of imaginative philanthropy inspired by the success of the Buñuel-Dali avant-garde film, *Un Chien andalou,*

---

[1] Photograph reproduced in Francis Steegmuller, *Cocteau: A Biography* (Boston and Toronto: Little, Brown & Co., 1970), 421.

provided both Luis Buñuel and Jean Cocteau with equal sums of money sufficient to finance a film apiece.[1] While Buñuel's new film, *L'Age d'or*, completed in 1930, was suffering censorship problems, Cocteau's *Le Sang d'un poète*, completed the same year, languished until 1932, awaiting an unthreatened première. Separately, both André Gide and Julien Green have recorded their impressions of the January 1932 screening of the film that at last took place before an invited audience.[2] Green's account is kinder than Gide's. Gide's version pays more attention to a speech by Cocteau than to the film itself. Always critical of Cocteau, Gide found on this occasion that Cocteau's performance was unacceptably mannered.

As for the film itself, it shall remain an indelible landmark in the history of French cinema. Although derivative to some extent of *Un Chien andalou*, it stands primarily as the first *filmic* expression of Cocteau's identification of himself as a poet, his first filmic use of the Orphic legend, and his first statements on film of such personal obsessions as voyeurism, opium-smoking, male beauty, immortality, trans-genderism, and angelic powers. Unsuitable in its 16mm format for commercial screenings in Europe, it is the first European art film to have played continuously in a Manhattan theatre for years.[3] It is also an ironic amalgam of mature themes and the fantasy world of children's literature: *Through the Looking Glass* (with an early Cocteau representation of a voyage through a mirror); *Peter Pan* (with a flying child); and *Tom Brown's School Days* (with schoolboys on a spirited rampage, a scene which is also a re-enactment of the Dargelos episode at the beginning of Cocteau's own 1929 novel, *Les Enfants terribles*). But perhaps most important, *Le Sang d'un poète* is one of the earliest examples of a sound feature film in France.

The weighty discussions that interpretation of the film arouse have often obscured the importance of the film's sound innovations. Cocteau's complete inexperience with the film medium found itself suddenly confronted not only with the challenge of photographing and editing moving images but also with thorny problems associated with recording and editing voice, music and sound effects. In the definitive film, the use of voice, though limited, is daring for the time. Cocteau

---

1 Jean Cocteau, *The Art of Cinema* compiled and edited by André Bernard and Claude Gauteur and translated by Robin Buss (London and New York: Marion Boyars, 1994), 57.

2 André Gide, *Journal 1889–1939* (Paris: Gallimard, Bibliothèque de la Pléiade, 1939), 1105, and Julien Green, *Journal 1926–1955* (Paris: Gallimard, Bibliothèque de la Pléiade, 1975), 156.

3 *The Art of Cinema*, 57.

himself pronounces the voice-over narrative, and perhaps the garbled Chinese of the man in the hall. A dubbed female voice intervenes for Lee Miller as the statue. The film boasts of the first of the Georges Auric musical scores that gave so many of the Cocteau films their distinctive aura. (All of the music in the film is extradiegetic.) The sound effects are limited to their extremely expressive role in a few episodes: a cock-a-doodle-do, some noises in the Hôtel des Folies Dramatiques, and a loudly beating heart at the card-game. Although the film functions primarily on a visual level, its director did not shrink from applying to its poetic expressiveness the latest devices for sound reproduction. By that token, Cocteau must be placed in film history beside Robert Florey (*La Route est belle,* 1929) and René Clair (*Sous les toits de Paris,* 1930) among the major French directors making early sound films.

By the time that Cocteau conceived *Le Sang d'un poète,* his desire to be reunited with his beloved Raymond Radiguet, deceased in 1923, had long ago firmly taken root. While male beauty is represented in the film by, among others, his newest lover, Jean Desbordes in an eighteenth-century wig, the protagonist poet's goal is clearly death, even though it carries with it mortal boredom: 'l'ennui mortel de l'immortalité' (the mortal tedium of immortality) as Cocteau says in the final speech of the film. Earthly immortality may be achieved through the superimposition of the poet's face on a statue, but in a peculiarly coctelian approach to the question of death, the poet enters into the after-life only after an Orphic divestment of his poetic paraphernalia, an earlier death having proved impermanent.

But the theme of *Le Sang d'un poète* that may strike the post-Freudian spectator as the most noteworthy is its voyeurism. For long before Alfred Hitchcock made such an elaborate illustration of the voyeuristic appeal of film in *Rear Window* (1954), Cocteau was underlining the parallel between spectator pleasure and film images indiscreetly glimpsed or savoured. The relationship between the protagonist as eavesdropping spy and the indiscretions he sees through the series of through-the-keyhole episodes in the hotel are echoed in the filmgoer's experience in viewing the whole personal world that the filmmaker candidly offers us here. As if this one analogy were not enough, Cocteau assembles spectators within the film to applaud without full comprehension —like most early viewers of his film— at the card-playing and the assassination that form the climax of the film's action. While images seen through the key-hole (such as an opium-smoker, a sadistic matron, and a hermaphrodite) as well as the diegetic audience's applause for a murder may seem only mildly outrageous to to-day's film audiences, one can understand that at the time of this film's release certain viewers could have been apprehensive about what lay in store for them in future films by this reputedly iconoclastic artist.

Viewers, however, would have to wait a long time before witnessing another film by Jean Cocteau. In the early 1930s, Cocteau was busy with other theatrical events, such as the creation of his most polished stage version of his ever-present Œdipus story, this time under the title *La Machine infernale* (1934). This was followed by his trip around the world with his very own Passepartout, Marcel Khill (who had replaced Desbordes in his personal life), his management of the prizefighter, Panama Al Brown, and his discovery and promotion of the young actor, Jean Marais. When Cocteau returns noticeably to film, it is first as an actor in *Le Baron Fantôme* (1942) for which he also wrote dialogue, and then as the full screenplay writer of *L'Éternel Retour*, a scenario especially designed to make of Jean Marais the movie star that his astonishing good looks seemed to have destined him to be.[1] The Marais vehicle, based on the Joseph Bédier version of the Tristan and Isolde legend, accomplished its goal, with both Marais (as Patrice/ Tristan) and his co-star, Madeleine Sologne (as Nathalie/Isolde), setting fashion and hair styles in occupied France throughout the summer of 1943.[2] Once again, the Cocteau script returned to a fantasy world, but unlike some of the grotesque moments of *Le Sang d'un poète*, this new film directed by Jean Delannoy took place mainly in exquisite settings such as a beautiful château, misty seascapes or a mountain chalet. When the action moved temporarily to a prosaic garage, critics' accusations of æsthetic inconsistency were met with Cocteau's defensive declarations about the garage's own special poetry.[3]

Delannoy had originally conceived this film as a costume-drama rather like Marcel Carné's equally poetic love story, *Les Visiteurs du soir* (1942).[4] When costumes were going to prove too costly, the film's setting was made contemporary. But certain grotesquely gothic elements remain in Cocteau's script, such as the hero's cousin, a malevolent dwarf named Achille. It is Achille who is the voyeuristic eavesdropping spy in this film, consistently using his acquired knowledge to sabotage the handsome hero's path to happiness. The study of a family in this film seems peculiarly indebted to both the Œdipus household and

---

[1] Jean Marais quotes Cocteau as saying, 'Jean, tu es Tristan,' in Marais, *Histoires de ma vie* (Paris: Albin Michel, 1975), 454.

[2] Steegmuller, 454.

[3] Cocteau, *The Art of Cinema*, 191.

[4] James Reid Paris, *The Great French Films* (Secaucus, N.J.: The Citadel Press, 1983), 97.

the Hubbard family in Lillian Hellman's *The Little Foxes*. In both *L'Éternel Retour* and *The Little Foxes,* three siblings are the mature propagators of a generation that is suffering the consequences of the earlier generation's greedy goals. Achille is an echo of Hellman's ineptly manipulative Leo Hubbard as much as of any source in the Tristan legend. Achille is also the character most closely associated with the supernatural. Cocteau, for instance, lends a magical aura to Achille's theft of Patrice's possessions by using Georges Méliès-style stop-action-photography for the disappearance of the objects.

Cocteau's contribution to the film's script is clear. Just as in *Le Sang d'un poète*, a *dédoublement* of deaths reinforces the importance of the theme of (im)mortality. The deaths of the hero and heroine are both more beautiful than fearful or sad, as Cocteau conveys the message that the lovers have achieved enviable immortal love through death. The oneiric quality of many scenes that take place in realistically photographed settings is more a quality of Cocteau's corpus than Delannoy's. Accounts of the filming attest to the spirit of Cocteau that pervaded the creative atmosphere once he appeared on the set midway through the shoot.[1] Moreover, Delannoy allowed Cocteau to participate in the editing of the final film.[2]

It was now time for Cocteau to direct as well as write a film for Jean Marais. Many consider the resulting film, *La Belle et la bête* (1946) to be his masterpiece. Based on a fairy-tale by the French Madame Leprince de Beaumont living at the time of its composition in Eighteenth Century England, the story reflects Cocteau's interest in children's literature. It also reflects his fascination with the legends that psychoanalysts like Freud and Jung have put to use. The heroine, Belle, is not only a kin of that other legendary drudge, Cinderella, like her, put upon by two demanding sisters, but also of Electra or Cordelia, closely attached to her father. This Cinderella does not attend a ball, but, rather, happens upon a mysterious castle in the woods where she is served a sumptuous dinner. Her Prince Charming must eventually emerge from a gentle beast's clothing — in the person of a curly-coiffed Jean Marais. The beast as object of love is a Jungian concept just as much as the father-daughter relationship is linked to the musings of Freud.

Even more clearly focused than in *L'Éternel Retour*, Cocteau's camera records realistically the activities of Belle's family and friends, blending here and there some molièresque touches of humour in his depiction of the episodic humiliations of the snobbish sisters. In the

---

[1] Claude-Jean Philippe quotes both Marais and Cocteau on this subject. *Jean Cocteau*, 57.
[2] *The Art of Cinema*, 190.

latter part of the film, Belle's rapid return to her home to retrieve her forgotten magic glove playfully emphasizes the imperfections that are possible in the most seemingly foolproof of magical schemes. Belle is a childlike creature, inexperienced yet curious in this semi-comic world of power-possessed keys, gloves, roses, horses and mirrors. The mirror is, in fact, the most specific means of spying in this film; it functions like a television screen, magically receiving transmitted images without the benefit of electronic equipment or wires! Other ludic eavesdroppers are a pair of curious caryatids on either side of the beast's luxurious hearth. The treasure in the beast's pavilion is, according to Clément Borgal, the treasure of childhood. 'If jealously preserved, it can enrich our interior worlds and thus become an inexhaustible source of poetry.'[1]

Poetry is, of course, what the film is truly about — as well as eternal love, realized in a heavenly ascent of the two lovers in the final sequence of the film. Descended from the fantasy traditions of French film originated by Georges Méliès, *La Belle et la bête* is the costume picture that Cocteau had imagined at the time of conceiving *L'Éternel Retour*. This is at last his own *Les Visiteurs du soir*. But in spite of its period look, the film manages to contain allusions to such more modern events in Cocteau's personal life as the fatal snowball thrown by Dargelos. For is the statue that kills not a transformation of that fascinating and lethal young boy? Furthermore, even Hellman's modern family from *The Little Foxes* is here in Belle's greedy siblings. In this case, Belle's brother Ludovic is the *rappel* of the dangerously feckless Leo Hubbard.

Jean Marais, it is said, once dared Cocteau to write a play for him in which he would not speak in the first act, would weep for joy in the second, and in the last would fall backwards down the stairs.[2] The Romantic melodrama *L'Aigle à deux têtes* (originally called *Azrael*), written in an old castle during a vacation in Brittany in the fall of 1944, is the answer to the dare. A Shakespearean-style blend of comedy within its potential tragedy, its happy ending prevents its classification as anything but a melodrama; for the lovers reunite, as in *L'Éternel Retour*, in the death that alone seems to permit the full joy of total love and its immortalization. Pathetic and passionate the story may be, but hardly tragic. The play was deliberately theatrical in its conception, designed to be an actors' showcase in an era when Cocteau feared that

---

1 Quoted by James Reid Paris in *The Great French Films*, 117.

2 Robert Phelps (ed.), *Professional Secrets: An Autobiography by Jean Cocteau* translated by Richard Howard (New York: Farrar, Straus and Giroux, 1970), 266.

stage acting was being too infiltrated by the more contained style of screen performers.[1] The love-story of a somewhat anarchical Queen with her slightly royalist would-be-assassin presents ironical anti-thetical possibilities that Victor Hugo had exploited in his 1837 play, *Ruy Blas*. (Hugo's heroic and love-stricken valet, Ruy Blas, describes himself in line 788 as a 'ver de terre amoureux d'une étoile' —or an earthworm in love with a star— in reference to his love for a Spanish queen.) But the fact that Cocteau's young political peasant is a clone of the Queen's husband who had been murdered by a parallel anarchist ironically multiplies the coctelian *dédoublements* for the audience's possible pleasure. In addition, the analogy with the Œdipus legend is obvious: after all, a young man echoing the murderer of the King is in all but name marrying the King's widow who is old enough to be his mother...

And what a widow she is: wielding a whip, drawing a gun, riding galloping horses, the Queen is a role that every mature actress would love to play! Understandably, this is a monarch who must be guarded and spied upon. Cocteau enjoys at last, then, the perfect opportunity to create the role of a professional spy in the person of Edith de Berg, an expert eavesdropper. This Queen has her own trustworthy adjuvant in the person of Tony, the black deaf-mute servant who is reminiscent of the black angel from *Le Sang d'un poète*. And the whole whirling polit-ical scene with its undercurrents of hypocrisy and deception reflects the politics of occupied France that Cocteau despised in the summer of 1944.[2] The Queen in this atmosphere is seen by certain characters to be already dead as the play begins, thus making her real death in the fi-nal scene the play's ultimate coctelian *dédoublement*.

The role of Stanislas, the young anarchist, is, of course, the reason for the creation of the play. Here again Cocteau has created for Marais a Peter Pan role. His youth and inexperience are emphasized as the Queen lectures him, molds him, profits from his youthful ideological pliability, in their brief time together. Like Peter Pan, Stanislas does not grow old; but in his case, it is death indirectly manœuvred by a mother-figure that stops him short. The Queen, thereby, can be likened to a perverse and destructive version of J.M. Barrie's mothering Wendy as much as to Shakespeare's Queen Gertrude. The deaths of Stanislas and the Queen remain surprisingly unmoving for most audiences. Neal Oxenhandler has suggested that this stems from the too formulaic op-

---

[1] Cocteau in Phelps, 266–7.

[2] Bettina L. Knapp, *Jean Cocteau* (updated edition) (Boston: Twayne, 1989), 112.

posing ideological stances that these two roles represent.[1] Just as theatrical as Cocteau originally desired, the Queen and Stanislas remain
dramatic functions rather than real people.

Cocteau's film version of *L'Aigle à deux têtes* (1947) resulted from
his delight in viewing the play's production from a variety of angles
backstage at the Théâtre Hébertot in Paris.[2] A film version would allow spectators to share the pleasure of different points of view. But his
backers insisted on more than this: a full opening-out of a play that
had taken place on only two interior sets.[3] Accordingly, the film opens
on a mountain-top and continues its dialogue in a moving carriage. A
fully staged ball takes place in the castle during the equivalent of the
play's First Act; the Queen is seen riding horseback at the beginning of
Act II; the Act III private conversation between Count Foehn and
Stanislas takes place in an elaborate tree-house. Other scenes take
place in the soldiers' barracks and in front of the castle where the entire horseguard regiment is assembled to salute the Queen standing
(fatally wounded) on her balcony. Some specifically filmic devices include the inevitable Georges Auric score, the Christian Bérard interiors, some exceptional close-ups, and the shortening of many speeches.
Most importantly, the narrative qualities of the film medium are emphasized by the occasional intrusion of Cocteau's voice where commentary or narrative summary seem appropriate. But the film retains the
extremely theatrical monologue in which the Queen indulges alone in
her boudoir in the First Act. Cocteau himself found this latter footage
of Edwige Feuillère to be breathtaking.[4] He also confessed that there
were no special effects used for Jean Marais' final tumble down the
staircase: he simply fell backwards for the turning camera.[5] To
Cocteau's surprise, in spite of the added realism provided by the film's
enlarged playing space, the film was criticized for its artificiality. In
particular, he needed to defend the scene in which the Queen addresses
Foehn while doing her gymnastics. The scene was, he pointed out, like
many others, based on actual documents referring to his historical inspiration for the role, the unpredictable Elisabeth of Austria. As for

---

1 Neal Oxenhandler, *Scandal and Parade: The Theater of Jean Cocteau* (New Brunswick, N.J.: Rutgers University Press, 1957), 225–6.

2 *The Art of Cinema*, 145.

3 Claude-Jean Philippe quotes Cocteau on the subject, 87.

4 *The Art of Cinema*, 150.

5 Ibid., 70.

the critical cries of anachronism in regard to the Queen's brass bed, this very model had belonged to Queen Victoria![1]

Some of the characters are altered in the film. Edith de Berg becomes a peculiarly nervous, fearful woman, for instance. Count Foehn acquires an accomplice or *confidant*; and an additional spy, Rudi, is operating in the court. The enlarged film budget was responsible, perhaps, for the bigger cast. As a result, the Queen seems all the more vulnerable, surrounded by so many enemies. Finally, followers of Cocteau's love-life may glimpse his new friend, Edouard Dermit, in a tiny role in this, the film that historians seem to collectively consider the filmmaker's most inconsequential.

While *L'Aigle à deux têtes* was written in 1944 to please Jean Marais, so had the play, *Les Parents terribles,* been composed at Marais' request in 1938. Marais had explained to Cocteau that he would like to play 'a young modern man with a high-strung temperament, who laughs, sobs, shouts, rolls on the floor; in short, a role set in some contemporary plot which could conceivably have been played by an old-time actor. For,' said Marais, 'nothing interested me apart from the Yvonne de Bray style, the holy terror style of former days.'[2] Marais had become enamoured of the stage work of de Bray, and after she was cast as his mother in the play Cocteau created for them, she reportedly replaced his own jealous mother in his emotional hierarchy.[3] The play is a series of confrontations in a Freudian-charged drama featuring a mother, Yvonne, who is driven close to madness when her son, Michel, falls in love with a young woman, Madeleine. The incestuous innuendoes were unsubtle enough to have the play banned both in its initial run in 1938 and in a 1941 revival.[4]

In addition to the Œdipal aspects of the story, Cocteau again emphasizes his Peter Pan motif. Michel is written as an especially immature young man, held back from full emotional development by his stifling mother. But he is aware that his parents, Georges and Yvonne, are also immature. When he affectionately calls them 'mes enfants,' he quickly realizes the too truthful implications of the normally harmless interjection. He has been instinctively right, and the play evolves into a dramatic contrast between opposites, with the orderly, sensible (and mature) Tante Léo and the equally orderly Madeleine in opposition to

---

[1] Jean Cocteau, *Entretiens sur le cinématographe* (Paris: Pierre Belfond, 1973), 62.

[2] Quoted in Frederick Brown, *An Impersonation of Angels: A Biography of Jean Cocteau* (New York: Viking, 1968), 329.

[3] Steegmuller, 475.

[4] Ibid., 441.

the disorderly, impulsive (and immature) Michel, Georges and Yvonne. In this play, it is the aunt who manipulates the action every bit as much as the infamous Achille did in *L'Éternel Retour*. One of the fascinating eternally unresolved ambiguities of the play is just how diabolical this woman may be.

Yvonne, the mother role, inspired by the real life mothers of both Cocteau and Marais,[1] bears kinship with literary women other than Jocasta. The formidable Agrippine in Racine's *Britannicus* springs readily to mind, as does the same playwright's incestuously-minded Phèdre. But more contemporaneous with Cocteau's Yvonne is the mother in *Génitrix* by François Mauriac, an author with whom Cocteau carried on a love-hate relationship over a period of six decades.[2] As for Michel, he can boast of a number of mythological cousins, such as Hippolytus, Adonis and Narcissus, as well as the countless attractive youths who were peopling the novels of such trend-setting novelists as Gide, Proust, Alain-Fournier, Martin du Gard, and the aforementioned Mauriac. The literary period had more than one handsome young hugoesque 'force qui va!' But, the critics agreed, there was only one Michel and only one actor to play him. This was the role of a lifetime for Jean Marais, at last released from the classical costumes of plays like Cocteau's *Œdipe-Roi* and *Les Chevaliers de la Table Ronde*. Censorship aside, the play was a resounding success.

Eventually, Cocteau wanted to record on film an expert ensemble cast playing *Les Parents terribles*.[3] His cast was so exceptional that, although by 1948 when the film was made they were in most cases too old for their roles, they earned the highest critical praise. Pauline Kael calls the film 'one of the best examples of group acting ever photographed'[4] and Cocteau considered it his greatest filmic success.[5] While he had tried with *L'Aigle* to make a theatrical film, here he wished to make a more purely cinematic work of art,[6] marginally lowering the level of the histrionic declamations and gestures for the cinema audiences while maintaining Marais' star 'glamour.' Once again the Auric score contributes to the now familiar Cocteau touch, and Cocteau's own

---

[1] Ibid., 450.

[2] Knapp, 95–6.

[3] Cocteau, *Entretiens sur le cinématographe*, 56.

[4] Pauline Kael, *5001 Nights at the Movies: A Guide from A to Z* (New York: Holt, Rinehart and Winston, 1984), 447.

[5] *Entretiens*, 55.

[6] *The Art of Cinema*, 36.

voice-over at the end of the film reminds us of the Cocteau authorship in every sense of the word.

Other aspects of the play are left fundamentally unaltered. The dialogue is modified less than in the film version of *L'Aigle*, and the action spills out no further than into other parts of Michel's family's apartment and into the mezzanine of Madeleine's, or into the stairway and corridor of her *immeuble*. Once again, though, Cocteau capitalizes on filmic close-ups; but he uses them so sparingly that the ones that do exist exert double the normal impact. Camera movement is equally sparing. The actors simply play the text. The result is a film that is clearly derived from a stage-play; but since the play has the merit of the most economical dramatic confrontations and of the least mannered dialogue in the Cocteau theatrical canon, the film has even been discussed in terms of 'realism.' Cocteau has argued that such terminology should be dismissed on the grounds that he has never in real life met a family like this one.[1] Realistic or not, from Œdipus to *The Little Foxes*, extraordinary families like this are the very stuff of major dramatic theatre.

In the summer of 1925, possibly inspired by the effects of opium, Jean Cocteau wrote his play *Orphée* at the Hôtel Welcome in Villefranche-sur-mer.[2] Supposedly derived from Racine's *Bajazet* or from the story of the Virgin Mary and the birth of Christ or even from some poems of Rilke,[3] the play is yet another of Cocteau's family dramas. Only one act (thirteen scenes) in length, the play is a study of a marriage in which the role of the manipulator is handled first (diabolically) by a horse who dictates poetry and later (angelically) by a window repairman named Heurtebise. These are earlier manifestations of Achille and Tante Léo. The comic elements are clear here from the first, inasmuch as the poet Orphée is more interested in his communicating horse than in his down-to-earth prosaic wife Eurydice. Eurydice, however, may not be as entirely conventional as she seems, since her abandonment of a lesbian circle led by the lethal Aglaonice causes a series of dramatic incidents in the plot. These include her own death (the first of two in an interesting network of *dédoublements* that pepper the play) as well as the death of her husband in an attack by Aglaonice's hysterical Bacchantes. As Cocteau tells us in his preface to the play, it should be played as taking place in the present time of whenever it is put on. In the production that the

---

[1] *Entretiens*, 57.

[2] Steegmuller, 349.

[3] Steegmuller thoroughly discusses the Rilke question, 42–3 and 353–4.

Pitoeffs mounted at the Théâtre des Arts in 1926, the costumes were, indeed, modelled on the trendiest Chanel clothes of Cocteau's recent young man, Jean Bourgoint, and his sister Jeanne.[1] In other words, while some classical version of the Orpheus myth is never far from the surface of the text of the play, Cocteau wanted it to be played in an eternally contemporary mood. Furthermore, to underline that this is *Jean Cocteau's* version of Orpheus, his signature is audibly explicit in the dialogue when the poet's severed head on the pedestal identifies itself as Jean Cocteau living at Cocteau's address.

The play, then, is fun-filled, including some nice satire of the police force as well as of bourgeois housewives and self-absorbed poets. Death appears in the form of an efficient beautifully dressed woman (inspired by the transvestite trapeze artist, Barbette)[2] assisted by two angels, one of whom is the epitome of incompetence and is obliged to borrow a watch from one of the spectators. Heurtebise floats in the air, and characters again disappear into an alternate life (or after-life) through a mirror. (A repeated scene that functions as book-ends to the timeless —and unplayed— voyage into the after-life reminds one of the crumbling smokestack shots at the beginning and the end of *Le Sang d'un poète*.) But is there a message? Well, yes. Certainly Cocteau is telling his audience that poets like Orphée are exceptional people and are sadly misunderstood — an old theme if there ever was one. This poet learns, however, not to accept as divinely inspired poetry just any message he hears from just any source ... Fresher still is Cocteau's attitude towards death, which is literally attractive — and preferable to life on earth as we generally experience it. After all, in the final scene, Orphée and Eurydice return to earth to continue their marital bickering. The poet's muse, the horse, has been replaced by the obliging presence of Heurtebise, but the couple is, ironically, not even astute enough to recognize the value of a new faithful servant in a bourgeois household!

Stylized, quirky, and fantastic, the play *Orphée* seems like an unpromising source for a mainstream French film. But in 1949 Cocteau profited from these very elements to make a film which is as distinctively his as the play. He began by abiding by his own advice to make the material representative of the period when it is produced. In the film, therefore, Orphée is a poet of the post-war Saint Germain-des-Prés set who is losing his popularity to a younger poet named Cégeste. It is clear that if the enemy group of poets in the play, the Bacchantes, had implicitly been Cocteau's real-life opponents of the 1920s, the Sur-

---

[1] Steegmuller, 371.

[2] Ibid., 364.

realists, the opposing poetic circle in the film (the Bacchantes, again led by Aglaonice) is the Existentialists. Aglaonice is even played by the musical mascot of Existentialism, Juliette Gréco. The concept of death is portrayed here as a mysterious Princess, an *agent* of death assigned especially to Orphée. She makes the grave error of falling in love with her victim and disposing of her rival, Orphée's pregnant wife, Eurydice, instead. Heurtebise, in a parallel plot, is a deceased student who is assigned to be the Princess's chauffeur. He also falls in love with a mortal, Eurydice; he is the one who guides Orphée through a mirror into the first plateau of the after-life that here is described as 'la zone.' The horse's messages are replaced by the voice of Cégeste on the radio of the Princess's automobile (an updated mode of communication in an updated mode of transportation), and the Princess's assistants are far from incompetent, but, rather, sleekly uniformed motorcycle agents reminiscent of the deft German gestapo. The Princess herself is the film's spy or eavesdropper who spends the night observing her love-object through the same painted eyelids that had become part of the Cocteau trademark.

The film version of *Orphée* is, then, ultra-modern in its style. Many years earlier, Diaghilev had urged Cocteau to astonish us; an older journalist repeats the statement to the seemingly upstaged Orphée in the Café des Poètes at the beginning of the film: 'Etonnez-nous.' Cocteau had himself just been excluded from Gaëtan Picon's *Panorama de la nouvelle littérature française* (1949) as being outmoded.[1] The film *Orphée* is Cocteau's astonishingly modern reply! Special effects abound, and again Cocteau's voice enters to carry the narration when appropriate, reminding the audience of his magisterial authorial role. Another Georges Auric score (with apologies to Gluck) enhances the Cocteau feel of the film. As the film ends, it is Orphée, the Cocteau *Doppelgänger*, rather than the young trend-setting Cégeste who survives, although his creativity seems to have been transferred to the area of fathering a baby as much as giving birth to poems. The Princess and Heurtebise have sacrificed themselves in the interest of poetic creation —and life— and depart in the final shot to be punished for their unprofessional earthly emotions and actions. Poetry and poets, just as in *Le Sang d'un poète*, inevitably achieve their own immortality even though it necessitates mortal boredom. In this misogynistic diegesis, Orphée has been condemned to marital stress and boredom with Eurydice. Have Hellman's Hubbards really left us? 'L'ennui mortel de l'immortalité' indeed!

---

[1] Ibid., 479–80.

After its release, *Orphée* won First Prize at the Venice Film Festival; Jean Marais, who played Orphée, moved out of his shared accommodation with Jean Cocteau, and Edouard Dermit, the actor who played Cégeste, moved in.[1] It was the handsome Dermit, claimed Cocteau, whom he had had in mind even in 1929 when he had created the character Paul in his novel, *Les Enfants terribles,* even though he did not meet the young Dermit until 1947. Similarly, Cocteau claimed to have imagined the actress Nicole Stéphane when he had conceived Paul's sister for the novel.[2] This was an appropriate thing indeed to say when these two performers played these roles in the 1950 film directed by Jean-Pierre Melville. But earlier it was accepted that the siblings in Cocteau's novel were inspired by Jeanne and Jean Bourgoint, those same two casually stylish young people whose clothes were cloned for the stage version of *Orphée* in 1926. Moreover, Cocteau says elsewhere that while he was describing Elisabeth on the final pages, he imagined an eighteen-year-old Greta Garbo in the role, a smoking revolver in her hand.[3] Cocteau also claimed that he had written the novel while obsessed by Jerome Kern's song 'Only Make-Believe' which he recommended that readers of the novel play (or hum?) while reading.[4]

What we know for certain is that in 1929 the Parisian publishing company Stock wanted another novel from Cocteau as a result of the commercial success of *Le Grand Écart* six years earlier, and that he obliged them by writing *Les Enfants terribles* rapidly in a clinic while recovering from a detox session.[5] The novel seemed to dictate itself, he found. Of course, his own memories helped. For in the novel, we find Cocteau's indelible snowball fight permanently incapacitating Paul and imprinting the image of Cocteau's own childhood hero, Dargelos, on the fictitious Paul's psyche in turn. Dargelos's white ball of snow at the beginning of the novel is echoed by the black ball of poison he delivers to Paul towards the end.[6] Dargelos thus becomes a unifier to the

---

[1] Elizabeth Sprigge and Jean-Jacques Kihm, *Jean Cocteau: The Man and the Mirror* (London: Victor Gollancz, Ltd., 1968), 188.

[2] Steegmuller, 476.

[3] Ibid., 397.

[4] Cocteau, in *Opium: The Diary of a Cure* translated by Margaret Crosland and Sinclair Road (London: Peter Owen, Ltd., 1947), 145.

[5] Steegmuller, 395–6.

[6] Cocteau spoke of the black bullet echoing the snowball, quoted by Steegmuller, 397.

circular structure of the novel just as he functions as one of the novel's two diabolical catalysts.

The disorder of the siblings' shared room recalls that of the Bourgoints, as does the closeness of their relationship. Their own private mythology takes shape in this room which contains talisman-like objects, and their private 'game' manifests itself in trance-like retreats, mischievous teasings and special language. Adults play little part in their lives. Instead, Elisabeth, every bit as much a manipulator as any other coctelian villain, Cocteau's second evil force in the novel, pulls the strings that lead her brother and their two key friends, Gérard and Agathe, to their various unhappy fates. Though briefly married, Elisabeth ages no more than her Peter Pan-like brother. But she becomes the centre of the action, the Queen Bee without whom all activity stops, all meaning vanishes. She and her brother must die together, like the lovers of *L'Éternel Retour* and *L'Aigle à deux têtes*. Having matured in spite of their companions, Gérard and Agathe may live on in an unhappy marriage like that of Orphée and Eurydice, having recognized the dull compromises that adult life demands.

The novel was an enormous success among readers of all ages in 1930. But it became the particular favourite of young people in search of new role models like Paul and Elisabeth.[1] Young readers must have felt too the impact of the economical style of its narrator's voice. The novel provided a short and thrilling read. A novel of adolescence to be sure, it was also a *roman policier* in which one could only imagine the police investigation that the discovery of the siblings' bodies would inspire. As a fictional tragedy, not only could its heroine recall Lady Macbeth; its hero could also recall Thomas Hardy's pitiful Tess Durbeyfield, whose letter, like Paul's to Agathe, went fatally astray. A psychological novel as well, it tells the story of multiple fascinations and obsessions and ambiguous sexual desires. The aura of immorality and incest hangs as heavy as opium fumes on the unventilated room that is the focal point of the novel's action. While the adolescents' 'Game' is clearly an escape as much as opium had been for Cocteau, it is never entirely clear from what they are trying to escape. Cocteau's ambiguity is tantalizing.

Claude-Jean Philippe believes that it was the constant presence of Edouard Dermit in his life that made Cocteau think of a film version of *Les Enfants terribles*.[2] Just as he had formerly planned vehicles for Jean

---

[1] Steegmuller, 397–8.

[2] Claude-Jean Philippe, pp. 129–30. Much of our factual data on the film version of *Les Enfants terribles* comes from Philippe's useful synthesis. We are much indebted.

Marais, so he would do for his new protégé. After seeing Jean-Pierre Melville's *Le Silence de la mer* (1947), Cocteau contacted the director. Much to his delighted surprise, he discovered that Melville had been an enchanted reader of the novel when he was thirteen in 1930. Melville, the only French filmmaker of the time who was being compared to Cocteau in the realm of originality, signed a contract which stipulated that the script would be primarily by Cocteau and Dermit would play Paul. The latter item did not please Melville immensely, and, indeed, Dermit's body remains too physically fit during Paul's debilitating illnesses. (It is difficult to say whether his performance itself is amateurishly wooden or deliberately equivocal.) Melville wanted to set the film in the 1925 décor of the novel. Cocteau stressed, however, that the now deceased Christian Bérard was the only designer who could have satisfactorily achieved the desired effect. The film was made, therefore, in actual locations and with styles of the moment, late 1949. Melville moved to a new flat in order to provide some of the interiors for Paul and Elisabeth's idiosyncratic life-style. Cocteau generally found the collaboration with Melville a happy one, was allowed to oversee many details of production, and was pleased with the film. He even said, 'Of all my writings which have been filmed, I feel it is the most faithfully presented.'[1] The critics were, however, suspicious of the moral message the film conveyed. Young people in particular were, on the contrary, impervious to such talk and flocked to its screenings.

René Gilson speaks enthusiastically of the voice-over narrative by Cocteau who thereby preserves the poetry of the novel.[2] To some extent, his voice serves as a Greek-chorus commentary, and provocatively leads to comparisons between 'les enfants terribles,' Paul and Elisabeth, and those meddling murderous mythological siblings, Electra and Orestes. The ritualistic aspects of the Cocteau-Melville world reinforce the comparison. The classical music of Bach and Vivaldi used here instead of Auric is also in keeping with the solemn tone. Cocteau's famous *dédoublements* multiply here. Not only do Paul and Elisabeth resemble each other; Dargelos and Agathe are played by the same actress! On screen Dargelos becomes the ultimate incarnation of insolence, but Cocteau remained uncertain that such casting was wise, Dargelos having always been for him the ideal of proud and virile young sexiness.

---

[1] Quoted from James Reid Paris, *The Great French Films*, 123.

[2] René Gilson, *Jean Cocteau*, translated by Ciba Vaughan (New York: Crown Publishers, 1969), 42.

Nicole Stéphane brings to her performance of Elisabeth strong and unsettling reminiscences of Maria Casarès as *Orphée's* Princess.[1] It is she, for instance, who obsessively observes her sleeping hero; it is she who utters the strident imperatives: 'Paul, Paul, écoute-moi. Regarde-moi. [...] Fais un effort. Ne lâche pas le fil.' ('Paul, Paul, listen to me. Look at me. [...] Make an effort. Don't let go.') Like the Princess, she is an instrument of death. But Elisabeth's victim is her very own brother. Stéphane's performance is highly theatrical, especially when compared with Dermit's. But could less be expected when playing one of the great villainesses of the screen? Regina Giddens of *The Little Foxes* seems to live again. But Elisabeth also recalls the selfish, destructive impulses of the hero of Claude Autant-Lara's *Le Diable au corps* (1947) played by Gérard Philipe. This landmark film was adapted from the novel by Raymond Radiguet, whose death at an early age is echoed as well in the death of the young and beautiful Paul. Pauline Kael appreciated *Les Enfants terribles* fully. She called it 'almost voluptuous in its evocation of temperament and atmosphere [...] one of the most exciting films of our time.'[2]

Close to ten years passed before Cocteau returned to directing. In September, 1959, at the age of seventy, he took his position not only behind the camera but also in front of it to film *Le Testament d'Orphée* with himself, at last, in the challenging role of Orpheus. This is the film that was financed by François Truffaut after commercial producers refused it.[3] (The sum involved was, fortunately for Truffaut and the other friendly backers, less than it might have been, the famous stars who appear in cameo roles having provided their services free.) As one prospective producer had reportedly said in 1958, 'I cannot produce a film in which nothing happens.'[4]

In actual fact, a great deal occurs in the film that Cocteau eventually made. Cocteau's narrative takes the spectator on a strange itinerary that makes this film a curiously picaresque visual poem. Most of the episodes refer directly or indirectly to events in Cocteau's own life. Working in conjunction with Claude Pinoteau, Cocteau found that one of his first obligations was to reduce continuously the wealth of material that he had originally conceived for his script. He had at first planned to centre the film on the pictorial art he had been pursuing since encountering his new patron, Madame Francine Weisweiller

[1] Claude-Jean Philippe agrees, 123.

[2] Pauline Kael, *Kiss Kiss Bang Bang* (New York: Bantam, 1968), 325.

[3] *Entretiens*, 128.

[4] Quoted in *The Art of Cinema*, 171.

(whose financial help is, naturally, also behind the production).[1] Thus, the film would have featured more prominently his decoration of the mayor's office in Menton or the chapel of Saint-Pierre at Ville-franche, or his Judith and Holophernes tapestry hanging in Madame Weisweiller's Villa Santo-Sospir. These remain briefly in the finished film, as does Madame Weisweiller herself, appearing as a distracted Countess whom Cocteau dressed in costumes reminiscent of his beloved mother's *fin-de-siècle* attire and whom Jacques Brosse believes Cocteau was relating to his recently deceased sister Marthe, another countess.[2]

Certainly the theme of death dominates *Le Testament d'Orphée*. But this is hardly a novelty in Cocteau's *œuvre*. It is more likely that his own aging and his heart attack in January 1959, a literal premoni-tion of more to come, could have inspired his contemplation of his own mortality and the poet's destiny more than did his mother's and sis-ter's deaths. One of the titles in the film reads: 'Pretend to weep, my friends, for poets only pretend to be dead.' Another states, in regard to the poet: 'The earth after all is not your domain.' Cocteau's flirtation with fascinating, enticing death is nearing its consummation. First there are the inevitable theatrical rehearsals of dying, assisted by Cégeste, who had already met death (in the film version of *Orphée*). Cégeste's dramatic rise from the sea is just one of the examples of the 'phénixologie' which characterizes the film. Even flowers die and are reborn in *Le Testament d'Orphée*. Cégeste, again played by Edouard Dermit, is the earthly heir to Cocteau/Orphée's poetic soul. Followers of Cocteau's life were aware on seeing the film that he would doubtless too be the heir to the poet's earthly fortunes, an event that did not take place until November, 1963. A touching appearance in the film is that of the ever loyal Jean Marais as Œdipus, here a helpless father-figure led by Antigone, perhaps recalling Cocteau's own father whose self-destruction at an early age had informed both the life and the themes of his son.

Cocteau's quotes in reference to the making of this film are numerous. 'This film shall be far more austere than *Le Sang d'un poète*,' promised Cocteau in January, 1959. 'The film opens with a kind of abstract farce à la Goldoni, on time and space. This sequence plunges me into a series of obscure intrigues from which Cégeste saves me ... It is a kind of Bach fugue with Godsent or Devilsent charm.'[3] Cocteau was as

---

[1] *Entretiens*, 127.

[2] Jacques Brosse, 'Présentation du *Testament d'Orphée*' in Jean Cocteau, *Orphée* (Paris: Bordas, 1985), 107.

[3] Quoted by Brown, 405.

good as his word. As the bewigged time-traveler at the beginning of the
film, Cocteau sets the tone for the rest of the episodes: whimsical and
philosophical; period and contemporary; personal and universal.
Cocteau, in fact, called the film 'a striptease in which bit by bit I
remove my body and reveal my soul quite naked.'[1] The young lovers
who take notes as they embrace may be references to Cocteau's public
acknowledgment of the lovers in his life. The audience he was seeking
was especially the young people who had believed in him. To them he
explained: 'In *Le Testament*, events follow one another as they do in
sleep, when our habits no longer control the forces within us or the logic
of the unconscious, foreign to reason.'[2] Cocteau here is confirming that
the poet is merely recording scenes on film that are dictated to him
while he is in a vague, sleepwalking state. Viewers of *Le Sang d'un
poète* thirty years earlier could have suspected the same condition.
Certainly the analogy between film and daydreams that modern film
theoreticians have exposed was already present in Cocteau's conception
of the film medium. Furthermore, the hypnotic impact of film and the
role of the filmmaker as hypnotist, taking the spectator into realms
where previously only sleep and dream had led him, prefigure the
concepts dear to the theoretician Christian Metz and his circle of the
1970s and after.[3] Even in the realm of film theory, Cocteau was ahead
of his time.

Too personal and abstract a film for wide commercial success, *Le
Testament d'Orphée* ran successfully in certain art cinemas[4] before
becoming the curious filmic document that concludes Cocteau's trilogy of
Orpheus films.

*   *   *

Jean Cocteau's film career included other enterprises besides these
eight feature films. We could have included, for example, the script he

---

[1] Quoted by Sprigge and Kihm, 238.

[2] *The Art of Cinema*, 165.

[3] See Christian Metz, *The Imaginary Signifier: Psychoanalysis and the Cinema*
(Bloomington: Indiana University Press, 1982), and two articles by Jean-Louis
Baudry reprinted in Philip Rosen (ed.), *Narrative, Apparatus, Ideology* (New
York: Columbia University Press, 1986), 286–318.

[4] Like La Pagode in Paris where it ran for eleven straight weeks. Its simultaneous
release on the Champs-Elysées lasted only two weeks. See Sprigge and Kihm,
243

wrote for Robert Bresson's *Les Dames du Bois de Boulogne* (1945) or for Pierre Billon's filmic adaptation of *Ruy Blas* (1947), starring Jean Marais. There is also his script for *La Princesse de Clèves* (1961), adapted for the screen from the novel by Madame de Lafayette and directed, like *L'Éternel Retour*, by Jean Delannoy. Shortly before his death, Cocteau wrote a screenplay from his own novel, *Thomas l'Imposteur*, which was respectfully filmed by Georges Franju in 1965. The voice of Jean Marais replaces Cocteau's for the voice-over narration in this film, while the score by Georges Auric and the on-screen presence of Edouard Dermit in a secondary role provide additional reminders of the creative and personal worlds of our poet. We could add here the short documentary that Cocteau made in colour about Madame Weiswseiller's Villa Santo Sospir, or the filmed version of his play, *La Voix humaine*, directed by Roberto Rossellini in 1948 with Anna Magnani doing the solo performance. After Cocteau's directing career was truly launched with *La Belle et la bête*, filmmaking remained a constant enthusiasm. Only the challenges of finding financing, of other commitments, and of failing health diminished his activity.

The importance of Jean Cocteau in film history is, however, normally judged by a more limited corpus: the six feature films that he directed himself. Even this restricted group defines him well. A pioneer in the earliest phase of sound cinema in France, he associated himself immediately with the most original of the avant-garde filmmakers through *Le Sang d'un poète*. His return to filmmaking during the Second World War was within the movement of literary films that were later pejoratively described as 'le cinéma de qualité.' But literary as he remained, Cocteau brought an individualistic lightness of touch to this script-heavy period. His love of fantasy, special effects, and imaginative photography in *La Belle et la bête*, *L'Aigle à deux têtes* and *Orphée* separated him from his contemporaries as the artist/poet that he was. Moreover, *Les Parents terribles* became a model of expert filming of successful stage plays. Finally, *Le Testament d'Orphée* stands as both a return to his ultra-poetic expression of *Le Sang d'un poète* and a comfortable companion to the indirect expression of the new generation of personal filmmakers in France and Italy. The presence of the young Jean-Pierre Léaud, fresh from Truffaut's *Les 400 Coups* (1959), discreetly conveys the kinship with the Nouvelle Vague and one wonders as well if the apparent incoherence or the overt personal allusiveness of Fellini's *8 1/2* (1963) would have taken place without the example of Cocteau.

The themes that distinguish Cocteau's films are, of course, highly literary: death, love, the family, artistic creation. Characteristically, his heroes' deaths are extraordinarily joyful, devoutly to be wished.

His love is overwhelmingly obsessive, total, even when it is impossible or even incestuous. Heirs of Œdipus, his families are as dysfunctional or as destructive as they come. Heirs of Orpheus, his artists are blessed with superhuman talent and all too human distress. Double deaths, fatal love, abject imprisonment in families, and unappreciated or misunderstood artistry abound. Moreover, all of the stories are told in structures that, even when experimental, have a classically identifiable beginning, middle, and end. In structure and in theme, classical æsthetic values are never far away.

Furthermore, these themes come packaged with the distinctive sets of a Christian Bérard or the musical score of a Georges Auric. Cocteau evidently recognized that even an artist of his genius needed to surround himself with the best empathetic talent available in the filmmaking business. Through repeated collaborations under his direction, his films do not deviate from the kind of consistent look that can make a filmic 'auteur.' That Cocteau was/is an auteur, the following essays by another team of adept collaborators will confirm, just as they will lead to clearer comprehension and new insights concerning each of the texts they address.

We are grateful to all the writers for their enthusiastic work on this project. Predominantly anglophones, they have given precedence to English-language versions of texts. The original French versions are provided whenever possible in the notes and bibliography. Special thanks goes to Dario Del Degan for his assistance in preparation of the text. Tanya d'Anger researched the original French sources and led us to our publisher. We would also like to thank the Department of French, University of Toronto, for its encouragement, both moral and financial.

Coctelian Neoplatonism: The Role of the Orphic Poet in Le Sang d'un poète[1]

Tanya d'Anger

> Poets, to live, must often die,
> leaving a trail not only of the heart's
> red blood but of the soul's white,
> by which they can be traced.[2]

Le Sang d'un poète is the earliest of Jean Cocteau's films. Made in 1930 during the *entre deux guerres* period, when linked with the later films *Orphée* (1950) and *Le Testament d'Orphée* (1959) it retrospectively forms part of a loose trilogy based on the Orpheus legend. The hermetic cult which sprang out of Orpheus' odyssey into the Underworld is key to Cocteau's poetic system, and the Orphic cosmogony is reflected both in the composition of *Le Sang d'un poète* and in Cocteau's preoccupation with the fecund conflict between order and disorder. His work

---

[1] Francis Steegmuller explains the development of *coctelian*: In the Figaro littéraire *for April 14, 1966, 'Aristide,' the author of the column 'Usage et grammaire,' wrote: 'Cocteau is a diminutive, a contraction of coqueteau, meaning "little cock." '* ('Cocteau...est un diminutif: contraction de coqueteau, il signifie petit coq. Par conséquent, les dérivés corrects ne peuvent en être que coctelisme et coctellien (eau égalant ellum).' 7) When a correspondent wrote in suggesting that 'Cocteau' might come rather from the Latin coctor (cook) —the term 'maître coq' being used for a cook on a ship— 'Aristide' expressed doubt (June 30, 1966). He suggested 'coctelien' as the proper adjective for 'cocteau.' Cocteau once described his own name as being 'the plural of "cocktail."' Cocteau, 206, footnote. All subsequent quotations from Steegmuller are from this source.

[2] *Professional Secrets*, 142. Quoted from *Le Cordon ombilical*, (1962). Also paraphrased in the talk given at the Théâtre du Vieux-Colombier, when the film was shown there in January, 1932. The English translation of this text is printed as a postscript to the screenplay of *Le Sang d'un poète* in *Two Screenplays: The Blood of a Poet/The Testament of Orpheus*, 66.

also contains significant use of Platonic imagery which is inverted to counter the great objection to subjective Art in Book X of the *Republic*, and the inaccuracy of the Platonic 'copy' which Cocteau viewed in terms of renewal rather than imperfection: 'I always advise the copying of a model. It is impossible to copy exactly; new blood is always infused, and it is by that that we can judge the poet.'[1] Reinterpreted in light of both his Orphic and his personal beliefs, Cocteau offers a *neoplatonic* alternative of universal harmony through the medium of poetry.

Neoplatonism, as opposed to Platonism proper, seeks a teleological purpose for mankind by drawing on all available cultures.[2] Unlike Plato's call for the homogenization of Art as an official reflection of the State's self image, it is an inclusive process which leads to spiritual harmony through the openness of artistic interpretation. It re-surfaced in modern times between 1905 and 1914 when Cocteau was intimately involved with Diaghilev and Les Ballets Russes, a period which Roger Shattuck describes as:

> ... a dynamic compound of renewed classicism, unbridled experimentation, cool scientific nihilism, and a rash of primitive devices and attitudes derived from African, Oceanic, folk, and ancient sources, as well as from the art of children and the insane.[3]

In Cocteau's work Neoplatonism takes the form of an avoidance of closure and a fascination with the mystical and artistic expression of the Orient. It is also part of the Orphic and Pythagorean mysticism

---

[1] Steegmuller, 483. 'Publicity folder (in English) distributed by Discina International Film Corporation, New York. Original French not available. A few changes made in the translation.' 558, footnote.

[2] Neoplatonism proposes a black hole theory of timeless history in which the supra sensible reality transforms first into time and space as we know it, and then into annihilation as the inevitable impetus of all matter. This sequence represents 'a type of causation radically different from causality in space and time.' It was 'the last creative effort of pagan antiquity (c. 250 to 550 A.D.) to produce a comprehensive philosophic system which could satisfy all spiritual (intellectual, religious, moral) aspirations of man by presenting an all-inclusive, logically coherent image of the universe and of man's place in it and by explaining how man can achieve salvation, i.e. be restored to his lost original condition.' *The Concise Encyclopedia of Western Philosophy and Philosophers*, 219–20.

[3] Roger Shattuck, 'A Native Son of Paris,' in Arthur King Peters (ed.), *Jean Cocteau and the French Scene*, 40. All subsequent quotations from this text are designated by 'Peters.'

which he embraced, and explains the surreal and 'magical' elements which punctuate his films.

The opening titles of *Le Sang d'un poète* identify it as a poetic riddle, 'a realistic documentary of unreal events' establishing a conscious difference between perceptual and conceptual reality.[1] The American composer Elliott Carter, an acquaintance of Cocteau's, explains the crumbling chimney which frames the film's narrative as a similar contrast between '... external time (measured by the falling chimney ...) and internal dream time (the main body of the work) — the dream time lasting but a moment of external time, but from the dreamer's point of view a long stretch.'[2] The riddle motif is in keeping with the mystical nature of the Pythagorean pentagram and its numerological symbolism which Cocteau chose for his emblem, as well as with his subsequent concept of poetry as a mathematical puzzle. 'Poetry is nothing but figures, algebra, geometry, operations and proofs' he wrote in *La Difficulté d'être*, and the numbers he assigns to the focal third and fourth hotel rooms in *Le Sang d'un poète* carry specific symbolism through which Cocteau offers a solution to Man's sense of mathematical displacement in the universe.[3]

Yet herein lies a tension. The Pythagorean pentagram is an icon associated with harmony and androgyny in that its fifth point harmonizes the 'gender' coupling of two and two, and in *Le Sang d'un poète* the Coctelian Star similarly represents the promise of harmony within the universe through the medium of poetry. In the *Symposium* Aristophanes explains the original existence of three genders —man, woman and the 'androgynous'— and Cocteau draws on this mythological gender void which now exists to represent the paradox of the Poet's inability to find spiritual resolution.[4] The notion of androgyny is specifically

---

[1] *The Blood of a Poet*, screenplay, 8. All subsequent quotations in English from *Le Sang d'un poète* and *Le Testament d'Orphée* are found in the translation: *Two Screenplays: The Blood of a Poet, The Testament of Orpheus*. '[U]n documentaire réaliste d'événements irréels'*, 22; all subsequent quotations from the original French screenplay are taken from *Le Sang d'un poète* (Paris: Robert Martin,1948).

[2] Ned Rorem, 'Cocteau and Music,' in Peters, 170.

[3] Neal Oxenhandler, *Scandal and Parade*, 33. '[L]a poésie n'est que chiffres, algèbre, géométrie, opérations et preuves.'* From *La Difficulté d'être* (Monaco: Éditions du Rocher, 1989), 89. All subsequent quotations from *La Difficulté d'être* are taken from this source.

[4] Plato quotes Aristophanes' discussion of the missing third gender in the *Symposium*: 'The sexes were not two as they are now, but originally three in number; there was man, woman, and the union of the two, having a name corresponding

associated with the Poet and the 'desperate' Hermaphrodite, both of whom are in search of a harmony which is denied them by the very nature of their exotic identities. This paradox highlights two things: Cocteau's belief in androgyny as a means of synthesizing the urges of his personal sexuality with the social norm, and society's parallel attitude towards the artist as something strange, fascinating but ultimately to be ostracized. This ostracization, in turn, echoes Plato's rejection of the poet, and Cocteau's quest to redeem him functions on both an æsthetic and personal level.

Cocteau's description of himself as an *'ouvrier'* is strikingly similar to Plato's privileging of the craftsman with skilled *technë* based on applied knowledge.[1] It is for lack of this that the poets are rejected from his Republic, yet Cocteau's call for intuition over logic under the same umbrella of 'craftsman' inverts the Platonic objection by championing aristic vision as a means of reaching out towards the greater truth which lies beyond rational deduction. In 1951 he wrote: 'Poetry comes from those who are not concerned with it. We are cabinetmakers. The mediums come afterwards, and it is their business to make the tables talk.'[2] The key difference is that where Plato distrusted the intangible nature of artistic intuition, and sought to assign a stable, closed meaning to the creative product based on logic or *logos*, Cocteau viewed this intangibility as the route towards the Platonic Ideal and emphasized the need to leave the semiotic implications of Art open to the individual imagination:

> People often look at me with incredulity when I truthfully tell them that I could not possibly confirm or reject their interpretations, because they are entirely a matter of individual comprehension and appreciation ...[3]

---

to this double nature, which had once a real existence but is now lost, and the word 'Androgynous' [a compound of the Greek words meaning 'man' and 'woman'] is only preserved as a term of reproach.' Plato, *Symposium*, 178–79.

[1] Christopher Janaway interprets *technë* as '[A] body of knowledge or a set of principles which guide an area of human activity towards a successful practical end-product.' 'Plato's Analogy between Painter and Poet,' 5.

[2] *Professional Secrets*, footnote, 147; also in Steegmuller, 407. *'Je ne cherchais qu'à emboîter les thèmes qui m'émeuvent, à m'introduire le moins possible dans ce déroulement de documentaires irréels. Il ne s'y rencontre jamais un symbole. C'est ce qui permet qu'on symbolise. Je suis ébéniste. Je construis une table, libre à vous de la faire tourner et parler.' Secrets de beauté* in *Œuvres complètes* vol. X (Geneva: Marguerat, 1946), 359.

[3] Steegmuller, 407. From an interview with Francis Korval, 'Interview with Cocteau,' in *Sight and Sound*, Vol. 19 (New Series), (August 1950), 229 *et seq.*

Marcel Proust wrote of Cocteau: 'You who enjoy representing the highest truths by a dazzling symbol that contains them all.'[1] Despite his denial of the use of symbolism, the recurring imagery and hermetic puzzles in Cocteau's work suggest that he laid great emphasis on both visual and mystical associations, and this seeming paradox can perhaps be explained by the differentiation which might now — in the late twentieth-century — be made between Symbolism and Semiotics. In the short essay 'No Symbols' Cocteau rejected their use as a facile escapism for the lazy spectator who avoids intuitive or emotional input by depending on the assigned meaning of an image.[2] He describes this in *Professional Secrets* as '... that craving to *recognize* which is the form of knowledge the public prefers, doubtless because it demands the least effort.'[3] The Coctelian Poet, then, is an archetypal figure whose role is to stir up what Cocteau refers to as the 'night' within the human soul, the creative obscurity out of which individuality and hence fulfilment spring:

> All of us contain in ourselves a night we scarcely know or do not know at all. This night tries to emerge from us, yet resists emerging. That is the drama of art, a real struggle between Jacob and the Angel.[4]

The metaphor of Night finds its source in a chaotic, Dionysian energy which Cocteau associates with childhood, and specifically with his youthful memory of the arrogant schoolboy Dargelos who represented for him:

> ... the type of all that is not taught or learned or judged, of all that is not analyzed or punished, of all that is singularized in a person, the first symbol of the wild forces which inhabit us, which the social machinery tries to extinguish, and which beyond good and evil maneuver the individuals whose example consoles us for living.[5]

---

[1] Steegmuller, 295. '*Vous qui pour les vérités les plus hautes vous contentez d'un signe flamboyant qui les rassemble...*' 'Lettres de Marcel Proust à Jean Cocteau,' *Cahiers Jean Cocteau*, no. I (Paris: Gallimard, 1969), 74 (dated 1918).

[2] In *Two Screenplays*.

[3] *Professional Secrets*, 268. '*...[C]e goût de reconnaître que le public préfère à celui de connaître, sans doute parce qu'il exige un moindre effort.*' From *Théâtre 2* (Paris: Gallimard, 1948), 301.

[4] Ibid., 295. From *Le Cordon ombilical*.

[5] Ibid., 27. '*...[L]e type de tout ce qui ne s'apprend pas, ne s'enseigne pas, ne se juge pas, ne s'analyse pas, ne se punit pas, de tout ce qui singularise un être, le premier symbole des forces sauvages qui nous habitent, que la machine sociale essaye de*

It is clear that Cocteau valued this chaotic source as vital to creative individuality, but paradoxically it is inevitably sacrificed in his work to the demands of Form to which Cocteau himself bowed. Only in coctelian images of childhood does this anarchy survive —in *Le Sang d'un poète*'s snowball fight and Dargelos; and the Poet's attempted theft of the Ace of Hearts from the dead boy's body during the card game sequence reinforces the comparative impotence of the adult who has lost the inspiration of childhood, and whose fate —like the Poet's— is to become a 'statue,' an empty icon like the busts of Diderot which frame the Woman-Statue's final exit through sumptuous golden doors.[1]

Cocteau contrasts this disturbing Dionysian energy with the metaphor of Light and its implications of Apollonian clarity as represented in the Woman-Statue. This dialectic foregrounds a tension between the artist's need for the disorder of creativity on the one hand, yet the order of structure and discipline on the other, a combustible combination which is harmonized in Cocteau's work through the necessary sacrifice of individuality to inspiration in line with the ancient Greek notion of *pharmakos*.[2] This theme of sacrificial death and resurrection in a new

---

tuer en nous, et qui, par delà le bien et le mal, manœuvrent les individus dont l'exemple nous console de vivre.' From *Portrait souvenirs*, in *Œuvres complètes*, vol. XI (Geneva: Marguerat, 1946), 71.

[1] This is an example of what might be called Cocteau's 'Peter Pan' complex, and is explored in greater detail in the novel *Les Enfants terribles* (1929) which immediately precedes *Le Sang d'un poète*. The visual reference to Diderot points to his responsibility for the replacement of verse by prose in eighteenth-century French theatre.

[2] Derrida describes the origin of *pharmakos* in 'Plato's Pharmacy': 'The word in question is *pharmakos* (wizard, magician, poisoner), a synonym of *pharmakeus* [poison] (which Plato uses), but with the unique feature of having been overdetermined, overlaid by Greek culture with another function. Another *role*, and a formidable one.

The character of the *pharmakos* has been compared to a scapegoat. The *evil* and the *outside*, the expulsion of the evil, its exclusion out of the body (and out) of the city — these are the two major senses of the character and of the ritual.' *Dissemination*, 130. 'Il s'agit du mot "pharmakos" (sorcier, magicien, empoisonneur), synonyme de pharmakeus (utilisé par Platon), qui a l'originalité d'avoir été surdéterminé, surchargé par la culture grecque d'une autre fonction. D'un autre rôle, et formidable.

On a comparé le personnage du pharmakos à un bouc émissaire. Le mal et le dehors, l'expulsion du mal, son exclusion hors du corps (et hors) de la cité, telles sont les deux significations majeures du personnage et de la pratique rituelle.' *Dissémination* (Paris: Éditions du Seuil, 1972), 149.

Le Sang d'un poète : The Poet and his Mirror (Enrique Rivero)
Courtesy of the Museum of Modern Art Film Stills Archive
© Jean Cocteau/SODRAC (Montréal) 1998

form is also part of the Orphic theogony (pre-dating Christianity by four centuries), and associated with the Great God Dionysus. In the Orphic reinterpretation Dionysus is no longer 'the rustic god of wine and jollity' or 'of orgiastic delirium ... from the Orient,' but in Plutarch's words 'the god who is destroyed, who disappears, who relinquishes life and then is born again' to become the symbol of everlasting life and renewal.[1] This is the source of what Cocteau termed 'phœnixology,' but varies significantly on one point from the ancient Greek interpretation.[2] Where in the work of Sophocles or Æschylus the *pharmakos'* role was to ensure society's renewal through the poet-hero's death, Cocteau's 'phœnixology' calls for the poet's surrender of his conscious individuality in order to become the vehicle for 'some unknown force' which lies beyond the social framework, and possibly beyond life itself.[3]

Cocteau identifies the power of this force in the artist's creative reflection of the world. However, instead of 'holding the mirror up to nature' in order to reflect perceptual reality, the Coctelian Mirror through which the Poet passes in stepping from his studio into the corridor of the Hôtel des Folies-Dramatiques compels a vision which passes beyond into the potent Coctelian Night and a conceptual, 'anti-reality.' This is suggested in Cocteau's use of masks and the metaphor of blindness which signals the presence of supernatural or 'poetic' characters with privileged insight, in line with the ancient Greek maxim 'Know thyself.'[4] It explains Cocteau's preoccupation elsewhere in his work with the myth of Œdipus, and in *Le Testament d'Orphée* where the Œdipal myth is referred to more directly Cocteau explains: '... [T]here is a considerable public interested in the world of shadows,

---

[1] *The New Larousse Encyclopedia of Mythology*, trans. Richard Aldington and Delano Ames, 160.

[2] 'The Original Sin of Art,' *Two Screenplays*, 78. Cocteau relates the notion of 'phœnixology' to *Le Sang d'un poète* itself: 'It is the resurrectional and, as Salvador Dali would say, the "phœnixological" quality of the film that makes it relive at every showing episodes that it was not aware of the night before.' See Cocteau's poem 'Phœnixology' which precedes the translated text of *Le Testament d'Orphée*, published in the same volume as the English language screenplay of *Le Sang d'un poète*, 79.

[3] *Two Screenplays*, 24. '...[O]n ne sait quel mistral incompréhensible...', *Le Sang d'un poète*, 46.

[4] The origin of this paraphrase lies in Shakespeare's *Hamlet, 1601*: III, ii, 76. In his exploration of the negative, or 'anti-reality,' Cocteau reaches back to Oscar Wilde and Lewis Carroll. The many similarities between Cocteau and Wilde, in particular, are worth study.

starved for the more-real-than-reality, which one day will become the sign of our times.'[1]

Cocteau continued to explore this theme of alternative reality in the photographically negative Zone of the Princess's world in the 1950 *Orphée*, and it is this that André Breton —the leader of Surrealism in Cocteau's day and a vituperative enemy— picks up on in his description of Cocteau as the 'anti-poet': 'Why must Cocteau be considered the anti-poet?/Because in his writing the mechanics of the image — the image being that element by which poetic ability can be measured — always works backwards ...'[2] In the 1930 *Le Sang d'un poète*, the Zone appears as a sleazy hotel corridor with doors through which the Poet 'spies' upon allegorical images of life, and the 'Folies-Dramatiques' of the Hotel's title highlights Cocteau's appropriation of the Sartrian dictum that one cannot play without playing at being.[3] The spying, or peeking motif is a throwback to the 'Fourth Wall' Naturalism of nineteenth-century theatre, but in Cocteau it becomes something far more surreal, with overtones of the 'forbidden' which tie into his direct association of the Poet with the bizarre figure of the Hermaphrodite, and his description of the corridor itself as 'a room of crime, a criminal anthropometry department, a prison courtyard.'[4]

Paradoxically, in his 1946 Preface to *Le Sang d'un poète* Cocteau rejected the description of 'surrealist' frequently applied to the film, along with any suggestion of assigned meaning, claiming that he alone among his contemporaries had avoided 'the deliberate manifestations of the unconscious in favor of a kind of half-sleep through which I wandered as though in a labyrinth.'[5] Where Plato in barring poets from his Republic privileged logic and what he believed was the stability of

---

[1] *Two Screenplays*, 83. '...[I]l existe un considérable public de l'ombre, affamé de ce plus vrai que le vrai qui sera un jour le signe de notre époque.' *Le Testament d'Orphée* (Monaco: Éditions du Rocher, 1983), 58.

[2] Quoted by Frederick Brown in *An Impersonation of Angels*, 402 from *Le Figaro Littéraire* (le 24 septembre 1960), 1: 'Pourquoi Cocteau doit-il être regardé comme l'antipoète?

Parce que chez lui la mécanique de l'image qui donne la mesure de la capacité poétique fonctionne constamment à rebours...'

[3] This is also part of Cocteau's fascination with childhood.

[4] *Two Screenplays*, 24. This motif of the 'criminal-poet' explains, partly, his later fascination with the criminal-playwright Jean Genet, whom Cocteau defended concerning an accusation of theft, during the Occupation. '[C]hambre de crime, de service anthropométrique, de cour de prison.' *Le Sang d'un poète*, 46.

[5] Ibid., 3. '[L]es manifestations volontaires de l'inconscient, au bénéfice d'une sorte de demi-sommeil où je labyrinthais moi-même.' Ibid., 13.

homogenization, Cocteau promoted the full development of personal individuality and intuition as a prelude to transformation and spiritual
revitalization as part of something greater: how can one participate in
the Other without first fully exploring the Self?

Le Sang d'un poète is an autobiographical exploration of the Self
and of Cocteau's notion of Art as a parthenogenetic construct. He establishes the autobiographical element quite clearly through voice-overs,
editorial projections linking the sequences, and explicit references to his
own past. With the projection of his signature under the legend 'The
surprises of photography, or how I was caught in a trap by my own
film,' Cocteau clearly identifies himself with the Poet who also bears
the coctelian 'stigmata' in the form of a star-shaped scar on his back.[1]
Like Plato, Cocteau draws on the ancient Greek term *poiesis* to desig-
nate the spirit of art in all its forms as 'poetry,' viewing the 'poet' as a
special, chosen individual having unique contact with the muses and
hence an obligation to create.[2] His self-image as a 'sniper' — like the
Socratic 'gadfly' in Plato's *Apology* — reinforces this impulse to inter-
rogate and prompt others towards questioning, clearly identifying the
Coctelian Poet's role in society as Socratic in impulse.[3]

Cocteau also draws on the shadow and light imagery in Plato's alle-
gories of the Sun and Cave to align the ancient Greek concept of *eikasia*
with the potent obscurity of his Night. It was the obscure perception of
eikasia which Plato associated with artistic inspiration, and rejected.[4] But Cocteau champions it as the unconscious expression of a
greater Truth in line with the Platonic Realm of Forms which should be

---

[1] Ibid., 17. '*Les surprises de la photographie ou comment je me suis laissé prendre
au piège par mon propre film.*' Ibid., 33. Cocteau's personal identification with
this Orpheus prototype becomes clear in his final film, *Le Testament d'Orphée*
(1960), where he himself plays the title role. The genesis of the Poet's scar is due
to chance: the actor had been in a fight and, typically, Cocteau incorporated this
unforeseen element into the subtext of his symbolism by giving it the appearance
of the Coctelian Star. As he wrote when he was filming *La Belle et la bête* in
1945: 'To reorganize chance. That is the basis of our work,' *Professional
Secrets*, 226. '*Réorganiser le hasard. Voilà la base de notre travail.*' From *La Belle
et la bête, journal d'un film* (Monaco: Éditions du Rocher, 1958), 168 (Mardi 13
— 7 heures du matin).

[2] B. Jowett explains: 'The Greek work meaning 'poetry,' *poiesis*, comes like our
own word from the Greek verb that means 'to make.' Hence the earliest meaning
of poetry was a making, a creating, and a poet might be a maker of other things
besides verse.' *Symposium*, 196, footnote.

[3] Cocteau in 'The Original Sin of Art,' *Two Screenplays*, 77.

[4] See Plato's *Ion*.

sensed rather than intellectually grasped, because true understanding is impeded by the conscious, intellectual functioning of the mind: 'Poetry imitates a reality of which our world possesses only the intuition.'[1] This conflict between intuition and logic, suggested in Plato's 'ancient quarrel between poetry and philosophy,' is represented in the opening scene in the studio where the Poet is still detached from his artistic creativity.[2] The gloves he wears while sketching symbolize this emotional detachment, and his Louis XV wig conveys overtones of the eighteenth-century's preference for literature over poetry and theatre. It is this rational 'third person' removal associated with prose rather than verse that the Woman-Statue arouses the Poet from through the ineluctable impulse of the artform when the living Mouth he has created is transferred from the Poet's canvas onto the Woman-Statue herself.

The recurring motif of negative and positive photographic frames which stems from this shadow-light dialectic signals the presence of supernatural activity in the 'natural' world of Cocteau's films. Privileged moments such as the Angel's mystical absorption of the dead boy's body towards the end of the card game sequence, in a gesture of protectiveness, are instances of the 'magic' which Cocteau incorporated into his filming, and convey an alternative reading to the limiting obscurity through which Plato represented mankind's perception of the world in the Cave Allegory. The logically inexplicable does not necessarily stem from confusion, because the overwhelming order of logic obstructs the greater insight of imagination which serves as the lifeline between the Ideal and human consciousness.

This dialectic between shadow and light is explored in *Le Sang d'un poète* within the opium den behind the hotel's third door. The room represents a 'celestial ceiling,' and is specifically given the number 19 which, in Pythagorean numerology, is a 'difficult' number suggesting Divine Order and the rejection of imperfection.[3] Unlike the second hotel room where the young girl 'flies' past the electric light bulb, the electricity has been turned off and the only light emanates from the glow of opium pipes being lighted, reflecting their shadows on the wall as in Plato's cave. The obscurity of this room echoes the potent darkness of the Coctelian Night which he associated with oriental mysticism, and leads to a Hegelian-like synthesis of opposites which is fundamental to the Orphic cosmogony of Night and Light which engendered hu-

---

1 'La poésie imite une réalité dont notre monde ne possède que l'intuition.' Le Mystère laïc (1928) in Œuvres complètes, Vol. X, 28. Quoted by Oxenhandler in Scandal & Parade, 33.

2 Republic, Book X, 1, 607b.

3 Two Screenplays, 28. '[P]lafond céleste', Le Sang d'un poète, 52.

manity.[1] The figure of the 'dark' Angel reinforces this when contrasted with the Woman-Statue who is both characterized by her 'whiteness,' and by her association with Light. Further, when viewed in the context of the positive-negative dialectic the Angel bears clear associations with the Platonic image of the divided human soul as visualized in the figure of a Winged Charioteer driving one good, white horse and one unruly, black one: Form in tandem with Chaos. This innate tension within the human soul —which Cocteau also identified between men and women in an intriguing echo of the English poet William Blake's concept of bigender angelism— informs the pessimism he felt concerning the possibility of human harmony outside of Art, a pessimism he expresses in the final transformation of the Woman-Statue herself into a frozen reflection of light at the end of the film.[2]

The Woman-Statue and the Angel represent different parts of the same supernatural force to which the Poet must eventually sacrifice himself in order to achieve artistic synthesis, and in the later Orphic films they would develop into the symbiotic figures of the Princess and Heurtebise.[3] In Le Sang d'un poète the Angel is played by Féral Benga, the black jazz dancer, chosen as a visible contrast to Lee Miller's Caucasian 'whiteness' of skin and (be-wigged) hair. Like the opium den he

---

[1] The dialectic of Night and Light ties directly into the Orphic cosmogony, which Cocteau uses to direct his contrast of positive and negative images, and a brief description may at this point prove helpful: '... [T]he first principle was Cronus, or Time, from which came Chaos, which symbolised the infinite, and Ether, which symbolised the finite ... Chaos was surrounded by Night, which formed the enveloping cover under which, by the creative action of Ether, cosmic matter was slowly organised. This finally assumed the shape of an egg of which Night formed the shell. In the centre of this gigantic egg, whose upper section formed the vault of the sky and whose lower section was the earth, was born the first being, Phanes — the Light. It was Phanes who, by union with Night, created Heaven and Earth.' The New Larousse Encyclopedia of Mythology, 90.

[2] There is no question of any negative, racial overtones in Cocteau's positive/ negative, black/white dialectic, but rather the two faces of the same force which ties into the tension between Fate and Justice which Cocteau explored through the Princess and Heurtebise in the later Orpheus films. Taking this allusion further, one cannot ignore Cocteau's development of the Horse-Muse in Orphée, or the frequent use of the horse motif in Le Testament d'Orphée to suggest artistic inspiration emerging from this 'chaotic' marriage of opposites.

[3] This dialectic of the male and female elements supports Cocteau's association of androgyny with harmony, as represented by the Pythagorean pentagram. For more on the possible influence of Nietzsche's Dionysian/Apollonian dialectic, see Micheline Meunier's Jean Cocteau et Nietzsche ou Philosophie du matin.

is representative of Night's fecund obscurity in contrast to the Woman-Statue's association with Light and the life-force of Art itself.

The Woman-Statue embodies order on the artistic level, blind response to the compelling force which directs creativity and ultimately the ominous 'mortal tedium of immortality' which lies beyond life.[1] She is the sole survivor at the end of the film, where only the white surfaces of her marble figure 'which become hard and stony and still hold the light' remain.[2] These elements are deliberately representative of the fabric of statues, reinforcing Cocteau's concern for the irrevocable spiritual loss which occurs during the transformation from childhood into adulthood, which Frederick Brown explains: '... [T]he theme of children foredoomed, their purity unable to survive outside its own playground, was eternally attractive to him.'[3] The red 'blood' of young human flesh inevitably transforms into the white 'blood' of the poet's spiritual destiny as a civic icon — ironically the very role which Plato sought to impose upon artists. Interestingly, Cocteau denied the notion of escapism in his work, but it is clear that like the Poet and Hermaphrodite he felt himself unable to attain harmony (or true androgyny) in the 'real' world.[4] In 1947 he expressed this angst in *La Difficulté d'être*: 'In the end, everything works out, except the difficulty of being, which does not work out.'[5]

In contrast to the cold dispassion of the Woman-Statue, the Angel's emotional response to the dead boy who is killed as a result of the snowball fight links it with the notion of a warmer 'disorder' which Cocteau associates with the riotous, vibrant energy of the schoolboys. The children represent Man's need for an emotional rather than intellectual answer to his existential questioning, and the fact that Cocteau associates this Dionysian chaos with childhood rather than adult-

---

[1] *Two Screenplays*, 60. '[E]nnui mortel de l'immortalité', Le Sang d'un poète, 94.

[2] Ibid. 'Cette femme fausse (cadrée en plan américain) confondue avec le noir du décor, sauf en ce qui concerne le profil et les accessoires, s'éloigne dans la nuit phosphorescente.' Ibid., 91–92.

[3] *An Impersonation of Angels*, 259.

[4] Arthur King Peters comments: 'Even for a public as relatively sophisticated as Cocteau's, the concrete representation of his homosexuality was inadmissible. (He certainly wasn't the least bit coy about it where his personal life was concerned.) Cocteau's solution, conscious or not, was to translate homosexuality into a kind of mystical male auto-eroticism on screen, from the serpentine posturings of Enrique Rivero, the Poet in his first film, through Marais to Dermit.' 'The Mask in the Mirror: The Movies of Jean Cocteau,' in Peters, 198.

[5] Jean Cocteau, *La Difficulté d'être*, 11. 'En fin de compte, tout s'arrange, sauf la difficulté d'être, qui ne s'arrange pas.' La Difficulté d'être, 8.

hood, depicting the schoolboys weighed down by their heavy satchels, suggests that they are spiritually 'deformed' by adult order, and that in maturity Man grows away from his instincts to become 'crippled' through the triumph of logic over intuition.[1] It is notable that the Poet, upon entering the hermetic world of the Mirror's corridor, is similarly 'weighed down and off balance.'[2] The suggestion of a world without the normal rules of gravity foregrounds the metatheatrical reality to which the Poet must now readjust in his growth away from the deforming effect of logic, into the receptiveness of an intuition which relies totally on illusion:

> ... [W]e are performing at a very high altitude and without benefit of a safety net. The least, untoward noise may cause us to lose our balance and result in the death of myself and my comrades.[3]

The symmetry of *Le Sang d'un poète* echoes the five-points of the Coctelian Star. Structurally there are five sections: the introduction in the Poet's studio and the four episodes which mark his progress towards his destiny as a civic icon, and the Woman-Statue's deathbed. The Second Episode, which follows the Poet's odyssey into and out of the corridor within the Mirror, is also constructed on the same five-point system: the corridor plus the four hotel doors where the Poet is forced to re-gain his 'balance' within the alternative reality of the Hôtel des Folies-Dramatiques. The themes of balance, flying and repetition signal the independent rules regarding logic and time which govern the world of Imagination rather than Reality, and represent the Poet's reluctant rites of passage in his development as an artist. In each replication of the pentagram structure the fifth sequence is the most important: the element which harmonizes the opposition of two and two. In the outer structure of *Le Sang d'un poète*, this moment of potential harmony occurs during the Woman-Statue's final transformation into a Sphinx-like figure before her 'death' scene. In the inner structure of the Mirror's anti-reality, it is represented behind the fourth door of the Hôtel des Folies-Dramatiques, by the Hermaphrodite.

---

[1] *Two Screenplays*, 39. *'[J]ambes nues, pèlerine, bosse produite par le sac de moleskine...' Le Sang d'un poète*, 71.

[2] Ibid., 22. *'Sa marche doit être insolite à force de déséquilibre et de lenteur lourde...'*, ibid., 43.

[3] Brown, 264. *'[N]ous jouons très haut et sans filet de secours. Le moindre bruit intempestif risque de nous faire tuer, mes camarades et moi.'* Prologue to *Orphée* (play) (Paris: Librairie Stock, 1930), 17.

Like the opium den, the Hermaphrodite's room is significantly given a mystical number: 23.[1] This number is deliberately placed after the 'difficult' number 19, and proffers a possible resolution in its representation of the harmony of equal division between male and female chromosomes which, in numerological terms, make up the universe: 46. The Hermaphrodite, like Cocteau's Angels, is an androgynous figure echoing this gender balance and is linked to the notion of harmony which lies at the centre of the Pythagorean pentagram, signaled through the projection of Coctelian Stars. It is psychologically revealing that the live elements of this bizarre figure are represented by living male limbs (the use of a live model), while the female elements are sketched onto the chalkboard which divides it. This dichotomy suggests a division within Cocteau's own psyche: his living, perceptual reality is masculine, tied up in his homosexual preferences; his artistic, conceptual reality — the 'more-real-than-reality' beyond the Mirror — is intriguingly female, suggesting the overwhelming influence of the various women who were associated with him throughout his life.[2]

Cocteau stresses that the Poet's response to the Hermaphrodite 'should be sensual,' recalling his sexual interaction with the living Mouth which transfers from the canvas to his hand in the opening sequence.[3] This reinforces the erotic fascination Cocteau obviously had with androgyny, and suggests a link between sexuality and parthenogenetic creativity in his work which he later articulated:

> Art is the child of a kind of incest, the lovemaking of self and self, a parthenogenesis ... How many geniuses appear to be 'poor specimens' because their creative instinct, satisfied in another domain, allows sexuality to function in the domain of the purely æsthetic, inclines it toward sterile forms.[4]

---

[1] Note that in the 1993 Marion Boyars edition of the screenplay, used for reference in this paper, there is an *erratum* which entitles the room '19' (like the opium den) instead of '23.'

[2] In his early days when Countess Anna de Noailles was a direct influence on him, Francis Steegmuller explains that '... it is not too much to say that Cocteau patterned much of his high style and his breathless deportment on the countess's. People noticed this and laughed, calling him an "*Anna-mâle*,"' 57–8. For more on the feminine influences on Cocteau's life and work —his mother, Misia Sert, Valentine Hugo, Coco Chanel and others— see Dominique Marny's *Les Belles de Cocteau*.

[3] *Two Screenplays*, 32, '[L]'image doit être sensuelle...', Le Sang d'un poète, 54.

[4] *Professional Secrets*, 295.

The Hermaphrodite, then, represents the possibility of Hegelian synthesis which lies at the end of the Mirror's corridor, but as already suggested it is also a figure of inherent confusion and angst. If androgyny equates with harmony in Cocteau's poetic system, this is obviously seldom possible in the 'real' world (in line with Aristophanes' account of the lost third gender), which explains his impulse to reach beyond it for an existential solution. This tension is revealed in the sign beneath the Hermaphrodite's loincloth which reads 'Danger of death.'[1] The forbidden nature of a sexuality outside of the social norm and its equation with the exotic nature of the Poet emphasizes the sense of social ostracization felt by Cocteau, and revealed in the sketches he published at this time.[2]

This inherent complexity contained in the figure of the Hermaphrodite is visualized in the 'confused jumble of shirts, petticoats, white ties and socks [which] appear, to the beating of drums, thrown about haphazardly.' Also, in the bickering male and female voices which argue —significantly— about whether or not to 'Turn the light off.'[3] Here we come to the crux of the coctelian æsthetic: the interminable dialectic between shadow and light, Dionysian chaos and Apollonian form, man and woman. It is also a direct reference to the Orphic cosmogony's union of Night with the first cosmic being, Phanes or Light, which engendered Heaven and Earth. It is the eternal balance and counterpoint of the Yang and Yin in Chinese philosophy, the active male versus the negative female principles of the universe, and explains Cocteau's 'celestial' association with the Orient and his dialectical representation of the Hermaphrodite's living versus artistic gender split. The sexual and pragmatic matters of life are masculine for Cocteau; the imaginative, photographically 'negative' matters of artistic creativity which lie beyond the Coctelian Mirror are feminine — and on the 'earthly' plane synthesis is eternally evasive.

Cocteau's solution is the harmonizing power of poetry which lies beyond ostracization and angst, thesis and antithesis. Its immortal qualities are embodied in the unending spiral which revolves near the Hermaphrodite's head, recalling the medieval notion of time as a vertical rather than horizontal construct and the Orphic belief in Time it-

---

[1] *The Blood of a Poet*, 32. 'Danger de mort,' *Le Sang d'un poète*, 55.

[2] For visual examples of this, see Cocteau's *Le Livre blanc*. The sketches it contains were first published in 1930.

[3] *Two Screenplays*, 35. '[U]n désordre de chemises, de jupons, de cravates blanches, de chaussettes, jetés n'importe où.' 'Voix d'homme : "Éteins." Voix de femme : "Non." Voix d'homme : "Si." Voix de femme : "Non...laisse..."' *Le Sang d'un poète*, 57.

self, or Cronos, as the first principle to exist in the universe.[1] Symbolically the Hermaphrodite is coiffed with a Louis XIV wig foregrounding
the seventeenth-century emphasis on poetry and theatre rather than
the Age of Enlightenment's preference for prose hinted at through the
Poet's eighteenth-century wig in the opening scene. But though the
Hermaphrodite may be Cocteau's ideal image of harmony, his innate
honesty acknowledges the impossibility of its acceptance in the 'real'
world, and leads him to represent an alternative figure of redemption:
pure Art as represented by the Woman-Statue. This becomes clear in
the fifth 'point' of the film's outer structure.

In terms of the male-female dialectic within Cocteau himself it is
fitting that the Woman-Statue should be the embodiment of both the
Platonic Ideal of Beauty and emotional frigidity.[2] Like the Coctelian
Poet she is an archetypal figure, and her power over events within the
film reinforces Cocteau's belief in the enduring qualities of Art which
outlast mortality, but —more importantly— are empowered to bring
harmony to mankind during its brief, ephemeral existence. Having succeeded in her mission of propelling the Poet towards his sacrificial destiny as *pharmakos*, her now superfluous human appearance drops off
her, and her symbolic power over the Poet's eighteenth-century friend
is evident in her magic appropriation of his cloak as she leaves the
'elegant' card game scene. The magic 'light metal ball' which moves
first to the spot where Dargelos last stood, and then to the point where
the Woman-Statue has exited at the top of the stairs, connects both as
potent symbols of the supernatural world of poetry and is itself a key
icon in Cocteau's work.[3] The spherical shape is semiotically reminiscent of the Orphic egg in which Light, represented here by the Woman-
Statue, was born through the union of Ether (the finite) and Night (the
infinite), directly linking poetry and artistic inspiration to the first
cosmic being.[4] This imagery enlarges on the shadow and light dialectic

---

[1] Cocteau's image of life was a flattened paper accordion pierced with a pin.
Frederick Brown explains: 'Unfolded, the accordion reiterates that puncture in
each of its folds, but the multiplicity is, he [Cocteau] contended, an illusion,' 331.

[2] The role of Woman in Cocteau's work is perplexing. His use of a young and
beautiful woman as Death or the Princess in the Orpheus trilogy has provoked
accusations of misogyny, but the fact that Art —which Cocteau revered above
all else— is also represented by a female image suggests the reverence he similarly felt towards the strong female influences in his own life and their harmonizing role in the mystical balance of the universe.

[3] *Two Screenplays*, 55. '[U]ne boule de métal léger,' *Le Sang d'un poète*, 88.

[4] The 'ball' or egg-shaped imagery can be traced throughout the Poet's rites of
passage within the Mirror's corridor: in the bullet which repeatedly kills the

already discussed, and reinforces the counterpoint of order and disorder which underlies all of Cocteau's work.

As the Woman-Statue moves back down the stairs of a now empty set, a bull mysteriously appears, and the cloak she wears spreads over it to combine them both in a sphinx-like union of woman and beast which holds a layering of meaning. This episode is particularly representative of the semiotic complexity in Cocteau's use of symbols. In the Orphic religion the bull is mythically linked to the Great God Dionysus whose influence in Cocteau's poetic system has already been considered, and its association with creativity and sexuality reinforces the Coctelian Dialectic. Dionysus was also given the epithet *Asterius* (the 'starry' one), which was similarly given to King Asterion of Crete who married the mythical Europa after she was seduced by Zeus in the form of a bull. The subtle, Orphic implications of the Coctelian Star gradually become apparent ...

Cocteau's message is far from ephemeral, however, and the 'torn, dismembered map of Europe' which appears on the Bull's back, pertinently stuck on with 'cow-dung,' transforms his private metaphysics into a stinging visual commentary on the recent World War.[1] The subsequent transformation of the bull's horns into a lyre and accompanying globe is an explicit reference to Orpheus' musical instrument and the power of poetry to charm the World away from the insanity of violence: 'We are never done destroying ourselves once the mechanism of thought begins to function.'[2] But this possible salvation is immediately contrasted with a deliberately crude transvestite parody of the Woman-Statue by two stagehands 'standing on the other's shoulders, draped like the woman.'[3] This 'false woman' is both a cynical self-parody of Cocteau's personal fascination with androgyny, and also a warning against 'false prophets' who mislead mankind in the name of

---

Mexican in the first hotel room, in the bells which cover the little girl in the second room, and in the ball of opium whose reflection creates the only point of light in the opium den. This symbolism is explored more deeply in the novel *Les Enfants terribles* which opens with a white (snow) ball and closes with a black (bullet) one, and barely pre-dates *Le Sang d'un poète*.

[1] *Two Screenplays*, 56, 58. '[U]ne carte géographique de l'Europe, arrachée, démembrée, collée avec de la bouse de vache.' *Le Sang d'un poète*, 90.

[2] *Professional Secrets*, 292. 'On n'a pas fini de se perdre dès que le mécanisme de la pensée se met en branle.' From *La Corrida du premier mai* (Paris: Grasset, 1957), 99.

[3] *Two Screenplays*, 58. 'Deux machinistes sur les épaules l'un de l'autre, drapés comme la femme...' *Le Sang d'un poète*, 91.

Art or moral principles.[1] As always, Cocteau leaves us with a question mark that the future alone can determine.

The final shot of the Woman-Statue foregrounds only those areas which are able to reflect light in a symbolic reference to its primeval power. Cocteau's representation of Art and Light as the film's sole survivors stresses the temporary, ephemeral condition of Man who thus needs to fulfil his life as he can:

> Our pessimism emanates from this void, from this non-being. Our optimism, from a wisdom which counsels us to take advantage of the parenthesis this void offers, to take advantage of it without seeking an answer to the riddle man will never answer for the good reason that there is no answer, that our celestial system is no more durable than our somatic sky, that duration is a legend, that the void is not a void, that eternity dupes us by offering a time which unrolls, whereas in reality the lump of space-and-time explodes, motionless, far from the concepts of space and time.[2]

Thus, though Cocteau rejects the 'escapism' of refusing to participate in life which he associated with Surrealism and Dadaism, he does seek a form of release from the nihilism of life's hermeneutic circle where lucid closure or synthesis are impossible: '... [A]s Goethe says, truth and reality are contradictory ...'[3] Like Plato he sensed that logic, when carried to its conclusion, leads only to insanity and the neoplatonic notion of annihilation as the ultimate impulse of all matter, when confronted with the existential paradox of Man's place in the cosmic equation. But where Plato sought to contain this by imposing a safe homogeneity on the artistic imagination, Cocteau turned to the 'obscure' power of poetry and imagination as the only possible means of synthesizing the symbiotic dialectic between order and disorder which controls human life.

---

[1] Ibid., 59. '[C]ette femme fausse'. Ibid., 91.

[2] *Professional Secrets*, 307. 'Notre pessimisme émane de ce vide, de ce non-vivre. Notre optimisme, d'une sagesse qui nous conseille de profiter sans chercher la solution d'un rébus dont l'homme n'aura jamais le dernier mot, pour la bonne raison qu'il n'y a pas de dernier mot, que notre système céleste n'est pas plus durable que notre ciel interne, que la durée est une fable, que le vide n'est pas vide, que l'éternité nous donne le change et nous présente un temps qui se déroule, alors que le bloc de l'espace et du temps explose, immobile, loin des concepts d'espace et de temps.' From *Journal d'un inconnu* (Paris: Grasset, 1953), 37.

[3] Ibid., 200. 'Selon le mot de Gœthe, la vérité et la réalité se contredisent.' From *La Belle et la bête*, 23 (Lundi matin — 7 heures 1/2).

Due to the impossibility of resolution on the mortal plane, the Coctelian Poet is necessarily doomed to suffer the fate of the ancient Greek *pharmakos* in line with the Orphic belief in regeneration. Though, like the Poet in *Le Sang d'un poète*, he may not perceive the ideal himself, he is a catalyst for others to sense the power of its existence.[1] He is the vehicle for Cocteau's Neoplatonism which necessarily reaches out beyond the confines of perceptual reality towards the possibility of a 'more-real-than-reality' which has now become the sign of our times in the late twentieth-century, an era of renewed existential questioning.

> His disciples said to him, 'When will the kingdom come?'
> Jesus said, 'It will not come by waiting for it. It will not be a matter of saying "Here it is" or "There it is." Rather, the kingdom of the father is spread out upon the earth, and men do not see it.'[2]

[1] This catalytic role is explored through Galaad in *Les Chevaliers de la Table Ronde*, premiered in 1937, who describes himself as 'only a poet': 'It [the grail] is within you. You see it once you are in harmony with yourself ... I shall never see it. I am the one who makes it visible to others.' *'Il est en vous. On le voit aussitôt qu'on est en règle avec soi-même. Vous le voyez tous, ma tâche est finie.'* *Œuvres complètes*, vol. 6 (Geneva: Marguerat, 1946), 281 (Act III).

[2] *The Gospel of St. Thomas*, in *Nag Hammadi Codex II*, 2–7, vol. 1, 'Saying' 113, 93.

Cinema Poetry: The Adaptation of Tristan et Iseult as L'Éternel Retour

Sara Maclean

After *L'Éternel Retour* was completed in 1943, Jean Cocteau boldly claimed that this film was the first instance ever of 'cinema poetry.' Although Cocteau did not direct the film, he took credit for its poetry, suggesting that it is to be found not only in the *mise-en-scène*, but also in the style and focus of his adaptation of the myth of *Tristan et Iseult*. Cocteau's conception emanates from his theoretical writings on theatre poetry. While he does not deny the possibility of visual poetry, he does propose that poetry must flow out from the very core of the work, which is the case with *L'Éternel Retour*.

Cocteau's concept of *theatre* poetry is outlined in the introduction to his play *Les Mariés de la Tour Eiffel* (1922) where he distinguishes 'theatre poetry' from 'poetry in the theatre':

> The action of my piece is pictorial, though the text itself is not. The fact is that I am trying to substitute a 'theater poetry' for the usual 'poetry in the theater.' 'Poetry in the theater' is a delicate lace, invisible at any considerable distance. 'Theater poetry' should be a coarse lace, a lace of rigging, a ship upon the sea ... The scenes fit together like the words of a poem.[1]

There are a number of important concepts contained in this passage. First, we have the implication that Cocteau's written text contains an ongoing action which is pictorial. On a basic level, Cocteau's screenplay for *L'Éternel Retour* contains extensive rubrics and specific de-

---

[1] 'L'action de ma pièce est imagée tandis que le texte ne l'est pas. J'essaie donc de substituer une "poésie de théâtre" à la "poésie au théâtre"[...] La poésie de théâtre serait une grosse dentelle; une dentelle en cordages, un navire sur la mer[...] Les scènes s'emboîtent comme les mots d'un poème.' Les Mariés de la Tour Eiffel, Œuvres complètes, vol. VII (Geneva: Marguerat, 1948), 14.

mands for the *mise-en-scène*. He supplied the director, Jean Delannoy, with a very specific vision of the world of the lovers. Cocteau's 'pictorial action' functions, however, at a deeper level, which corresponds but is not limited to the *mise-en-scène*. Instead, we are to understand that theatre and cinema-poetry are possessed of a visual action, a strength and tangibility which transcend text. Poetry is not just to be found in the language or meter of the film (the dialogue, the beautiful flourishes of the camera, dialogue or actor). The film as a totality is the poem; its construction should be tight and solid, its beauty deriving from the way in which it treats grand themes.

The choices that Cocteau made in his adaptation are consistent with his vision of cinema-poetry. This poetry is not only indicative of Cocteau's vision of how art should work, but is also telling of certain trends in his *œuvre*. Not only does Cocteau transpose elements of *Tristan et Iseult*; he also adds features of his own mythical world which come to light through our comparison of the original story to Cocteau's film. Jean Marais explains in his biography of Cocteau that 'as the myth is transferred from pen to pen, it is distorted, it gains strength ... enriched or obscured according to the author's personality.'[1] In *L'Éternel Retour* Cocteau gives rebirth to a grand, eternal narrative which features the poet's favourite themes: love and death, and eternal recurrence. These themes, combined with the distinctive camera work and *mise-en-scène*, some of which was Cocteau's doing and some the work of others, create the cinema poem that is *L'Éternel Retour*. The solidity of Cocteau's rigging in *L'Éternel Retour* can be attributed to his obsession with exactness and his faithfulness both to the spirit of the myth itself and to his vision of poetry. The uniqueness of this particular adaptation, however, stems from the bizarre and wonderful additions from Cocteau's personal arsenal.

Determining the extent of Cocteau's contribution during the filming is not easy. Few accounts of the project consider it to be the sole creation of Delannoy despite the fact that he directed the film. Some suggest that the resulting film was due to the union of the two different styles of Cocteau and Delannoy.[2] Most, however, almost ignore Delannoy altogether by claiming that Cocteau was responsible for decisions regarding casting, *mise-en-scène*, acting and camera work. While it is unlikely that we will ever know the exact extent of Cocteau's influence over the making of the film, Jean Marais (who played the role of Patrice in the film) provides us with an important clue in his autobiography *Histoires de ma vie*. He explains that Jean Cocteau joined the production

[1] Marais, *Jean Cocteau*, 111–12.

[2] Millecam, 154.

group fifteen days into filming and took a back-seat to Delannoy. Marais suggests that although Cocteau had little to do with the *mise- -en-scène* on site, he had made most of the decisions regarding casting, costumes and locations during pre-production. He had also contracted Georges Auric[1] to compose the soundtrack. According to Marais, Cocteau's presence affected every element of production.[2]

When comparing *L'Éternel Retour* to the Tristan myth, it is important to note that the edition from which Cocteau was working was that of Joseph Bédier (1864–1938), the French medievalist and literary historian.[3] Interestingly, Bédier himself tried to avoid a blending of modern concepts into older forms of thinking.[4] Bédier lists his sources: he culled segments of the story from different versions, attempting to make his rendition as complete as possible. He relied heavily on the works of Béroul, Anglo-Norman Thomas of Britain, and Eilhart von Oberg, with the addition of fragments from Gottfried von Strassburg and other ancient poets.[5] While, as Bédier himself admits and Cocteau explains, there can be no definitive version of the Tristan and Iseult myth, Cocteau's version is clearly indebted specifically to Bédier's work of 1900 and not earlier versions. Thus, we shall compare it with this particular version alone.

The first major difference between *Tristan et Iseult* and *L'Éternel Retour* is their starting points. The myth provides significantly more background than the film, starting with Tristan's birth. The myth explains that Tristan is the son of King Rivalen of Lyonesse, and his wife, Blanchefleur, who is the sister of King Mark of Cornwall.[6] King Rivalen is killed in battle and Blanchefleur dies shortly after giving birth

---

[1] Auric wrote the music for *Le Sang d'un poète* (1932), *L'Éternel Retour* (1943), *La Belle et la bête* (1946), *L'Aigle à deux têtes* (1947), *Ruy Blas* (1948), *Les Parents terribles* (1948), and *Orphée* (1950). His music contributes significantly to our sense of Cocteau's style.

[2] Marais, *Histoires de ma vie*, 147.

[3] Gilson, 21.

[4] Bédier, *The Romance of Tristan and Iseult*. Trans. Hilaire Belloc and Paul Rosenfeld (New York: Random House, 1965), i. All subsequent quotations in English are taken from this source. Bédier's preface was not available to us in French, but all other quotations in the original French are taken from: *Le Roman de Tristan et Iseult* (Paris: H. Piazza et Cie., 1910).

[5] Ibid., ii.

[6] Ibid., 3. Ibid., 22.

to her son, naming him 'sadness' before dying of sorrow.[1] Patrice of *L'Éternel Retour* is also an orphan because his parents drowned.[2] When Tristan's parents die, he does not become a ward of his uncle as we assume Patrice did. Instead he is raised by the loyal Marshal Rohalt, and taught the 'arts that go with barony' by the squire Gorvenal.[3] Tristan is abducted by Norwegians and, after a storm at sea, he finds himself lost in Cornwall. His hunting and musical skills convince a band of huntsmen to bring him to their lord, King Mark, in his castle Tintagel.[4] He lives there as a knight until one day three years later Rohalt arrives in Cornwall and tells King Mark that Tristan is in fact his nephew.[5]

While Patrice is also living with his uncle Mark in a castle, already there are pertinent differences between the two stories. First, the family in *L'Éternel Retour* is obviously rich and important enough to worry about scandal and, thus, feel obligated to have weddings with great pomp and legions of cheering townspeople.[6] Cocteau uses these moments to depict a family that lives like royalty, but he does not recreate the structure of Tristan or Iseult's family or their backgrounds. Furthermore, Patrice and Mark's relationship seems strong and stable: they are the only two who have formed a friendship within the family. Tristan, by contrast, has to prove his loyalty to King Mark.

The first proof of Tristan's loyalty to King Mark is established after he avenges the death of his father and seizes Lyonesse from his murderer, Duke Morgan.[7] Instead of staying and ruling over his land, he leaves it to Rohalt and returns to Cornwall to serve his uncle. Patrice clearly need not prove his loyalty to his uncle. Cocteau effectively

---

[1] Ibid., 4. '*Triste j'accouche, triste est la première fête que je te fais, à cause de toi j'ai tristesse à mourir. Et comme ainsi tu es venu sur terre par tristesse, tu auras le nom Tristan.*' Ibid., 23.

[2] The parents of Nathalie, the Iseult of the film, were also drowned, making the lovers, as Cocteau calls them, 'children of the sea.' Film: '*Nous sommes enfants de la mer.*' By making the family Norwegian, perhaps Cocteau is making a reference to Tristan's Norwegian kidnappers.

[3] Bédier, 5.

[4] Ibid., 8.

[5] Ibid., 10.

[6] When Mark sends Patrice away, he explains that he 'doesn't want tongues wagging.' Film: '*Il ne faut pas donner prise aux mauvaises langues.*' Earlier at their wedding, Mark and Nathalie wave from the castle balcony to an adoring throng of well-wishers.

[7] Bédier, 10.

L'Éternel Retour : The Modern Iseult and her Tristan
(Madeleine Sologne and Jean Marais)
Courtesy of the Museum of Modern Art Film Stills Archive
© Jean Cocteau/SODRAC (Montréal) 1998

replaces Tristan's fidelity and King Mark's paternal love and trust by creating a mutual affection between Patrice and Mark. While the former relationship might seem outdated and distant to a modern audience, the latter communicates a bond just as strong and more relevant within the film's context.

Tristan's next proof of loyalty takes place during his battle with the giant knight Morholt of Ireland who threatens to claim six hundred of Cornwall's young people.[1] When Tristan flees victorious, he ends up at the castle of Morholt's cousin, Iseult the Fair. She tends to his wounds for forty days until he is restored to good health and he leaves, '[knowing] himself to be in a land of peril'.[2] This part of the myth is recreated quite differently by Cocteau. Patrice leaves in his boat to find a wife for his Uncle, hoping thus to find him happiness. Patrice crosses the sea with his dog Moulouk aboard, a moment when the direction of Delannoy is especially successful. The two face ahead, exemplifying knights on a journey, as they advance towards the mountainous island. Like Tristan, Patrice arrives to be threatened by a giant warrior named 'Morholt,' but this time he isn't a knight but a raging drunk in the local pub. As Morholt abuses his fiancée Nathalie, holding her face to the bar and commanding her to 'drink!', our hero enters. Patrice (like Tristan) nobly fights Morholt; he is the only person brave enough to stand up to him. He is victorious, smashing a bottle over Morholt's head, but suffers a knife wound to his leg. He is carried out horizontally, his head lolling backward, with Nathalie following close behind. The effect created is reminiscent of a noble procession for a wounded knight. This image is a favourite symbol of Cocteau's (although he denied that he used symbols at all). The image of the wounded knight creates the 'wounded angel' image reminiscent of the limping black angel in Le Sang d'un poète.[3] Furthermore, Patrice seems as undefeatable as one blessed by heaven. Tristan is both beloved of and protected by God. Also like Tristan, Patrice displays his humanity when he is wounded, needing the mythical powers of healing administered by a beautiful woman.

Unlike Tristan, Patrice need not hide his identity from Nathalie. She and her guardian Anne heal him like Iseult did Tristan.[4] Like

---

[1] Ibid., 13.

[2] Ibid., 18. '[I]l comprit que les flots l'avaient jeté sur une terre de péril.' Ibid., 48.

[3] Patrice's later leg wound not only echoes the earlier wound, but also recalls that other limping legend, Œdipus.

[4] Both Iseult and Anne are 'skilled in philtres', Bédier, 18. '[H]abile aux philtres,' 48.

Tristan, Patrice, once healthy, cannot stay for he is endangered by re-venge-seekers. In the film, they take the form of Morholt, who comes to find Patrice to finish him off. Again, Nathalie saves Patrice, this time by skilfully using reverse psychology. She convinces Morholt that she would be happy to see him hurt Patrice but that it would be unwise con-sidering his position (Patrice's uncle owns the island). She tells Morholt that she will marry him the very next day provided he leaves at once. Thus, Nathalie saves Patrice twice. This doubling is an impor-tant feature of Cocteau's work that one encounters throughout the film. It is also a reproduction of a similar doubling in *Tristan et Iseult*.

When Tristan leaves Iseult and returns to King Mark, it is not long before he must face peril to serve his lord again. This time, King Mark's treacherous knights have counseled him to have a child to replace Tristan as heir, for they mistrust him. King Mark refuses, but capitu-lates at Tristan's urgings. When two white birds bring a golden strand of hair to his window, King Mark tells Tristan to find the woman with the golden hair. Tristan, realizing the danger, sets sail for Ireland once more to seek Iseult the Fair. Tristan slays a great dragon, winning Iseult's hand. Once more he is healed by Iseult but when she realizes who he is, she brandishes his own sword while he bathes and threat-ens to kill him to avenge the Morholt. Tristan talks his way out of the situation by claiming that he sought her from afar to marry her, prov-ing so by showing her the golden hair still attached to his armour.[1] Iseult begs a pardon from her father on his behalf, saving him from the court's vengeance.[2] This moment is replicated nicely when Nathalie endangers Patrice by telling Morholt to kill Patrice if he wants, direct-ing him to his room where he rests in his bed. Nathalie spares the life of *her* helpless 'knight' by talking Morholt out of killing Patrice, sav-ing him twice from death.

The next part of *Tristan et Iseult* has already been played out in *L'Éternel Retour*. When Tristan stands before the King of Ireland to claim Iseult, he announces that he will not marry her, but will deliver her to his uncle, King Mark. Iseult is shamed and angry. Likewise, ear-lier when Patrice asks Nathalie to marry his uncle, she is furious. He shames her further when later he laughingly asks if she thought he was going to propose to her. Like Iseult who became angry with 'hate swell[ing] her heart',[3] Nathalie exclaims 'you're such a child!'[4]

---

[1] Ibid., 27.
[2] Ibid., 28.
[3] Ibid., 32. '[E]t la haine gonflait son cœur.' Ibid., 74.
[4] Ibid. Film: 'Vous avez cinq ans.'

The circumstances in which the sets of lovers consume the philtre of love differ considerably. First of all, it is Iseult's mother who brews the potion, entrusting it to her maid Brangien: 'For this is its power: they who drink of it together love each other with their every single sense and with their every thought, forever, in life and in death'.[1] Unfortunately, once aboard the ship, Tristan and Iseult are 'athirst' and in Brangien's absence a serving maid gives them the potion to drink. When Brangien learns of the unhappy accident, she cries 'Cursed be the day I was born ... Iseult, my friend, and Tristan, you, you have drunk death together'.[2]

Cocteau lengthens the time between Patrice and Nathalie's departure from the island and the drinking of the potion. The potion has tellingly been put in a bottle labelled 'poison' by Anne who explains that 'those who drink it will love each other all of their lives and after.'[3] Patrice and Nathalie's nighttime journey is brief and uneventful. After docking, they travel up a steep hill leading to the castle on a single horse. As Nathalie's long white dress flows behind them, one is again given a visual glimpse of the myth. Within the modern setting, Cocteau demonstrates once again the pictorial quality of cinema-poetry. Upon arrival, Achille, Gertrude and Amédée watch through a window as Nathalie is led into the castle. She unpacks in her new room featuring high rafters, an enormous bed, and a fireplace; the room emits a foreboding atmosphere (it was, after all, the room of Mark's late wife Edithe). She places the bottle of 'poison' in a medicine cabinet ready for use despite the fact that she clearly does not believe in its power. Once Cocteau establishes the family's ill will towards Nathalie, the scene is set for the drinking of the potion. One stormy night the family leaves the young people (as well as Achille who gets drunk in the cellar) alone in the castle. Patrice and Nathalie are ensconced in front of a fire when Patrice decides that they shall consume a magic potion (meaning alcohol) to lift Nathalie's spirits. Achille, hiding behind the bar with a look of evil in his eyes, pours the 'poison' into the drinks at the moment when Patrice turns his head. As Nathalie lies on her back, we are treated to a point of view shot of upside down Patrice holding the glasses while chirping like a bird. The moment duly heightened, they drink together and a magical scene ensues. They lie on their backs in front of the fire, Nathalie in a flowing white gown

---

[1] Ibid. *'Car telle est sa vertu: ceux qui en boiront ensemble s'aimeront de tous leur sens et de toute leur pensée, à toujours, dans la vie et dans la mort.'* Ibid.

[2] Bédier, 33. *'[M]audit soit le jour où je suis née...Iseult, amie, et vous, Tristan, c'est votre mort que vous avez bue!'* Ibid., 76

[3] Film: *'Ceux qui le boivent s'aiment toute la vie et après la vie.'*

and Patrice in a sweater with a pattern resembling a coat of arms. They watch the shadows of the fire on the ceiling and Nathalie wonders 'What's wrong with me? It's not marvelous and it is marvelous, I'm afraid.'[1] Patrice responds by comparing himself to Ben Franklin chasing lightning; he reassures her that he will protect her from evil. As Nathalie discovers 'c'est toi, c'est toi,' the poison bottle is discovered. 'We got off well'[2] she tells Patrice, thankful that Achille did not use real poison.

After Tristan and Iseult drink the potion, it is not long before they fall in love and consummate the relationship realizing that they shall never 'know joy without pain again'.[3] It takes their modern counterparts a little longer since neither of them believe in the potion. What Cocteau has done, apparently realizing that his audience with their modern sensibilities may well not believe in the potion either, is create an effective psychological motivation for what ensues. We have watched Patrice and Nathalie spend time together, enjoy each other's company and already have had hints that they have feelings for each other. When they fall in love not long after spending a romantic evening together, it is believable.

The difference in the traitors' relationships to the pairs of lovers is also an important distinction between the myth and the film. In *Tristan et Iseult*, it is the King's knights Denoalen, Andret, Gondoïne, and Guenelon who urge King Mark to stop trusting Tristan. While he does not believe the knights, and sees no proof of the affair, King Mark 'could not kill his uneasy thought'[4] and banishes Tristan, telling him that he will doubtless be recalled soon. This event is replicated in *L'Éternel Retour*. After finding Nathalie out of bed claiming to be unable to sleep, Mark goes to Patrice who is smoking at his window. He tells him to take a trip 'to prevent tongues from wagging.'[5] It is important to note that it is his sister Gertrude and her son Achille the dwarf (and her husband Amédée, half-heartedly) who have planted the 'bug' in Mark's ear. This is a smooth replacement for the knights who are jealous of Tristan's power and sway over the King. Instead, Gertrude feels that her son Achille, whom she treats like a baby despite his 22 years of age, deserves to have a more prominent position in the house-

---

[1] Ibid: *'Qu'est-ce que j'ai? [...] Non, ce n'est pas merveilleux et en même temps c'est merveilleux. [...] Patrice, j'ai peur.'*

[2] Ibid: *'Nous l'avons échappé belle.'*

[3] Bédier, 35. *'[E]t jamais plus vous n'aurez de joie sans douleur.'* 80.

[4] Ibid., 44. *'[N]e put secouer le maléfice...'* Ibid., 93.

[5] See p. 46, note 6 *supra*.

hold. She wants Mark to treat the three of them with warmth and respect despite the fact that she complains incessantly and plots end-
lessly against him and the more urgent fact that her son listens at doors
and has murdered at least one neighbourhood pet. In fact, our first encounter with Achille shows him stealing a gun from his father's collection in order to shoot a dog. Thus, we immediately realize that he has
a great capacity for evil; the opening shots of the film show him manipulate, steal, lie, eavesdrop and kill. No other character possesses
the power that Achille does. Significantly, when King Mark wishes to
know whether or not Tristan is sneaking back to the castle to see Iseult,
he consults an evil little dwarf named Frocin whom Bédier refers to as
an evil little man.[1] The borrowing of the evil dwarf figure from *Tristan
et Iseult* adds a great deal to the atmosphere of medieval magic and
mystery which Cocteau was fostering. Achille possesses a boundless capacity for evil, an air of unnaturalness and an ability to evade the family's 'eyes,' hiding who-knows-where only to reappear magically at
opportune moments. Achille resembles Frocin who effectively flees
King Mark's wrath twice. Frocin is a seer who reveals damning information about the couple to King Mark, struggling to provide evidence
much like Achille. Achille is not only a powerful figure in *L'Éternel
Retour*; he is also a psychologically complex and believable modern
character who evokes the dark force of evil at work in *Tristan et Iseult*.

The character of Gertrude is one of Cocteau's stock women. She hates
happiness and youth, and controls her son and husband. Amédée is all
but absent in the film, characteristic of Cocteau's fathers. They plot
against their own family, with some success. Frocin and the knights
convince King Mark, and Achille and Gertrude convince Mark to wait in
the garden by the pond where the lovers will meet. In the myth Tristan
and Iseult see King Mark's reflection in the stream and pretend that
Tristan has summoned Iseult to ask her to beg pardon from the king.
This encounter is transposed into the film. Patrice signals knowingly to
Nathalie with his cigarette while he loudly asks her to convince Mark
that they are blameless. Luckily, Tristan and Patrice are successful and
their uncles ask them to stay.

L'Éternel Retour continues to replicate *Tristan et Iseult* at this point.
While Tristan stays, the dwarf devises a further test. He sprinkles
flour between the beds of Tristan and the Queen to catch his footprints
if he goes to her to bid her farewell before he leaves on a journey. King
Mark plans to burn both Tristan and Iseult at the stake in retaliation,
but they escape. Likewise, Patrice's family devise a test of his honour.
They all pretend to leave one night and when Patrice and Nathalie fi-

---

[1] Bédier, 47–8.

nally meet in her bed, the lights are turned on and the family surrounds them. Mark decides to send Nathalie back to her island while Patrice is banished. When the pairs of lovers reunite, it isn't until after Tristan rescues Iseult from a band of lepers and Patrice steals Nathalie out of the car that Gertrude and Achille are driving to the island. Iseult, Tristan and his dog Hodain live in a hut in the forest for one year and have many adventures before they are discovered by the King. Nathalie, Patrice and his dog Moulouk end up in a small hut in the snow where they are truly happy. Cocteau does not spend much time developing this period; instead, we are only witness to their last morning in the hut before they are discovered.

Stephen Harvey remarks that Cocteau's love stories are particularly sexless. Indeed, at this point in the film, when the lovers can be open with their love, nothing is shown; while we may assume that they make love, Cocteau is not being explicit. The erotic imagery of L'Éternel Retour, explains Ashton, is 'bound up with the self — or its idealization ...'.[1] The story Jean Marais tells in Histoires de ma vie about Cocteau insisting that he and Madeleine Sologne visit the hairdresser together to be certain that they obtain the identical shade of blonde takes on new significance.[2] This explanation only takes us so far, however, as Tristan and Iseult also have striking blonde locks. But Ashton is right to point out the sexlessness of the film. One does not get the sense that the lovers ever consummate their relationship, except, perhaps, when they flee to the log cabin. Tristan and Iseult on the other hand, clearly have a sexual relationship. From their first voyage together, after drinking the potion, Bédier recounts: 'The lovers held each other; life and desire trembled through their youth ... [a]nd as evening fell ... they gave themselves up utterly to love'.[3] Later, on Iseult's wedding night, 'to conceal the Queen's dishonour and save her from death,' her maid Brangien took her place in the wedding bed.[4] It seems clear that there are striking differences in Nathalie and Patrice's characters. She seems more sad but often more wise than Patrice who is light-hearted and extroverted. Physically, however, they could be brother and sister and this, judging from Cocteau's body of

---

[1] In "The Mask in the Mirror: the Movies of Jean Cocteau", Arthur King Peters (ed.), Jean Cocteau and the French Scene (New York: Abbeville Press, 1984), 202.

[2] Marais, 148.

[3] Bédier, 35. 'Les amants s'étreignirent; dans leurs beaux corps frémissaient le désir et la vie... Et, quand le soir tomba... ils s'abandonnèrent à l'amour.' 35.

[4] Ibid., 37. '[A]fin de cacher le déshonneur de la reine et pour la sauver de la mort...' Ibid., 82.

work (especially *Les Enfants terribles*), is no accident. As Ashton points out, one is struck by the fact that the lovers could be mirror images of each other. Interestingly, in the film's publicity poster, Marais appears with his natural darker hair, perhaps because the couple looks better together that way. Cocteau's mirror-image lovers, who barely touch each other, might seem surprising to the uninitiated, but looking back at his work as a whole, it would have been odd had the characters been any different.

The happy times end suddenly when both Iseult and Nathalie discover Mark's glove. King Mark sees Tristan and Iseult sleeping together with the naked blade of a sword between them, proof of their chastity. He forgives them and leaves his glove, sword and ring to show his forgiveness. Mark on the other hand, comes to take Nathalie back to the castle. She finds the glove before Patrice leaves the cabin and waits for Mark to arrive. Both Nathalie and Iseult are dreadfully unhappy. When Tristan and Patrice find their love-huts empty, they set off on voyages.

At this point, Cocteau finds a controversial way to deal with the introduction of the second Iseult figure. He has Patrice end up living for a while at a garage managed by a friend of his. The friend's unconventional sister, Nathalie, who smokes and cavorts with the men, lives with them and falls in love with Patrice. Many criticized the garage scene claiming that it did not fit the rest of the film. Cocteau defended his choice, stating that:

> ... it was precisely in that garage that poetry functioned the best. In understanding the desertion of the brother and sister, in their innate and almost organic failure to understand grace, I touch poetry and approach the terrible mysteries of love.[1]

Indeed, condemning the garage scene ignores the very essence of *L'Éternel Retour*. What is marvelous about this particular scene is the way in which it typifies the reality of the time in which the film is set, in addition to its adherence to the legend. In *Tristan et Iseult*, Tristan (after a long journey), ends up in the castle of Kahedrin, a new friend, and his beautiful sister Iseult aux Blanches Mains. Upon hearing that Iseult the Fair is happy with King Mark, he agrees to wed his friend's sister. The rest of the story unfolds similarly in the myth and the film with a few important exceptions. Tristan does wed Iseult aux

---

[1] *Journals*, 129. '[C]'est justement dans ce garage que la poésie fonctionne mieux. En effet, à comprendre l'abandon du frère et de la sœur, à leur méconnaissance innée et comme organique de la grâce, on la touche du doigt et j'approche des terribles mystères de l'amour.' *La Difficulté d'être* (Paris: Éditions du Rocher, 1989), 60.

Blanches Mains but lies and says that he can not embrace her due to a vow he made.[1] Kahedrin is angered, as is Patrice's friend when he learns that he covets another woman. Both friends agree, however, to return to the relevant castles with the hero for one last proof that Iseult/Nathalie no longer loves him. While Patrice is convinced because Nathalie doesn't come to the window as he chirps, Tristan is foiled by an ugly rumour that he fled an enemy who challenged him in Iseult's name. Tristan is later wounded in battle.

Patrice's fate is somewhat different. As he whistles at the castle window, the evil dwarf Achille appears and takes aim with a shotgun. As Patrice retreats, Achille fires, his second murder attempt in the film. Thus the film is opened and closed with the ruthless act of a bitter little man. Yet another doubling is used in the film; this one owes nothing to the myth. It proves, however, that even when injecting his own elements and characters, Cocteau picks up the meter and poetry of the myth and reshapes it successfully. The stories end the same way, with the mortal lie of Iseult/Nathalie II. As the boats return bearing Iseult and Nathalie, their doubles lie about the colour of the scarf tied to the boats' masts, convincing Tristan and Patrice that their loves have not returned to them. They both die almost instantly, having lost all hope.

L'Éternel Retour adapts Tristan et Iseult quite successfully. The themes of consuming love that extends beyond death and of evil that can exist due to jealousy are picked up by Cocteau and modified, to create a fascinating study of the family and forbidden love. But his adaptation is not simply a faithful rendition with injections of his style or characters. Instead, he modernizes elements of the myth, adding elements of his personal mythology, with an eye to the poetry and spirit of the original. He is able to blend diverse elements, some of which are personal, some universal, some ancient and some modern. His fusion of these seemingly incompatible components is possible due to his concept of cinema-poetry. As the title of the film suggests, heroes and their myths are reborn eternally without their knowing it. The fact that Patrice and Nathalie are sometimes unrecognizable as Tristan and Iseult, and at other times are identical to them is essential. Cocteau is yet again playing with mirrors that never reflect exactly what one expects.

---

[1] Bédier, 115.

The Beauty of the Philosophical Beast: Towards the Existential Poetry of La Belle et la bête

Dario P. Del Degan

In his film *La Belle et la bête* (1946), Jean Cocteau reveals that the beauty of being human is possessing freedom of choice. Cocteau's film subtly, yet clearly, explores the existential concept of human freedom by employing cinematic magic to situate the viewer simultaneously within two worlds. The film features characters who create their own destinies through the decisions they make as opposed to having their outcomes prescribed by fate. The subject of ontology in *La Belle et la bête* arises from a phenomenological reading of the film. By considering one's experience of entering the world of the film and then returning to the world of so-called objective reality, the transcendental viewer is compelled to explore the nature of human existence after leaving a realm which shatters preconceived notions of what constitutes reality. This examination positions Cocteau's æsthetic within the greater theoretical cinematic context, compares his æsthetic to phenomenological cinematic discourse, and examines the existential content of the film arising from this æsthetic positioning. By using the medium of cinema to broach the subject of human freedom, Cocteau's *La Belle et la bête* can be considered 'existential poetry' because he utilizes artistic significant form to explore ontology.

In *La Belle et la bête*, Cocteau exploits the medium of cinema to create a world which obfuscates reality and illusion. To succeed in creating a dream-like fantasy world, Cocteau asks the viewer to be receptive to the concept of miracles. In a projection at the outset of the film, the poet asks the viewer to adopt a childlike naïveté:

> Children believe what they are told and doubt it not.
> They *believe* that a rose that is picked can bring on trouble in a family.

> They *believe* that the hands of a human beast that kills begin to smoke
> and that this beast is ashamed when a maiden dwells in his house. They
> believe a thousand other very naïve things.
>   I am asking of you a little of this naïveté now, and, to bring us all good
> fortune, let me say four magic words, the veritable 'open sesame' of child-
> hood:
>   Once upon a time ...[1]

Cocteau's skilful use of cinematic magic makes it easy for the viewer
to surrender his or her imagination to the world on the screen. The well
paced immersion of special effects into the film transforms scenes of
seeming reality into fantasy almost without notice. The visual impact
of the film is undoubtedly affecting. However, according to Cocteau, for
art to be considered 'poetry,' it must be more than affecting; it must engage the recipient's imagination within the world of the creation.[2]
    Cocteau's use of special effects in *La Belle et la bête* engages the
viewer's imagination. His manipulation of reality in the world of the
film metaphorically suggests that one can also manipulate one's own
reality through the decisions one makes. The existential poetry of *La
Belle et la bête* arises from Cocteau's orchestration of special effects to
create a new, magical reality. Cocteau's poetics veers closely to phenomenological æsthetic discourse because he emphasizes the importance of both the emotional and intellectual response of a recipient to a
work of art. What becomes enlightening, by analysing Cocteau's æsthetic function within *La Belle et la bête*, is discovering the way in
which the film simultaneously situates the viewer within two reali-

---

[1] Jean Cocteau, *Beauty and the Beast: The Shooting Script*, edited by Robert M.
Hammond. (New York: New York University Press, 1970), 4. '*L'enfance croit ce
qu'on lui raconte et ne le met pas en doute.*

Elle croit *qu'une rose qu'on cueille peut attirer des drames dans une famille.*

Elle croit *que les mains d'une bête humaine qui tue se mettent à fumer et que
cette bête en a honte lorsqu'une jeune fille habite sa maison.*

Elle croit mille autres choses bien naïves.

*C'est un peu de cette naïveté que je vous demande et, pour nous porter chance à
tous, laissez-moi vous dire quatre mots magiques, véritable "sésame ouvre-toi" de
l'enfance:*

IL ETAIT UNE FOIS...' La Belle et la bête (Moulins: Éditions Ipomée, 1988),
23.

[2] Jean Cocteau, *Cocteau on the Film*, conversation recorded by André Fraigneau,
translated by Vera Traill. (New York: Dover Publications, 1972), 64. *Entretiens
sur le cinématographe* (Paris: Pierre Belfond, 1973), 45. All subsequent quotations from the original French are taken from this source.

ties: the world projected onto the screen, and the world of the spectator watching the screen. The artistic choices Cocteau makes to displace reality has implications on one's interpretation of the film. A consideration of Cocteau's poetics offers an ideal starting point for any interpretative journey into the film because it was his poetics which informed his æsthetic choices. The methodology used in this voyage starts with the roots of Cocteau's æsthetic and then proceeds to build upon various cinematic theories used to enlighten his æsthetic.

The atmosphere of *La Belle et la bête* invites the spectator to become emotionally engaged within the fantasy on the screen. Cocteau claims in *Diary of a Film* that the viewer determines whether *La Belle et la bête* is poetic:

> My method is simple; not to aim at poetry. That must come of its own accord. The very word whispered will frighten it away. I shall try to build a table. It will be up to you to eat at it, to criticize it, or to chop it up for firewood.[1]

Cocteau's film encourages the viewer to search for poetry by presenting a montage of phenomenal, magical images painted with beautiful special effects. Poetry enters the film because Cocteau strives to create a charming spectacle that will transport the viewer to a state of elation.

Cocteau's poetics seems to be congruent with philosopher Clive Bell's æsthetic notion that the function of art is to elevate one from daily concerns by manipulating artistic form. Bell, in 'The Æsthetic Hypothesis,' defines art as the use of significant form to produce a subjective æsthetic emotion. He describes an æsthetic emotion as a feeling of leaving the world of human activity for a world of exaltation and bliss because '[f]or a moment we are shut off from human interests; our anticipations and memories are arrested; we are lifted above the stream of life.'[2] Cocteau's *La Belle et la bête* seems to correspond with Bell's notion of æsthetics because it elevates the viewer from his or her daily concerns into a world of dreams. Although dreams lack the significant form of art works, Cocteau's artistic waking dream fulfils

---

[1] Jean Cocteau, *Diary of a Film (La Belle et la bête)*, translated by Ronald Duncan (London: Dennis Dobson, Limited, 1950), 15. '*Ma méthode est simple: ne pas me mêler de poésie. Elle doit venir d'elle-même. Son seul nom prononcé bas l'effarouche. J'essaie de construire une table. À vous, ensuite, d'y manger, de l'interroger ou de faire du feu avec.*' *La Belle et la bête, journal d'un film* (Monaco: Éditions du Rocher, 1958), 17. All subsequent quotations in French are from this source.

[2] Clive Bell, 'The Æsthetic Hypothesis,' *Art* (London: Chatto and Windus, 1949), 25.

Bell's depiction of art by using cinematic significant form to create a dreamlike reality. *La Belle et la bête* resembles a dream because it contains beautifully integrated special effects juxtaposed with scenes of seeming reality. Bell seems to be correct in identifying one's emotional reaction to a work as central to its consideration as art. However, in *Cocteau on the Film*, Cocteau cautions against regarding art only from its emotive qualities because doing so could reduce it as a means to escape the world.[1]

In discussing *La Belle et la bête* Cocteau claims that 'genuine poetry has no use for evasion. What it wants is *invasion*, that is, that the soul be invaded with words and objects which ... impel it to plunge deep into itself.'[2] Cocteau argues that poetry is detached from art proper because 'poetry is that "something else" in great art that moves us, something that is not of the art itself.'[3] When discussing the poetry of his films, Cocteau claims that the scenes which he feels best express his poetry, citing the garage scene in *L'Éternel Retour* and the farm-yard scene in *La Belle et la bête*, often disappoint audiences because they require the viewer to actively search for the poetry. Cocteau complains that 'it's through sheer frivolous laziness that the public prefers poetic poetry, fantastic fairy plays, and rebels against anything that requires a personal effort of fantasy and magic.'[4] Although Cocteau's comment may be construed as harsh, it stresses the importance of the recipient's participation with a work of art.

La Belle et la bête begins and ends with the flight of an arrow. Cocteau employs a similar technique in *Le Sang d'un poète* by enclosing the events of the film between a shot of a smokestack at the beginning of the film and its crumbling to pieces at the end. One could argue that this technique attempts to break temporal unity by claiming that the events of the film occur during the short time it takes for the arrows to hit their targets or for the smokestack to crumble to the ground. By manipulating time, Cocteau highlights the paradox in which the viewer

---

[1] *Cocteau on the Film*, 64. *Entretiens*, 45-46.

[2] Ibid. '*Or, l'évasion n'a que faire avec la poésie véritable. C'est l'invasion qui compte, c'est-à-dire que l'âme soit envahie par des termes ou des objets qui, ne présentant pas un aspect ailé, l'obligent à s'enfoncer en elle-même.*' Ibid., cited in René Gilson, *Jean Cocteau* (Paris: Seghers, 1964–69), 117.

[3] Lynn Hoggard, 'Writing with the Ink of Light: Jean Cocteau's *Beauty and the Beast*,' *Film and Literature*, edited by Wendell Aycock and Michael Schoenecke (Lubbock: Texas Tech University Press, 1988), 130.

[4] Cocteau, *Cocteau on the Film*, 64. '*C'est donc par simple paresse frivole que le public préfère la poésie poétique, la féerie fantastique et répugne à ce qui exige de lui un effort personnel de fantastique ou de féerie.*' *Entretiens*, 46.

finds him or herself when viewing a film. In 'A Sense of Magic: Reality and Illusion in Cocteau's *Beauty and the Beast*,' David Galef explains that the camera, recording objectively, projects an appearance of reality while the experience of viewing a film, producing innumerable illusions, creates a dream-like quality.[1] Cocteau's manipulation of temporal reality, by enclosing the events of *La Belle et la bête* during the flight of an arrow, suggests that Cocteau consciously sought to have the viewer ponder issues of reality by manipulating conceived notions of it. For instance, Beauty and the Beast's temporal realities are reversed; he tells her that when it is morning in her domain, it is night in his. This challenges the viewer's preconceived notions of time and his or her relation to it. The technique suggests that time is only a subjective construct of human understanding.

It seems clear that Cocteau utilizes the tools of cinema to engage the viewer's imagination and to transcend the material world. The question then becomes: how does film transform the viewer into a transcendental subject? The answer lies in the way in which cinema creates this strange existence between reality and illusion. Jean-Louis Baudry, in 'Ideological Effects of the Basic Cinematographic Apparatus,' argues that film transforms the viewer into a 'transcendental subject' because the continuous unfolding of a universe before one's eyes disconnects one's mind from one's body allowing one's imagination to roam freely within the world of the spectacle.[2] He states that film, like the plastic arts, creates a metaphysical reality by creating a space of an ideal vision 'and in this way asserts the necessity of a transcendence — metaphorically (by the unknown to which it appeals ...) and metonymically (by the displacement that it seems to carry out; a subject is both "in place of" and "a part for the whole").'[3] According to Baudry, Western easel painting (from which film is derivative) presents 'a motionless and continuous whole'; it 'elaborates a total vision which corresponds to the

[1] David Galef, 'A Sense of Magic: Reality and Illusion in Cocteau's *Beauty and the Beast*,' *Literature Film Quarterly* 12:2 (1984), 96.

[2] Jean-Louis Baudry, 'Ideological Effects of the Basic Cinematographic Apparatus,' *Movies and Methods Volume II*, translated by Alan Williams, edited by Bill Nichols (Berkeley: University of California Press, 1985), 536. '[S]ujet transcendantal', 'Effets idéologiques produits par l'appareil de base' in *L'Effet cinéma* (Paris: Éditions Albatros, 1978), 20. All subequents quotations from Baudry are taken from these sources.

[3] Ibid., 534–5. '[E]t assure, de la sorte, métaphoriquement (par l'inconnu qu'elle appelle, et il faut rappeler ici la place structurale qui tient le point de fuite) et métoniquement (par le déplacement qu'elle semble opérer: un sujet est à la fois un "à-la-place-de" et "une partie-pour-le-tout")'. Ibid., 17.

idealist conception of the fullness and homogeneity of "being."[1] Baudry's theory suggests that art works engage recipients by depicting a universal subject with which all recipients can identify. Baudry transfers the notion of subject identification in art to film by citing André Bazin's claim that '[b]ehind what the film gives us to see ... [is] the existence of an "other world" of phenomena, of a soul or of any other spiritual principle. It is in this revelation, above all, of a spiritual presence, that I propose we seek Poetry.'[2] An amalgamation of Baudry and Bazin's theories suggests that while film engages a viewer through identification with a universal subject, once the viewer is absorbed within the world of the film, the viewer exists in a daydream state and is receptive to accepting the world on the screen as the 'real' world.

Cocteau would probably concur with Bazin that cinematic poetry reveals itself only once the viewer enters the daydream state since Cocteau utilizes cinematic magic to create the world of *La Belle et la bête*. Baudry and Bazin's notion of the 'daydreaming viewer' illuminates the way *La Belle et la bête* can be both emotionally mesmerizing and intellectually stimulating at the same time. The daydreaming viewer accepts the magic of the film by becoming the transcendental subject, yet retains his or her cognitive faculties with respect to subject identification with the characters of the film. For instance, one accepts the magic of Beauty being able to appear in different locations by putting on a magic glove while still being able to question whether Beauty makes the correct decision to stay with her Father rather than returning to the Beast. The daydreaming viewer accepts the world of magic but always retains his or her ability to contemplate within that world. Thus, Cocteau's use of cinematic magic serves to engage the viewer.

Galef illustrates that there are three types of magic integral to creating atmosphere in Cocteau's film. The simplest form of magic includes the dematerialization or animation of inanimate objects: for instance, the transformation of Beauty's magic necklace into a burned rope when in the hands of her greedy sister.[3] A second type of magic consists of the ordinary effects of cinema: a breeze blowing leaves produced by a fan, or the eerie glare created from an arc lamp. A third type of magic falls be-

---

[1] Ibid., 535. '[U]n ensemble immobile et sans intervalle élabore une vision pleine qui répond à la conception idéaliste de la plénitude de l'homogénéité de l'"être".' Ibid.

[2] Ibid., 535. 'Derrière ce que le film donne à voir, ce n'est point l'existence des atomes que nous sommes conduits à rechercher, mais plutôt celle d'un au-delà des phénomènes, d'une âme ou de tout autre principe spirituel. La poésie, c'est dans cette révélation, avant tout, d'une présence spirituelle que je vous propose de la chercher.' Ibid., 18.

[3] Galef, *Literature Film Quarterly*, 97.

tween cinematic effects and cinematic tricks: scenes which could be staged theatrically but would lose their impact. For instance, the Beast on stage would appear like a person in a beast suit. However, in Cocteau's film, the Beast is huge, fearsome, and believable; in some close-up shots the Beast's growling face takes up the entire frame. 'Many of the effects in the Beast's castle are also semi-magical'; in the world of the film the viewer accepts the reality of, 'for example, a human-arm candelabra.'[1] Galef notices that although these effects are intermingled throughout the film, the film does exhibit a subtle progression in its use of special effects. At the beginning, the film uses ordinary cinematic effects to heighten the awareness of the setting. As the fantasy becomes more prominent, Cocteau employs more and more special effects. Galef's cognizance of the paced immersion of special effects into the film strongly suggests that Cocteau intentionally sought to make the fantasy appear as reality by slowly immersing the viewer into the world of the film so as not to draw attention to the fact that this world is a product of cinematic magic and manipulation. Cocteau's moderate and appropriate use of cinematic magic creates, temporarily, a metaphysical reality for the viewer. It may not be an empirically tangible world, but rather, a spiritual and emotional world where tears turn into diamonds and disembodied hands pour wine.

Cocteau's use of cinematic magic not only affects the viewer emotionally but also intellectually. Baudry describes the camera as a roving eye which can capture different images from different angles.[2] Baudry claims that the 'movability of the camera seems to fulfil the most favorable conditions for the manifestation of the "transcendental subject."'[3] Through image and sound, the camera produces a fantasized reality which manifests, 'in a hallucinatory manner the belief in the omnipotence of thought.'[4] The moving camera creates a new world; but it is a transformed world of objective reality. For Baudry, the cinematic image will always be an image of something by which the viewer, through a deliberate act of consciousness, derives meaning. The roving eye of the camera provides the images while the viewer provides the meaning. Cocteau seems to implement Baudry's theory by aiming for verism in his film.

---

[1] Ibid., 97.

[2] Baudry, *Movies and Methods Volume II*, 536. *L'Effet cinéma*, 19.

[3] Ibid., 537. '*Les mouvements de la caméra semblent réaliser les conditions les plus favorables à la manifestation d'un sujet transcendantal.*' Ibid., 20.

[4] Ibid., 537 and 541, note 10. '*Le cinéma manifesterait d'une manière hallucinatoire la croyance en la toute puissance de la pensée...*' Ibid.

In *La Belle et la bête* Cocteau strives to create a work of art that is able to transcend itself and achieve unreal realism ('le réalisme irréel') in order to lead the viewer 'to glimpse [at] the mystery and marvel of life.'[1] Cocteau creates a waking dream which focuses on realistic detail but which aims for verism ('vérisme') to reveal 'a truth that, because it combines consciousness with unconsciousness, becomes more true than truth ('plus vrai que le vrai').' Verism is particularly suited to cinema because in film the viewer sees as fact 'not only the world of the real, but that of the unreal as well.' Cocteau creates this double world using trick shots such as the scene where Beauty is pulled along on a dolly to create the effect that she is floating through the Beast's castle. The effect creates an image absorbed by the senses but which the mind must interpret. Lynn Hoggard, in 'Writing with the Ink of Light: Jean Cocteau's *Beauty and the Beast*,' notices that in adapting the short story for film, Cocteau consciously sought to 'transform verbal narrative into visual form.' Images drive the narrative of the film; for instance, 'Beauty's words of love were changed to a look of love.'[2] Cocteau attempts to circumvent reason in order to reach emotion by suggesting that the viewer must provide the context for the images.

To achieve this higher truth of verism, Cocteau transforms the eye of the camera into the eye of the viewer. He refers to the camera as the most indiscreet and immodest eye ('La caméra est l'œil le plus indiscret et le plus impudique.')[3] Thus, Cocteau shoots the film with the viewer's reaction in mind. For instance, 'when Beauty's father is about to pluck the forbidden rose in the Beast's garden,' the viewer realizes that it is he or she who takes on the gaze of the Beast 'looking at the father as potential prey.'[4] Another instance where the camera acts as the eye of the viewer occurs in one of the scenes featuring the Beast's magic mirror. When Beauty enters her room in the Beast's castle for the first time, she discovers a mirror on the vanity table. In this scene, the viewer possesses a multi-leveled viewing position since the camera can portray the world like a mirror or transcend objective reality. The question becomes: who is viewing whom? Cocteau provides the viewer with a privileged keyhole view of the Beast's castle; however, once inside, statues open their eyes and stare at the intruder, disrupting the distanced gaze of the viewer. As the statues look at the intruder in the

---

[1] Hoggard, *Film and Literature*, 132.

[2] Ibid., 132.

[3] Jean Cocteau, *Entretiens autour du cinématographe* (Paris: Editions André Bonne, 1951), 106.

[4] Hoggard, *Film and Literature*, 132.

castle (Beauty's Father), they also transform the viewer into the intruder. Suddenly, it is the viewer who has penetrated the castle.

Entering the world of film provides an interesting experience for the viewer. Dudley Andrew, in 'The Neglected Tradition of Phenomenology in Film Theory,' argues that the foremost function of cinema is to create an experience for the viewer. Andrew speaks of the 'pressing tasks of describing the peculiar way meaning is experienced in cinema' (the phenomenological analysis of film).[1] Andrew conceives of phenomenological cinematic discourse as being concerned with the 'perceptual, imaginative, and æsthetic experience' of watching a film.[2] For Andrew, the value of applying phenomenology to cinema is that it attempts to embrace the receptive experience of watching a film:

> [F]rom the most primitive descriptions of the peculiarities of perception in cinema, to our emotional involvement in the image, to the momentum of a narrative, to the constitution of a cinematic world, to the description of types of worlds (or genres) and to the life of our interpretation of them, phenomenology claims to be closer, not necessarily to truth, but to cinema and our experience of it.[3]

Andrew seems to assert that the experience of viewing film is the connective tissue which links the viewer and the viewed. Cocteau maintained a similar poetic æsthetic. When the statue opens its eyes in *La Belle et la bête* and turns to the viewer, or blows smoke as it turns its head, Cocteau seeks to intrigue the viewer within this strange, new world and not have him or her scrutinize the kinetic signs. Cocteau's creation of a world of magic exists to provide an experience for the viewer.

Christian Metz, in *The Imaginary Signifier*, utilizes phenomenological discourse to explain a viewer's transformation when watching a film. Metz calls the viewer the 'shifting spectator' because he considers watching a film to be a process of having the viewer move in and out of the world of the film with the dimming and raising of theatre lights:

> In order to understand the fiction film, I must both 'take myself' for the character (= an imaginary procedure) so that he benefits, by analogical projection, from all the schemata of intelligibility that I have within me,

---

[1] Dudley Andrew, 'The Neglected Tradition of Phenomenology in Film Theory,' *Movies and Methods Volume II*, edited by Bill Nichols (Berkeley: University of California Press, 1985), 627–8

[2] Ibid., 628.

[3] Ibid., 632.

and not take myself for him (= the return to the real) so that the fiction can be established as such (= as symbolic): this is *seeming-real*.[1]

Metz's concept of the shifting spectator serves well to assemble the various cinematic elements which make up *La Belle et la bête*. The roving eye invites the transcendental subject to a game of æsthetic play. The shifting spectator leaps into the world of the film, experiences a number of viewing positions, and then leaps out of the world at the end of the film. Having determined the way in which the viewer participates within the world of *La Belle et la bête*, it is now possible to determine how this process leads to an interpretation of the film.

This study of Cocteau's *La Belle et la bête* has so far considered the way in which the viewer is engaged within the film. Cocteau creates the emotional experience while the viewer provides the interpretation. The question remains: what can the viewer interpret from such a film? One prominent interpretation, arising from Cocteau's use of cinematic magic, is that the film explores universal æsthetic questions as Galef notices:

> When Beauty cries, her tears turn to diamonds, an illusion of film, but also a metaphor for the film itself: the film as exquisite artifice, a multi-faceted surface created out of simple materials.[2]

In conjunction with the questions raised by Cocteau's artistic choices and those raised by the medium itself, the characters in the film also explicitly raise the issue. For instance, Beauty ironically refers to herself as a monster on one occasion while her name and appearance suggest otherwise. On another occasion, the Beast claims that he has a soul. Cocteau's film certainly challenges notions of beauty by having Beauty fall in love with the ferocious Beast. Another persuasive æsthetic interpretation of the film comes from Michael Popkin, in 'Cocteau's

---

[1] Christian Metz, *The Imaginary Signifier: Psychoanalysis and the Cinema*, translated by Celia Britton, Annwyl Williams, Ben Brewster, and Alfred Guzzetti (Bloomington: Indiana University Press, 1977), 57. '*Pour comprendre le film de fiction, il faut à la fois que je "me prenne" pour le personnage (= démarche imaginaire), afin qu'il bénéfice par projections analogiques de tous les schèmes d'intelligibilité que je porte en moi, et que je ne me prenne pas pour lui (= retour au réel) afin que la fiction puisse s'établir comme tel (= comme symbolique): c'est le semble-réel.' Le Signifiant imaginaire: Psychanalyse et cinéma* (Paris: Christian Bourgois, 1977), 80.

[2] Galef, *Literature Film Quarterly*, 102.

La Belle et la bête : The Look of Love (Jean Marais and Josette Day)
Courtesy of the Museum of Modern Art Film Stills Archive.
© Jean Cocteau/SODRAC (Montréal) 1998

Beauty and the Beast: The Poet as Monster,' who suggests that the Beast represents the poet. Popkin argues that the death and rebirth of the Beast symbolizes the poet who 'must die in one form in order to be reborn in another.'[1] According to Popkin, Cocteau's film identifies 'not with the young girl but with the monster' who represents his 'dilemma as a poet.'

Cocteau's adaptation of the short story features several changes from the original narrative which also contribute to the question of interpretation. In the original story, the Beast is placed under a curse because 'a wicked fairy condemned me to keep this appearance until a beautiful woman agreed to marry me.' Cocteau reacted against this arbitrary punishment by devising a more elaborate explanation: 'My parents didn't believe in fairies, so the fairies punished them through me as a result. I could only be saved by the look of love.'[2] Cocteau's adaptation of the Beast's situation maintains the fairy-tale atmosphere of the story but significantly alters the context so that this unfortunate situation becomes the result of choice; the Beast's parents chose not to believe in fairies and thus, the fairies punished them by turning their son into the Beast.

While this alteration features more self-directed characters who create their situations from the choices they make, it simultaneously indicates the limitations of free will. The Beast is not punished as a result of his own actions or choices, but those of his parents. His parents' 'wrongful' act was to not believe in things beyond human control, such as fairies or the miracles they can be seen as representing. The Beast's salvation from the curse is dependent on another person's love — an emotion which is thought to be beyond one's control and choice. However, it is from the background of these uncontrollable elements that the Beast must transcend and make himself into a being Beauty can love. Rebecca M. Pauly, in *'Beauty and the Beast*: From Fable to Film,' illustrates the way Cocteau's fairy-tale source used fate-oriented means to drive the same story. Mme. Leprince de Beaumont's original narrative features characters who allow situations to happen to them. For instance, Beauty waits all day in the original tale for the Beast to make his appearance, indicating that the character will wait to see what transpires from her situation. In Cocteau's version, Beauty rushes into the garden to confront the Beast with her feelings. Furthermore, the Beast in the short story is depicted as stupid while Cocteau depicts a more intelligent Beast with human emotions. Finally, in the fate-driven story,

---

[1] Michael Popkin, 'Cocteau's *Beauty and the Beast*: The Poet as Monster,' *Literature Film Quarterly*, 10:2 (1982), 100.

[2] Ibid., 105.

no one is exchanged for the Beast when he transforms back into a prince, whereas in the film Avenant dies in the pavilion for his attempt at stealing the Beast's source of power. Although he based his film on a famous fairy-tale, Cocteau initiated major changes in plot, cast of characters, characterization, atmosphere, and symbols. By carefully considering the distinctions between the short story and the film, one can argue that Cocteau's version features more active characters who decide their own course of action despite the magical elements of fate imposed on the narrative. This tension between facticity and transcendence, fate and human freedom, that is derived by entering within the world of the film, leads to an existential interpretation of *La Belle et la bête*. An examination of Cocteau's use of cinematic magic to invite the viewer into the film leads to questions of æsthetics which, in the treatment of the subjects within the world of the film, produce questions of existential ontology.

Jean-Paul Sartre argues in *Being and Nothingness* that human beings, as free agents, do not have fixed essences, but are 'characterized by a constantly renewed obligation to remake the *Self*' by continually making new decisions among future possibilities.[1] Cocteau captures the spirit of Sartre's manifesto by creating 'a primordial place where everything lives and wants to become.'[2] One of the most striking characters in the film who remakes himself by making decisions amongst future possibilities is, ironically, the Beast. If the Beast were truly a beast, he would act according to instinct. But this Beast *decides* to spare Beauty's father in exchange for his daughter. Out of love, respect, and trust for Beauty, the Beast *decides* to give her a chance to visit her father; he entrusts her to such an extent that he *decides* to give her his Pavilion key to his treasure. His decisions are an attempt to transcend his situation as Beast. Sartre recognizes that a human being's past constitutes his or her facticity, but he also argues that humans are able to transcend their facticity.[3] 'Being a creature that is both noble and murderous who is torn by conflicting desires, Cocteau's Beast achieves tragic dimensions' because he represents both the glory and disgrace of humankind.[4] Part of his facticity is that he physically takes what he

---

[1] Jean-Paul Sartre, *Being and Nothingness*, translated by Hazel E. Barnes (New York: Washington Square Press Incorporated, 1953), 72. '[S]e caractérise par une obligation perpétuellement renouvelée de refaire le Moi qui désigne l'être libre.' *L'Être et le néant* (Paris: Gallimard, 1968), 72. All subsequent quotations in French are taken from this source.

[2] Hoggard, *Film and Literature*, 126.

[3] Sartre, *Being and Nothingness*, 64.

[4] Hoggard, *Film and Literature*, 128.

wants. When he is hungry, he kills for his food. But he tries to overcome aspects of his facticity. He does not force Beauty to love him, but rather waits until her love is freely given. The Beast's dual existence as human being and beast raises the distinction between objects, what Sartre calls Being-in-itself, and humans, what Sartre calls Being-for-itself.

A Being-in-itself 'is an immanence which can not realize itself, an affirmation which can not affirm itself, an activity which can not act, because it is glued to itself.'[1] The in-itself can only be discussed on the basis of its appearance; it is an entity which is full positivity, it has no possibility of being anything else. The Being-for-itself has no fixed essence. The for-itself engages in constant motion and change; human consciousness engages the for-itself in purposeful activity.[2] In the original narrative, Beauty's father, who is supposedly so fond of Beauty, agrees rather quickly to let her take his place as the Beast's victim. The film more sharply etches the concept of choice by having Beauty slip away without her father's notice or consent. Beauty represents a constantly changing for-itself who redefines herself by the decisions she makes: she *decides* to go to the castle, she *decides* to stay at the castle, she *decides* not to marry the Beast, she *decides* to ask the Beast to visit her father, she *decides* to love the Beast. One could argue that love is one emotion that one can not turn on and off according to one's whim. Even so, for love to cast its magic spell, the for-itself must be receptive to being spellbound. Cocteau's film aptly shows the transformation in the relationship between Beauty and the Beast as blossoming because Beauty overcame her fear and prejudice and began to look at the Beast with compassion and humility. Upon the first sight of the Beast, Beauty shrieked in horror. It is only once she *decides* to get to know the Beast a little better, that love can then work its magic. The for-itself creates its own destiny and thus must be responsible for its own destiny.

The concept of anguish enters into the for-itself because human beings must choose between a multiplicity of possibilities and are responsible for their choices. One must choose; one can never relinquish responsibility and relax in a determinism where all is done for him or her. Anguish is only a condition of the for-itself because, as Sartre writes, 'anguish is the mode of being of freedom as consciousness of being; it is in

---

[1] Sartre, *Being and Nothingness*, 27. '[I]l est une immanence qui ne peut pas se réaliser, une affirmation qui ne peut pas s'affirmer, une activité qui ne peut pas agir, parce qu'il s'est empâté de soi-même.' 32.

[2] Ibid., 28, 119–55.

anguish that freedom is, in its being, in question for itself.'[1] Perhaps one of the most pronounced scenes in the film which reveals anguish occurs when Beauty must choose between returning to the Beast, who will die without her, and staying with her father, whom she loves. Each choice has its positive and negative circumstances; and yet, she must choose. The film also illustrates the consequences of those who do not consider the responsibility for their actions. Ludovic foolishly gambles away his father's money with the consequence that all his father's goods are taken away. Avenant, urged by Ludovic and his two selfish sisters Félicie and Adelaide, attempts to break into the sacred Pavilion to steal the riches. Not realizing that his decision will have consequences, he is shot dead by the statue protecting the space.

Cocteau and Sartre both offer humanity a renewed sense of freedom. Both posit conceptions of human existence which emphasize the power one has to create oneself. For one caught within the trappings of daily life, the existential outlook on life offers a little bit of reassurance. Unfortunately, many people misconstrue the anguish associated with freedom of choice as something unfavourable. Beauty does reveal the pain of anguish when she has to choose between the Beast and her father. But she also reveals the potential for happiness that freedom of choice can bring: Beauty chose love and set the Beast free. By inviting the viewer to participate within the world of the film, Cocteau illustrates the way in which film can inform one's own reality by being situated in another reality. Cocteau's *La Belle et la bête* presents a world where magic occurs, but does not dictate the actions of the characters. The poetic magic serves to intrigue the viewer into entering this new environment. But, after all the tricks have been played out, what drives the narrative is the decisions of the characters. Cocteau's film not only allows the viewer to transcend objective reality, it also engages the viewer to transcend the limitations of his or her own existence.

---

[1] Ibid., 65. '[L]'angoisse est le mode d'être de la liberté comme conscience d'être, c'est dans l'angoisse que la liberté est dans son être en question pour elle-même.' Ibid., 66.

The Play as Star Vehicle: Actors Interrupt the Art of L'Aigle à deux têtes

Wade Lynch

More than any of his other works, Jean Cocteau's *L'Aigle à deux têtes* has suffered from the direct and indirect influence of actors. Since its conception in late 1944, the play has been troubled by the whims and actions of self-serving thespians and those who seek to pander to them.

As World War II was coming to an end, poet, playwright, filmmaker and illustrator Jean Cocteau was exhausted, confused, broke and juggling his on-again, off-again relationship with opium. Depressed and artistically constricted by the waning German Occupation, he sought refuge in a gothic castle in Brittany. There he hoped to find inspiration for a new work that would be both artistically pleasing and commercially viable. Physically weak and intellectually numbed by his narcotic of choice, Cocteau answered what would come to be recognized as an order from his great friend and lover, Jean Marais, to write him a play.

Jean Marais, the beautiful young actor, twenty-four years Cocteau's junior, gave specific dimensions to the piece he requested:

> Marais asked for a drama in which he would remain 'silent' in the first act, 'cry with joy' in the second and 'fall down the stairs backwards' in the third. Intrigued by the challenge, Cocteau's 'theatrical' mechanism was set into motion almost immediately.[1]

---

[1] Knapp, 131. '*Il m'avait demandé, il m'avait pour ainsi dire posé des colles ; il m'avait dit : "je voudrais une pièce où je me taise au premier acte, où je pleure de joie au second acte et où je tombe d'un escalier à la renverse au troisième acte..."*

Moi, j'aime beaucoup qu'on me donne des ... qu'on me commande, parce qu'alors le mécanisme se met beaucoup mieux en marche, le mécanisme qui nous permet de sortir de nous des choses inconnues.' Entretiens avec André Fraigneau (Meaux [Seine-et-Marne]: Michel-Claude Jalard, 1965), 139.

The actor's involvement in the inception of *L'Aigle à deux têtes* was direct as well as indirect. Directly, he can be said to have 'ordered' Cocteau to write the play to his specifications. Indirectly, he served as the role model for the young Stanislas.

L'Aigle à deux têtes touches the autobiographical when it reflects in its love story the tale of an older, tragic Queen and the young poet whose romantic notion of her is ideal and awesome (fifteen years separate the couple in the 1946 adaptation of Duncan's script for Tallulah Bankhead's New York production; six years in the 1964 Wildman script). This perspective can be nicely fitted to Cocteau's own vision of himself in his relationship with Marais (and previously with Raymond Radiguet and others), where he finds himself lusting for the vigour and physical beauty of youth possessed by the young actor and where the actor seeks in Cocteau the wisdom, passion and worldliness of his experience. Where the relationship between Stanislas and the Queen is anarchical, passionate and ultimately doomed, the Cocteau/Marais relationship could be called equally anarchical and passionate, and if not doomed, at least unhealthy. In *An Impersonation of Angels*, Cocteau biographer Frederick Brown repeats an incident described by writer Ronald Duncan when he called on Cocteau at his home in Paris' Palais Royal to discuss the possibility of translating *l'Aigle* into English. It reveals the extent of the obsessive, symbiotic nature of the Cocteau/Marais relationship and the degree of Cocteau's opium abuse:

> When the door opened I looked up to see a very handsome young man standing framed in it. He looked like a Greek statue — and knew it.
>
> 'Jean's expecting you,' he said languidly; then he called 'Jean, Jean, quick, look what we've got.'
>
> I couldn't think whether he referred to me, or, if not, what this last remark meant. But before I could fathom this, Cocteau came running out into the hall. I was shocked: he looked emaciated and raddled. He seemed oddly pleased to see me, demonstrably affectionate.
>
> 'Let me introduce you to Jean Marais. Isn't he beautiful?'
>
> I glanced at the Apollo now standing posed on a white sheepskin rug and had to agree, but couldn't think how to say so. Then I noticed that Marais and Cocteau were regarding me with nothing less than a predatory glint in the eyes. I followed their look, then realized they were both focusing intently and silently on a carton of Chesterfields ...
>
> ... I studied Cocteau. My first impression was confirmed. He looked wizened and this effect was heightened by the spruce and youthful style of his dress. My own casual diagnosis was that he was either suffering from yellow fever or jaundice.
>
> 'I suppose this is the result of your diet during the Occupation?'

'No,' he answered with clinical detachment. 'You're looking at the effects of opium'..[1]

Cocteau completed the play and Duncan agreed to pen the translation. Duncan's translation of *L'Aigle* was, in fact, the first version of the play to be produced. His English language adaptation premiered in London in September, 1946, under the title *The Eagle Has Two Heads*, a title that would subsequently be adapted back to French. *L'Aigle à deux têtes* replaced the original title, *Azrael*, a name critics dissuaded Cocteau from using due to its phonetic similarity to 'Israel.' Duncan was a well-known poet and verse-dramatist in his own right. He wrote plays like *Don Juan* and *The Death of Satan* and the libretto for the opera *The Rape of Lucretia* among many other works. In addition to the translation for *L'Aigle*, he also translated Cocteau's play *La Machine à écrire* and the sub-titled translation for Cocteau's film script for *La Belle et la bête*.

In his translator's notes to the play, published in 1947, Duncan wrote:

> In fairness to my friend Jean Cocteau, I must emphasize that this text is an adaptation and not a literal translation.
> When I was approached by the Company of Four to translate 'L'Aigle à deux têtes,' I hesitated, although the play intrigued me greatly.
> A few weeks later, I saw Jean in his little red room in the Palais Royal. Flapping his arms like an Eagle, I gathered that Jean didn't mind what I did so long as his original play still flew.
> However, as I worked, I even exceeded this generous mandate. The original was in prose; much that I wrote was verse. Miss Eileen Herlie, who eventually realized the part so successfully must be blamed for this. As a poet, I was interested in her opinion that verse on the stage gives an actress a flying start. And what has gratified me considerably is that the contemporary audience's resistance to poetry was not aroused. It is surprising what you can do behind their backs — and it is this perhaps which is worth doing..[2]

In this instance, the translator —as Cocteau himself did with Marais— took the lead directly from the actor: the medium manipulated by the artist, instead of the artist manipulating the medium. Duncan wrote to please Herlie. The result is, as one might guess, uneven as a selection of dramatic literature. The stylistic jumps from verse to prose are not always smooth and are contradictory to the musical rhythms

---

[1] Brown, 367–68.
[2] *The Eagle Has Two Heads*, 5.

and intent Cocteau assigned to the play. In his *Interviews with André Fraigneau*, Cocteau said:

> My play is written in the form of a fugue. It opens on the theme of the Queen. In the second Act the Stanislas theme takes its place and the two themes resolve by fitting into and struggling against each other in the final chord with the double death..[1]

Duncan's adaptation, tailored to suit Herlie's wishes, did not fulfil Cocteau's musical intention. On September 5, 1946, the *Times* reviewer reported, 'The piece ... fails to come off. Its dialogue is rhetoric masquerading as poetry'..[2] Joseph Wood Krutch, commenting on the same adaptation for *The Nation* on April 5, 1947, wrote:

> What is really painful about *The Eagle Has Two Heads* is not merely the theatrical claptrap but the leaden march of bad poetic prose, the thin whine of inflated *pensées* as they go flat, and the dull thud of epigrams falling dismally on their faces. What are we to think of a poet who offers us 'you were fleeing like a hunted beast' as though it were a striking metaphor? Of an epigrammatist who can make his royal heroine explain her lack of fear of lightning by declaring that 'it sometimes strikes trees but not family trees,' or can allow his Machiavellian statesman to rebuke a political poet with the pronouncement that 'it is one thing to split an infinitive, but it is quite another to divide a state?'[3]

For the actors however, the altered *The Eagle Has Two Heads* was a resounding triumph. The play was a huge commercial success. It was extended three times and played at three different theaters before concluding its near year-long run in July, 1947. The play, adapted to suit the ambitions of its lead, succeeded in making her a star and launching a long and respected career. The play's opening was an international news item. On September 16, 1946, *The New York Times* reported:

> The outstanding theatrical event in London last week was the presentation at Hammersmith's Lyric Theater of Jean Cocteau's new play *Azrael*, adapted by Ronald Duncan under the title *The Eagle Has Two Heads*.

---

[1] Knapp, 130. '*Ma pièce est écrite en forme de fugue. Elle s'ouvre sur le thème de la Reine. Au second acte le thème de Stanislas prend sa place et les deux thèmes se résolvent pour s'emboîter et lutter ensemble jusqu'à l'accord final de la double mort.*' *Cocteau par lui-même* (Paris: Éditions du Seuil, 1957), 91.

[2] *The Times*, 6.

[3] Krutch, 403.

The play is outstanding for two reasons — because it has not yet been produced in Paris, and because it has brought fame overnight to a young actress, Eileen Herlie, who four years ago was a typist..[1]

Herlie was properly launched on an admirable career path (thanks to Cocteau and Duncan), but at the expense of the play. She was, nonetheless, very forthcoming in her praise of the piece, and particularly the playwright(s). In an interview for *Le Figaro*, published on November 6, 1946, Herlie declared:

> I adore the play. I spent six months studying it. Some excessively kind critics have suggested that I was the sole reason for the play's success. But one does not create a play without a text. In the England of to-day, plays are no longer being written with such dramatic intensity, with such subtlety.[2]

The play was an ideal showcase for Herlie despite poor reaction to the Duncan treatment of the script. If Cocteau was disappointed at Duncan's translation, he was at least philosophical about its ultimate success on the London stages and probably grateful for the attention and revenue it afforded him. In his *Diary of an Unknown*, he recorded his thoughts on translations:

> The initial thrust must be strong enough so that something of the translated work remains at the end of the trajectory, and so that a foreign audience can recognize us in it. *L'Aigle à deux têtes*, in an inaccurate adaptation, triumphed in London because of the leading lady. In New York, it flopped in an even more inaccurate adaptation, taken from the British adaptation by the actress who played the queen.
> If we were miraculously to receive the gift of a new language, we would not be able to recognize the books we love. And if personal memories are connected to the errors in these translated works, and mingle with them, we would surely be sad to have lost them..[3]

---

[1] *The New York Times*, 9.

[2] *Le Figaro*, le 6 novembre 1946, 4. *'J'adore la pièce. J'ai passé des mois à étudier. Des critiques trop bienveillants ont suggéré que j'en ai fait tout le succeès. Mais on ne fait pas une pièce avec rien. En Angleterre, on n'écrit plus aujourd'hui de pièces d'une pareille intensité dramatique, d'une semblable subtilité.'*

[3] *Diary of an Unknown*, 122–23. *'Il importe qu'un jet soit robuste au départ pour qu'en fin de courbe quelque chose subsiste d'une œuvre traduite, et qu'un public étranger nous y aperçoive. L'Aigle à deux têtes triomphait à Londres dans une adaptation inexacte, à cause de l'actrice. À New York, il échoua dans une adaptation encore plus inexacte, faite d'après l'adaptation anglaise, par l'actrice qui interprétait la reine. Si le don d'une langue nous venait par miracle, nous ne reconnaîtrions pas les livres qui nous charment. Et si des souvenirs personnels s'atta-*

When *L'Aigle à deux têtes* opened in Paris in 1946 before its New York run, it was successful enough commercially to enjoy a healthy initial run and subsequent remount, but was at best uneven artistically. The new post-war cultural climate in Europe was discovering revolutionary new literary works such as Jean-Paul Sartre's essay *L'Être et le néant*, Albert Camus' novel *La Peste*, and was analysing recent wartime plays like Sartre's *Huit Clos* and Jean Anouilh's reworking of *Antigone*. A melodramatic perspective of an historic mystery could find no solid refuge in a community nurturing a new wave of introspective and intellectual artist-citizens..[1] In his Cocteau biography, *Jean Cocteau: The History of a Poet's Age*, Wallace Fowlie commented:

> *L'Aigle à deux têtes* ... was only a partial success. It is an intelligent but far too cerebral attempt at playwriting, a virtuoso piece which seems more the vehicle for an actress than a play capable of holding audiences in successive generations ... In the writing of this play which was obviously destined for the large theatre-going public, Cocteau omitted all elements that might have seemed strange or disconcerting or obscure.[2]

Although somewhat of a disappointment for Cocteau, the play very nicely served for whom it was created. Jean Marais' star rose higher up in his actors' heaven by virtue of Cocteau's efforts. When the play opened in Paris on December 20, 1946, after a two month try-out in Brussels and Lyon, Jean-Jacques Gautier of the Paris newspaper, *Le Figaro*, glowed about Marais:

> One could not award a greater tribute to Jean Marais. He is excellent in the violence, the anger, the frenzy of the Second Act, and we admire the visual quality of his great bold death [Note that, in Act Three, Cocteau wrote, as Marais requested, a dramatic event in which Marais' character, Stanislas, would 'fall down backwards' to his death.] He plays by the rules of the game and wins..[3]

---

chent aux fautes de ces livres traduits et se confondent avec eux, sans doute serions-nous tristes de les perdre.' *Journal d'un inconnu* (Paris: Bernard Grasset, 1953), 125.

[1] Knapp, 130.

[2] Wallace Fowlie, *Jean Cocteau: The History of a Poet's Age* (Bloomington: Indiana University Press, 1966), 75.

[3] *Le Figaro*, le 26 décembre 1946, 4. 'On ne saurait décerner de plus beau compliment à Jean Marais que de reconnaître qu'il ne fait pas tache à côté d'une telle partenaire; il est excellent dans la violence, la colère, le délire du deuxième acte et nous admirons la valeur plastique de sa grande mort audacieuse. Il joue la règle du jeu et gagne.'

He played by the rules of the game and won indeed. After the play completed its first Parisian run and during the filming of the subsequent movie, Marais talked publicly about the appeal of the Stanislas character and his passion for him. In an interview written by Roger Cantagrel and published in *Le Figaro* on November 7, 1947, Marais commented, 'Stanislas, an anarchist and poet, put his purity, his loyalty, and his enthusiasm at the service of an ideal. The good of the people guides his thoughts. Politics is for him merely a means of setting his deeds at the service of the cause he is defending'.[1]

If the play was good for Marais, it was even better for his co-star, Edwige Feuillère. Already a well established and respected artist, Feuillère enjoyed rave reviews for her performance:

> This 'reine morte' from the banks of the Rhine is the unforgettable Feuillère, she of the caressing, imperious, smooth, serious and laughing voice, the voice that comes from the head and from the throat, strident, unctuous and slippery, clear and veiled, ironic and poignant, a musical instrument, to be sure. And her acting, her bearing, her class and her ease ... What she does deserves and releases our enthusiasm which leaves us at a loss for words..[2]

Feuillère was at no loss for words herself when expressing her gratitude and admiration for Cocteau and the play. In *Edwige Feuillère*, the 1991 biography by Alain Feydeau, Feuillère said, '*L'Aigle à deux têtes* was a great experience. At that time, its author was really in control of the show, for he was also the director. With Cocteau one only had to let oneself go. He took what was good from the suggestions one gave him. It was marvellous...'[3]

---

[1] Ibid., le 7 novembre 1947, 4. '*Stanislas, anarchiste et poète, a mis sa pureté, son loyalisme, son enthousiasme au service d'un idéal. Le bien du peuple guide ses pensées. La politique n'est pour lui qu'un moyen de mettre ses actes au service de la cause qu'il défend.*'

[2] Ibid., le 26 décembre 1946, 4, Gautier: '*Cette reine morte des bords du Rhin, c'est l'inoubliable Feuillère, à la voix caressante, impérieuse, roulante, grave, rieuse, voix de tête, voix de gorge, stridente, onctueuse et glissante, claire et voilée, ironique et poignante, cette voix qui est un instrument de musique. Et son jeu, et sa démarche, et sa classe, et son aisance... Ce qu'elle fait mérite et déclenche cet enthousiasme... qui ne trouve plus ses mots.*'

[3] Feydeau, 239. '*L'Aigle à deux têtes a été une grande expérience. À ce moment-là, l'auteur était vraiment le père du spectacle, car lui-même faisait la mise en scène. Avec Cocteau, on n'avait qu'à se laisser aller. Il prenait ce qu'il avait de bon dans les suggestions qu'on lui faisait, c'était merveilleux...*'

The New York flop Cocteau referred to in his *Diary of an Unknown* is the production of a variation of the Duncan script in which the famous and infamous thespian, Tallulah Bankhead, starred at New York's Plymouth Theater in March, 1947. It is this effort which strays the furthest from Cocteau's original vision and is the most potent example of the danger of a production pinning its success on the name of a celebrity — particularly a celebrity with artistic control and a healthy disregard for art.

Tallulah Bankhead was forty-five years old when *Eagle* opened in New York City. By then, she had already been a Broadway star for over two decades. She had made a name for herself playing wild, scandalous women in a series of productions which, with rare exceptions, would be unremarkable except for her presence. In her youth, her glamorous looks, throaty voice and natural athleticism on stage, coupled with her legendary party-girl escapades offstage made Bankhead a darling of the Great White Way and a guaranteed box office draw. As she aged, her performances became somewhat repetitive as she played characters that were more along the lines of caricatures and self-parodies. Her fans were many and loyal, but even they could not keep Tallulah's *Eagle* aloft for longer than 29 performances. In his April 12, 1947 review of *The Eagle Has Two Heads* for *The Saturday Review*, critic John Mason Brown focused principally on the phenomenon that was Bankhead:

> The truth is Miss Bankhead is a show in herself — and something of a side-show, too. She has enough temperament to share with whole stagefuls of more tepid performers; enough energy also to permit Niagara to take a well-earned rest. She can at times be victimized by her blazing virtues. Although vastly exciting, the boldness of her ease upon the stage is on occasion as uncomfortable to watch as it is to see a guest making himself too much at home in another person's house ... But even Miss Bankhead, brilliant as she is, profound as is my admiration for her blazing gifts, and magnificent as she looks all dressed up as a queen in Aline Bernstein's costumes, cannot keep M. Cocteau's play from seeming more like a six-months' night in the Arctic Circle than a lively evening in the theater.[1]

The reviews for the American debut of *The Eagle Has Two Heads* reveal much about Broadway's 'star' system. Both Brown and *The New York Times'* Brooks Atkinson discussed Bankhead's 'choice' in selecting the role of the Queen for herself, asserting the post-war consumer-sensitive environment wherein a star's name frequently carried more clout

---

[1] J.M. Brown, 41–43.

than the project to which it was attached. In his March 20, 1947 review, Atkinson observed, 'Not that anyone should wonder about Miss Bankhead's interest in the part. Our Tallulah is an actress, and the rôle of the Queen fairly bulges with richness — tragedy, passion, nobility, imperiousness, bravado, cruelty and loneliness ... [and] Donald Oenslager has nailed together a grand staircase where a dying Queen can shuffle off and topple magnificently'.[1]

Stars could choose the projects that appealed to them, and alter them to suit themselves. This is certainly the case in Bankhead's *Eagle*. Brendan Gill, in his 1972 biography of the actor, *Tallulah*, recounts Bankhead's liberties with the Cocteau (Duncan) play:

> Tallulah's opening speech in the play is said to be the longest soliloquy ever written ... [I]t took her thirty minutes to deliver it in Wilmington. In Boston, it was clocked at twenty-two minutes, and on its opening in New York it was down to seventeen minutes. To hold an audience with an uninterrupted speech of that length, and at the very start of the play, was a remarkable feat of acting; not content with this, Tallulah added a scarcely less remarkable feat of acrobatics. At the moment the Queen was shot, she was standing at the top of a long flight of stairs, and John Lardner was prompted in his review of the play to speak of her performance in sporting terms: 'Miss Bankhead spared herself nothing on opening night at the Plymouth. In a plunge that I would hesitate to make with football pads on, she toppled headfirst, majestically and in a pure line, down several stairs. She was fresh as a daisy, however, for her curtain calls, which were up to the standards of the Bankhead public'.[2]

That Tallulah had little regard for Cocteau and his play was evident in the inappropriate decision to act in the production and in the liberties she took with the story. There was, as Gill's book indicates, extreme editing and liberal rewriting as the play travelled from out-of-town trials to Broadway. In order to provide her audience with the theatrical tricks they expected of her, Bankhead changed Cocteau's method of death from a knife to a gunshot and (in strict defiance of Jean Marais' 'order') saved the 'tumble down the stairs backwards' for herself.

Tallulah Bankhead however, was not the only New York actor whose personal agenda would take precedence over Cocteau's poetry in the North American debut of the play. Before the New York opening, where Bankhead would co-star with Helmut Dantine as Stanislas, *The Eagle Has Two Heads* was performed in out-of-town try-outs with up-

---

[1] Atkinson, 39.

[2] Brendan Gill, *Tallulah* (Toronto: Holt, Rinehart and Winston, 1972), 74.

and-coming actor Marlon Brando in the role. Brando hated the production and Tallulah Bankhead in it and set out to sabotage the play before its New York debut. Richard Maney, Tallulah's friend and press agent, recalled the Brando *Eagle* in his autobiography, *Fanfare*:

> I first encountered this fakir [Brando] when John C. Wilson engaged him to shoot Tallulah Bankhead in *The Eagle Has Two Heads* ...
>
> Throughout the rehearsals, Wilson had interpreted Marlon's trance-like conduct as a manifestation of genius. He hesitated to correct him lest he upset his mood. That night Wilson's mood was addled while watching Brando during Tallulah's soliloquy.
>
> He squirmed. He picked his nose. He adjusted his fly. He leered at the audience. He cased the furniture. He fixed his gaze on an offstage property man instead of his opponent. But these didos were nothing compared with his surprise finish. On cue he plugged the Queen and watched her pitch headlong down the stairway. Then, in defiance of Cocteau, Wilson, and Equity's Board of Governors, he refused to die. Instead he staggered about the stage, seeking a likely spot for his final throe.
>
> The audience was in convulsions. Spread-eagle on the stairway, head-down, Miss Bankhead was having a few convulsions of her own ... The curtain came down with the audience in hysterics. If Tallulah could have gotten her hands on a gun, the coroner would have had a customer then and there.[1]

Marlon Brando's antics served him well enough. He was released from his contract and went immediately into rehearsals for Tennessee Williams' *A Streetcar Named Desire* and a long, successful career. *The Eagle Has Two Heads* went on to New York and died a dismal death.

Broadway had over 300 professional houses up and running in the month that *Eagle* was on the boards. It was an era of incredible growth for the professional theater in the mid-1940s in New York City. Postwar America was basking in a fiscal renaissance; money was being made and much was being spent. There was theater available for every taste and, for the most part, audience for every theater. Musical reviews, musical comedies, modern drama, Edwardian comedies and social satires were all running and making money. In the same week that *Eagle* opened at the Plymouth Theater in March, 1947, a random sampling of theater-going options would reveal a selection as varied as: *Carousel* and *Oklahoma*, Lunt and Fontanne in *O Mistress Mine*, Ruth Gordon's comedy *Years Ago* beside husband Garson Kanin's comedy *Born Yesterday*, John Gielgud's production of Oscar Wilde's *The Importance of Being Earnest*, Lillian Hellman's *Another Part of the Forest*, and An-

---

[1] Ibid., 72–73.

toinette Perry (namesake of Broadway's 'Tony' awards) directing Mary Chase's *Harvey*.[1]

Even amidst Broadway's colourful bounty of theatrical tastes, the spectacular paradox that *The Eagle Has Two Heads* had become could not find a public hungry enough to swallow Cocteau's melodramatic prose fugue *Azrael*, distorted at the insistence of actors, into a sometimes-prose, sometimes-verse, chopped-down, camped-up curiosity.

To carry the concept of paradox, and even irony, further, it is worth noting that Cocteau's art had, to this point, never been particularly consumer-driven. Cocteau, the poet, had always placed the 'art' of his work first, over any potential revenue it might generate. When he finally wrote a piece specifically designed to have a broader public (and therefore, ticket-selling) appeal, the actors, in whose faith and fate the play had been entrusted, couldn't make it work in the United States of America, the most capitalistic, consumer-driven country in the world.

Jean Cocteau recalled his impressions of the New York debut of *Eagle*, and particularly his feelings about Tallulah Bankhead in his published diaries, *Past Tense*. In an entry dated July 13, 1953, he detailed a radio interview he and friend and fellow playwright, Tennessee Williams, were giving for a broadcast out of Barcelona, Spain. The interviewer asked Williams who he felt were the two greatest American actors. Williams said Marlon Brando and Greta Garbo. Cocteau then commented that, '... Garbo had passed through the wall of fame and that she was disintegrating. That she would never appear again, either in a film or on stage. It was my bad luck that she wanted to do *The Eagle Has Two Heads* when Tallulah turned it into a disaster in New York'..[2]

America would not experience a major attempt at a production of *Eagle* for another decade. The New York theater scene of the 1950's would witness a phenomenal growth of new and daring theater apart, physically and philosophically, from mainstream Broadway. As increasing costs and the rapid development of other sources of entertainment were sky-rocketing, Broadway shows were becoming greater financial risks. Television, cinema, drive-in movies and Rock and Roll meant Broadway had to compete in a much bigger arena and would have to become

---

[1] Advertisements in *The Saturday Review* (April 12, 1947), 41.

[2] *Past Tense*, vol. II, 165 (13 July, 1953). '[G]arbo avait traversé le mur de gloire et qu'elle se désintégrait. Qu'elle ne paraîtra plus ni dans un film, ni sur les planches. Ma déveine est qu'elle voulait jouer L'Aigle à deux têtes, lorsque Tallulah m'en fit une catastrophe à New York.' *Le Passé défini*, vol. II (Paris: Gallimard, 1985), 194.

increasingly cautious and conservative in order to survive (Greenberger, Chapter 1). Big name stars in well-suited projects would take precedence over the new, the controversial and the unproved.

Off-Broadway, as the new trend would come to be called, is defined in the Actor's Equity rulebook as professional theater relegated to under-300 theater houses outside the borders of the Times Square theater district (Little 14). Philosophically, it is defined by its artistic mandate. Stuart W. Little, author of *Off-Broadway: the Prophetic Theater* explains it as '... a showcase for new actors and directors, a place where new talent can be discovered. It is a place to revive Broadway failures and restore the reputations of playwrights who may have been ill served in the regular commercial theater.'[1]

There is no doubt that Cocteau and *The Eagle Has Two Heads* had been ill served in its first incarnation in New York. Could a new production in the dynamic Off-Broadway environment gave it new life? The Actors Playhouse and Colleen Dewhurst seemed to think so. Cocteau's works were historically known for their cerebral, intimate, claustrophobic nature; certainly a production in a smaller venue mounted by a company committed to the art of the poet would fare better than one headed by a self-serving actor bent on starring in a Broadway hit.

Alas, the actor would once again intervene to mold Cocteau's play into a vehicle designed to carry its driver to a self-aggrandizing destination while relegating the art of the original creator to the back seat.

Colleen Dewhurst's career was at a precarious point in 1956. After a series of much-heralded Off-Broadway performances, peaked by a brilliant 'Kate' in a Joseph Papp-directed production of Shakespeare's *The Taming of the Shrew*, the actor seemed poised on the brink of stardom.[2] When she then took on the role of the heroine in an adaptation of Alexandre Dumas fils' *Camille*, things went slightly awry. Dewhurst, a tall, tanned, deep-voiced fury, was far too healthy for the role of the frail girl/woman, Marguerite, dying of consumption. Critics panned the production, saying, for instance: 'Last night at the Cherry Lane they laughed and laughed and laughed'.[3] Colleen Dewhurst knew she needed a role which would both utilize her powerful instrument and adhere to Off-Broadway's artistic mandates. Encouraged by her new and powerful agent, Jane Broder, Dewhurst signed on to play the Queen in yet another adaptation of *The Eagle Has Two Heads*.

---

[1] (New York: Coward, McCann and Geoghegan, 1972), 15.

[2] Howard Greenberger, *The Off-Broadway Experience* (Englewood Cliffs: Prentice Hall, 1971), 126.

[3] Kerr, *New York Herald Tribune*.

The play opened at the Actor's Theater on December 13, 1956. The 'new' script was adapted by Stanley Bosworth and Miles Dickson. Dickson also directed. In addition to Dewhurst, the cast featured Anthony Vorno as Stanislas and, as the mute servant, Tony, an actor who would in the years ahead become very well known for his voice, James Earl Jones.

The play flopped. For a role of which Dewhurst asked, 'Who could resist ... such a grande dame?', the audience resisted mightily.[1] The play ran for 38 performances only, beating out Bankhead's run, a decade earlier, by nine.

Once again, it was Cocteau who endured the most criticism for a production that was removed, by yet one more generation, from his original. In a December 14, 1956 review headed by, 'Miss Dewhurst "Dies" in Cocteau Revival,' Arthur Gelb of *The New York Times* wrote:

> The new Stanley Bosworth-Miles Dickson adaptation is endlessly talky, pretentious and cryptic. (This is not to be confused with Ronald Duncan's adaptation in 1947, which was endlessly cryptic, pretentious and talky. Could it be that this is just bad Cocteau?) ... The play can boast ... the kind of dialogue that beats mercilessly upon the ear for three long acts. [2]

For Dewhurst however, the play served its purpose. While the play was panned, the actor was praised for her work. Gelb found her, '... lovely to look at ... has a nice rich voice, a graceful carriage and admirable stage presence ...' and Frances Herridge, in the December 14, 1956, *New York Post* wrote simply, 'Cocteau Play Is a Waste of Talent.' The actor and her agent would ultimately be pleased with the fruits of the production's labours. Dewhurst's performance in *Eagle*, coupled with those in *Camille* and *Shrew*, would earn her the 1957 'Obie' award for Best Actress..[3] Dewhurst would go on to further her brilliant career in Off-Broadway, Broadway, films and television. The Bosworth-Dickson script would not go on to either publication or a second production.

That actors were, in a large part, responsible for the disappointing outcome of *The Eagle Has Two Heads* in its principal productions is an interesting, though not unprecedented, phenomenon. In virtually all theater, the success of any given performance depends on the symbiotic relationship between poet and performer. What appears to have

---

[1] Greenberger, 129.

[2] Gelb, 37.

[3] Little, 292.

thrown *Azrael/L'Aigle/Eagle* off balance was the degree to which the actors influenced the play from its initial stages through its closing curtains. But if actors are to be blamed for having too much influence in these instances, any judgment of that influence must be seasoned with the thoughts of Jean Cocteau himself who, in a post script to his preface to the play wrote:

> It is hardly necessary to add that a great part has nothing to do with a play. Writing plays and great rôles is one of Racine's strong points. Sarah Bernhardt and Mme. Réjane, de Max and Mounet-Sully gained renown through a series of mediocre plays where the great rôles were only a pretext to show their genius. To unite these two —the human play and the great rôle— might this not be a means of saving the theatre and restoring its power?
> It is a dangerous undertaking. The true audience turns away from too intellectual a theater. But a large élite, unaccustomed to violent action, full of high-sounding phrases, is risking a bad shock from this trumpet reveille as well as the danger of confusing it with melodrama.
> Never mind. The risk will have to be taken.[1]

Few other companies would risk a major production of Cocteau's *Eagle*. Another New York attempt in December, 1964, would close after 30 performances at the Royal Playhouse. Carl Wildman wrote the (published) adaptation and this time called the play *The Eagle With Two Heads*. The production was unreviewed by the New York press and unattended by the New York public. The damage done to the play by the actors who used it to further their careers apparently persists.

---

[1] *The Eagle Has Two Heads*, 8–9. 'Ajouterai-je qu'un grand rôle n'a rien à voir avec une pièce ? Écrire des pièces et de grands rôles est un des prodiges de Racine. Mmes Sarah Bernhardt et Réjane, MM. de Max et Mounet-Sully s'illustrèrent par une multitude de pièces médiocres où de grands rôles ne furent que prétextes à mettre leur génie en vue. Marier ces deux forces —la pièce humaine et le grand rôle— n'est-ce pas le moyen de sauver le théâtre et lui rendre son éfficacité ?

L'entreprise est dangereuse. Il est vrai que le véritable public s'écarte d'un théâtre trop intellectuel. Mais une grosse élite déshabituée de l'action violente, bercée de phrases, risque de prendre fort mal ce réveil en fanfare et de le confondre avec le mélodrame.

Peu importe. Il le faut.' *L'Aigle à deux têtes*, in *Théâtre* vol. I (Paris: Gallimard, 1948), 303–04.

The Story with Two Lives: The Filmic Narrativity of L'Aigle à deux têtes

Andrea Scott

Tired of the theatrical trends of the mid-twentieth century, Jean Cocteau reacted by writing *L'Aigle à deux têtes* in the fall of 1944. For Cocteau, the 'fashionable' plays of the time were boring; so he had decided that a good old-fashioned melodrama was needed: 'I brought the public back quite bluntly to the *theatre of action* — action that saves the audience from the boredom which most of them take for seriousness'.[1] In 1948, *L'Aigle à deux têtes* was released as a film starring Jean Marais and Edwige Feuillère. Although the film received considerable praise in Europe, it was not well received in the United States. Part of the reason for the film's failure in North America may have had to do with the terrible reception it received as a play in New York. Another reason may have been its particular cinematic style. Often when a play is converted into a film, the result is unsatisfactory because the director may have difficulty transferring the *dramatic* text to the screen in a comprehensible *narrative* mode. Sometimes when a play is adapted to the screen, an unimaginative director makes the end product appear merely a stage-play filmed by a workmanlike camera crew on a sound stage. This was not the case with *L'Aigle à deux têtes*; the playwright was also the film director, and he was able to present the story on film the way he wanted it to be perceived. Jean Cocteau managed to turn a claustrophobic three-act dramatic play about a Queen's death-wish into a sweeping, romantic, melodramatic, particularly coctelian film

---

[1] *Cocteau on the Film*, 88. *'Je ramenais le public, sans l'ombre de ménagements, au théâtre d'actes. Actes qui empêchent l'ennui que la plupart de nos spectateurs prennent pour le sérieux.' Entretiens sur le cinématographe* with André Fraigneau (Paris: Pierre Belfond, 1973), 60. All subsequent quotations in the original French are taken from this source.

complete with location shots, interesting camera movements, and emotionally charged music.

The reason the film may not have wooed American audiences, then, could have been their discomfort or confusion with the style of Jean Cocteau. He operated by his own rules and nobody else's. The standard Hollywood films of the time featured goal-driven protagonists and were shot in a certain manner, with prescribed camera angles, distances, rules (such as the 180 degree rule) and predictable shot orders. Cocteau's film was different. Thematically, Cocteau conformed to the objectives of the classical mode by having all the parts of the narrative work together to create a unified whole, and by having the conflict resolved at the end. Technically, however, Cocteau's film flouted the established formal rules. In France, Cocteau was freer to follow his own vision (a kind of pre-ordained auteurism). The French sense of directorial freedom grew out of a poetic sensibility rooted in the nationalism of France. Hence, while *L'Aigle à deux têtes* was a film that thematically followed a standard Hollywood formula in its use of a goal-driven protagonist within a cause and effect narrative, the style of the film was purely coctelian.

The prime æsthetic behind the filmmaking style in the classical American cinema of the post war era is its discretion, its unselfconsciousness. Cocteau disregards this rule in his play-turned-film about the fate of an Austrian Queen and her would-be assassin. Indeed, Cocteau once remarked that his 'primary concern in a film is to prevent the images from flowing, to oppose them to each other, to anchor them and join them without destroying their relief'..[1] But his comment does not quite hold for this film which does, indeed, flow. Cocteau was a poet who inserted his personality and poetry into every art form he explored. A coctelian element in *L'Aigle à deux têtes* apparent upon first viewing is the impeccable decadence surrounding the Queen. Although such grandeur is expected when depicting royalty, this Queen, veiled and cloistered, finds herself in a period of extended mourning. One might think that somebody in mourning would care little to be surrounded by luxury. But his film gave Cocteau, in conjunction with his esteemed set designer Christian Bérard, the opportunity to create a majestically decorated set (a set far removed in beauty from the environments of *Le Sang d'un poète* or even the more similar *La Belle et la bête*). However, some critics tried to fault the set design by claiming that the bed the Queen slept in was anachronistic, when, in fact, 'that

---

[1] Ibid., 15. '*Mon premier soin, dans un film, est d'empêcher que les images ne coulent, de les opposer, encastrer et joindre sans nuire à leur relief.*' Ibid., 14.

bed was the one young Queen Victoria had slept in'..[1] Despite Cocteau's claim that his inspiration for the character of the Queen was modelled after the real Empress Elisabeth of Austria, who was assassinated in 1898, some viewers could not believe that a Queen would have a trapeze in her home to alleviate periods of boredom. While this bizarre fact is true, there is good reason for viewers to have believed that the trapeze was a peculiar coctelian feature added to the film. After all, Cocteau had maintained a lifelong fascination with the circus and in 1917 had created the ballet, *Parade,* with Pablo Picasso and Erik Satie, which featured a circus theme.

Other coctelian features found in *L'Aigle à deux têtes* include the many statues and candelabra scattered throughout the set. Past films by Cocteau, like *Le Sang d'un poète* and *La Belle et la bête,* were peppered with statues that came to life and candles that created a hazy, muted, romantic atmosphere. One might conclude that the naked male statues, mirrors and candles were included because of Cocteau's fascination with the mysterious, sensual, and beautiful. The theme of *L'Aigle à deux têtes,* whereby a poet is the focus of a Queen's quest to die to escape from her grief and tortured, lonely life on earth, is reminiscent of Cocteau's feelings when his young companion Raymond Radiguet died from typhoid on December 12, 1923 at the age of twenty. After Radiguet's death, Cocteau expressed his feelings, similar to those of the Queen, in a letter to a friend:

> ... The death of my poor boy has been the finishing blow for me. Death would be better than this half-death ... Friends, religion, bring me no comfort; you know what I need, and it is not something to be had for the asking ... I suffer night and day[2]

One can draw parallels between the character of the Queen and Cocteau even though he generally insisted that one should not attempt to draw such parallels from his creations. Due, in part, to Radiguet's death, Cocteau became fascinated with the concept of the romantic and tragic as inseparable entities. Love and death are themes foregrounded in all of Cocteau's works, including *L'Aigle à deux têtes,* as illustrated in the variable emotional state of the relationship between the Queen and Stanislas.

Although the emotional tenor of the play and the film of *L'Aigle à deux têtes* remains the same, the presentation of the action which

---

[1] Ibid., 90. '[C]elui de la reine Victoria dans la jeunesse...' Ibid., 62.

[2] Steegmuller, 316. Letter to Abbé Mugnier, c. December 1923, reported by Mme Singer.

L'Aigle à deux têtes : The Anarchist and the Queen
(Jean Marais and Edwige Feuillère)
Courtesy of the Museum of Modern Art Film Stills Archive
© Jean Cocteau/SODRAC (Montréal) 1998

evokes the passions of the story is necessarily different due to their belonging to two separate art forms. In the play, all the scenes are set in either the bedroom or the library, spaces which have the potential to create a static performance if the actors are unable to control either the space or an overwhelming text. For another director the obstacles of the text and the sparseness of scenes could prove to be a problem in the adaptation from stage to screen. Cocteau was able to excise a significant amount of the text by creating new, shorter bits of dialogue and by adding more spatial variety. The large monologues were kept but shortened to keep the film from exceeding two hours in length.

To initiate a comprehensive analysis of *L'Aigle à deux têtes*, it seems obvious to commence with Cocteau's decision not to begin the film in the Queen's bedroom as written in the play. Instead, the film opens with a beautiful, outdoor setting sweeping across a landscape which the audience should presume to be in Austria. This helps to suggest the location that would otherwise not have been clear in the play until Stanislas enters in mountaineer's attire. The opening shot of the film helps to establish several points of reference that would otherwise not have been clear until much later in the action. For instance, the presence of Felix and Edith in the carriage next to the Queen gives the Queen the opportunity to explain to the characters (and hence the viewer) that she is having a ball to commemorate the ten year anniversary of the King's assassination and their wedding day. The opening shot also sets up the Queen's entrance to the Krantz castle that helps to reveal one of her character traits. The Queen does not stay in any one castle for more than a few days because of a paranoid belief that she will be assassinated like her husband. The opening sequence visually highlights the Queen's idiosyncrasy by showing her arrive at a new location. In the play, this character trait is only mentioned, due to practical considerations; thus, the medium of film, in this case, serves to provide a stronger depiction of a character-trait. The Queen's arrival at the castle is filmed, incidentally, with considerable pomp expressed in elaborate terms. An overhead shot looking down on the proceedings as they happen is accompanied by grand processional-like music suited to royalty. The musical score of the film adds an interesting dimension which was not suitable in the stage-play.

The music in *L'Aigle à deux têtes* illustrates some interesting points in regard to Cocteau's notions of the function of a film score. The use of processional music in the opening sequence represents the second incidence of music being used to direct the audience's feelings and emotions. The music used in *L'Aigle à deux têtes* is flagrantly manipulative, just like the music used in 'typical' Hollywood films. Surprisingly, the use of music in the film is contradictory to what Cocteau said regarding the use of music in movies: 'Nothing, it seems to me, can be more vulgar than the musical synchronism in films'.[1] Yet, the music in this film is synchronized to complement the emotional tone of the scene in the same way that any Classical Hollywood director would attempt. The music of *L'Aigle à deux têtes* succeeds fully in directing the spectator's emotions most dramatically in the scene where the Queen rides into Krantz, with soldiers standing on guard, accompanied by royal processional music which evokes feelings of pomp and circumstance. Georges Auric composed the music for the film and though Cocteau said that he and Auric agreed to 'accidental synchronism' such 'accidents' seem to be quite predetermined in this film.[2] Another example of synchronizing specific music with specific action occurs during the scene where the Queen and Tony, her servant, are racing their horses. She is happy, saying that she cannot believe she avoided happiness for so long. The music that underscores the riding scene is raucous, loud and pounding. At this point, the viewer cannot tell if the Queen and Stanislas had been intimate at the conclusion of the scene prior, but the viewer would know that her love for him has blossomed, inasmuch as the music which accompanies the scene ties in neatly with the image of the galloping horses, an established symbol for sex and bursting passion. The combination of the music and the image gives the viewer the impression that *something* has transpired between the Queen and Stanislas.

As for the outdoor landscapes used periodically as settings in the film, one can see that Cocteau utilizes location shooting to help the film's story flow with more visual variety. The outdoor shots expand the vision of the audience to see the world which the Queen inhabits; they help to create a context which the story inhabits. These outdoor shots also provide new space for the members of the Queen's staff to have discreet discussions, discussions which could only take place in the play when the Queen is offstage. In addition to the first outdoor establishing shot, there is another scene where soldiers go to Stanislas' stepmother's home and question her about his whereabouts, a scene which was not included in the play but was created specifically for the film. Similarly, the first fifteen minutes of the film that occur outside constitute an entirely new beginning not found in the original play. But such changes do not detract from the story; rather, they enhance it. By the time one witnesses the bickering scene between Felix and Edith, the first scene of the play, the film viewer is immersed in the story.

---

[1] *Cocteau on the Film*, 71. 'Rien ne me semble plus vulgaire que le synchronisme musical dans les films...' 50.

[2] '[L]e synchronisme accidental'. Ibid., 51.

In the play, Act Two starts in the Queen's library; but in the film, additional material is added. The shots outdoors leading up to the film's library scene show Count von Foehn arriving at the Krantz castle only to discover a ball has taken place. By this time the viewer is aware that the Queen's would-be assassin is in the castle and is being attended to by the Queen herself. In the conversation, the Count learns how the assassin escaped from the guards and police. Following this explanation, the Count is seen in a carriage discussing what a nuisance the Queen has become, thus establishing that, though it is his job to protect the Queen, he and the Archduchess have hopes that the assassin will kill the Queen once in the castle. With these added scenes, the film viewer is privy to information not immediately revealed in the play and, in particular, becomes aware more explicitly of the Count's disloyalty to the Queen. The film more clearly suggests that the assassin was allowed to enter the castle with the help of security, an idea only alluded to in the play when the Queen merely suggests the possibility of the Count's involvement in the break-in. She says to Stanislas in the play:

> How amusing if, unwittingly, you were his secret tool? That would explain your escape, the slackness of the police, and with what else you slipped out of their clutches. It is unusual for Foehn to miss his man..[1]

Outdoor shots not only provide new insights for the viewer but also draw the narrative outside cramped quarters. Due to the physical limitations of the theatre, all the scenes in the play were situated in either the Queen's library or bedroom; thus, secondary characters could not offer new information unless the Queen was offstage. With new outdoor scenes added in the film, the dramatic devices for arranging confrontations become less necessary and the story becomes almost plausible. 'Almost' plausible because the scene which takes place in the King's former tree-house may be considered a stretch of the imagination; it seems unlikely that a tree-house built for a ten year old boy maybe fifteen or twenty years earlier could sustain the weight of a forty-five year old man and another adult.

The final outdoor scenes of the film feature the soldiers and the band moving into formation to prepare for the Queen's unveiled appearance. These scenes work well for the end of the film because the

---

[1] Cocteau, 252–53. 'Il serait drôle, sans le savoir, que vous fussiez son arme secrète. Cela m'expliquerait votre fuite, la mollesse de la brigade, et avec quelle aisance vous avez glissé entre ses mains. D'habitude, Foëhn ne rate pas son homme.' *L'Aigle à deux têtes* (Paris: Gallimard, 1946), 63 (Act I, scene vi). All subsequent quotations in the original French are taken from this source.

cross-cut editing between what is happening outside the castle (order, control) and what is happening inside the castle between Stanislas and the Queen (chaos) is contrasted with rhythmic balance. The cross-cutting, in conjunction with the highly anticipatory music, creates a heightened anxiety which builds suspense in the audience.

In addition to the use of location shots, the film medium also provided Cocteau with several camera angles from which to frame each scene. The overhead shot used at the beginning of *L'Aigle à deux têtes* is echoed many times later to create different effects. During the aforementioned processional scene the viewer is treated to a bird's eye view of the situation. When the ball is in progress, in a subjective shot, the Queen watches from a special curtained window in her bedroom. One almost feels as if the Queen is spying on her own party. This perspective is returned to as the guests leave the ball. These various points of view were, of course, not possible for an audience viewing the play. Cocteau said in an interview that through the use of high-angle shots he was able to 'catch some glimpses of my play from another angle than the dead angle of the stalls ... the cheap seats do to some extent the job of the film camera, giving the audience some very curious viewpoints, as though they were indiscreetly peeping through portholes, key-holes or trapdoors into cellars'.[1] The viewer sees what Edith sees when she enters the library from the top of the stairs and looks down on the scene of Stanislas reading *Hamlet* to the Queen. What this scene tells the audience to feel is difficult to articulate. It seems to indicate that the audience should be surprised at what Edith sees as someone usurping her position in the Queen's life. Or she could be, literally, looking down on Stanislas because she knows that his intention is to murder the Queen. This elevated position is reversed when the viewer sees Stanislas look down on Edith in the library. He is on a ladder arranging the Queen's books as Edith enters. It makes sense that he would now figuratively look down on her as well because, by this time, he knows that she is working with the Count and against the Queen; loyalty to the Queen has been switched between two unlikely characters.

Subjective camerawork is even more crucial in other shots. Cocteau achieves the 'peeping through portholes' effect perfectly in two scenes of this film. The first event is one that is merely recounted by Felix in the play. It occurs when he watches the Queen visit the room dedicated

---

[1] *Cocteau on the Film*, 89. 'J'y avais découvert ma pièce sous un autre angle que l'angle mort des fauteuils d'orchestre... les petites places faisant à l'avance le travail d'un appareil de prise de vues et présentant le spectacle avec une singularité qui ressemble au coup d'œil indiscret à travers des trous de serrures, des œils-de-bœuf ou des soupiraux de cave.' 61.

as a shrine to the King. In the film, the viewer sees Felix sneak up the stairway that was supposed to be off limits during the ball. The camera directs the viewer to notice the sneakiness of Felix but then immediately switches to Felix's point of view. The switch has been from an objective perspective to a subjective one. Felix (and the viewer) crouch, unobserved by the Queen, behind a statue and watch as she walks from her bedroom to the shrine. The scene proceeds with a subjective shot from the Queen's point of view as she enters the room. The spectator sees the room as she sees it. This very brief shot is followed by an objective shot of the Queen dwelling over a picture of her husband. The next cut returns to Felix's subjective view as he (and the viewer) watch the Queen retreat to her bedroom. By observing this scene through Felix's eyes, one may feel particularly intrusive, for Felix and the viewer are witnessing someone's private grief and suffering. The invasion of the Queen's privacy could not be as strongly represented on stage since Felix merely verbally recounts the event to Edith some time after it happened. In the film the immediacy and impact of his breach of trust is brought to the forefront.

The second 'peeping' scene occurs when the Count arrives to talk to the Queen about the assassin's capture. In the play, the Queen tells Stanislas to hide in the gallery so he may listen and observe the conversation. In the film, Stanislas is not told to hide in the gallery but behind a two-way mirror where he can see and hear what is happening in the room. In between the conversation of the Count and the Queen there are point of view shots from Stanislas' perspective. This is an eavesdropping scene where the audience can be both a distant observer and the eavesdropper himself. The substitution of the two-way mirror for the gallery as the place of hiding can be contextualized in light of Cocteau's past works. In *Le Livre blanc*, the narrator speaks of attending male brothels where peep shows took place:

> You enter a dark booth and open a shutter. This reveals a metallic cloth, through which you find yourself looking into a small bathroom. On the other side, the cloth is a mirror, so completely reflecting and highly polished that it is impossible to guess that it is being stared through..[1]

Another feature that one may call coctelian is the scene where Felix watches the Queen walk down the hallway to the shrine. In this scene

---

[1] Steegmuller, 17–18. *'On s'installe dans une cabine obscure et on écarte un volet. Ce volet découvre une toile métallique à travers laquelle l'œil embrasse une petite salle de bains. De l'autre côté la toile était glace si réfléchissante et si lisse qu'il était impossible de deviner qu'elle était pleine de regards.' Le Livre blanc* (Paris: Passage du Marais, 1992), 55–56.

the door magically opens by itself. This image is reminiscent of *La Belle et la bête* wherein the Beast's home was a place of magical activity. Doors open by themselves, bed covers pull back without help, and wine is poured from disembodied hands. The self-opening door in *L'Aigle à deux têtes* is indeed an example of a signature moment in the film.

Cocteau never claimed to be a great filmmaker. He said, 'I didn't know anything about film art. I invented it for myself as I went along, and used it like a draughtsman [sic] dipping his finger for the first time in Indian ink and smudging a sheet of paper with it'..[1] Though he attended many films himself, he did not follow the techniques of the popular directors in his time. This is not to say that his films looked as if they were directed by an amateur. Cocteau possessed a gift for picking up trades quickly; as a new film director he did well. But Cocteau had a tendency to ignore basic rules in order to realize his vision. He constructed films the way he constructed poems — without any regard for how 'things should be done.' This may be part of the reason American audiences did not respond favourably to *L'Aigle à deux têtes*. While there are not many anomalies in the film-making of *L'Aigle à deux têtes*, there are enough for one to distinguish between the style of Cocteau's film and those filmed in the Classical Hollywood style. Some of Cocteau's camera movement may be questionable because it was not always motivated by conventional methods and expectations. For instance, the camera shots after Stanislas has broken into the Queen's bedroom and during the time she speaks to him at length are typical shot-reverse-shots of the two of them. The audience sees her speak, then the camera cuts to Stanislas' reaction. But quite unconventionally, during the Queen's monologue the camera focuses on Stanislas and slowly tracks in on him, ending in close-up. During this shot he does not say anything nor does his face reveal anything he may be thinking. In a standard Hollywood film a slow tracking shot may be used to show the audience a gradual shot of a character's change in facial expression such as the transformation from passivity to tension. Or it may be used to show that the character is, literally or figuratively, a target as the camera moves closer. Since nothing of the sort happens here, the viewer is confused. Typically, tracking in on somebody's face invites the viewer to take a closer look at that character. Stanislas' impassive reaction to the monologue seems hardly worthy of such stylistic attention.

---

[1] *Cocteau on the Film*, 16. '[J]'ignorais tout de l'art cinématique. Je l'inventais pour mon propre compte et l'employais comme un dessinateur [sic] qui tremperait son doigt pour la première fois dans l'encre de Chine et tacherait une feuille avec.' 15.

Immediately following this questionable shot is what seems to be a mistake on the part of the editor. Preceding the slow tracking into Stanislas' face, the Queen has walked away from him as she spoke and stopped a few feet from him; then the slow tracking shot occurs. The next cut displays a shot of her facing him and then of her walking away. There has been no transition shot showing the Queen cross back over to Stanislas as she is speaking; she suddenly appears with her back to the camera. The sequence is slightly disorienting and seemingly unmotivated. One could almost forgive Cocteau this edit when he repeats a shot in three variations shortly thereafter. The shots occur when the Queen tells Stanislas what he symbolizes to her:

> 'You are not a man for me. You know who you are? You are my death. Yes, my death.'[1]

This scene is punctuated by a repetition of variations on that last line three times proceeding from a medium close-up of the Queen, to a close-up of her face, followed by an extreme close-up of just her eyes. This privileging artistic technique underlines the Queen's desire for a quick and easy death at the hands of the man who has broken into her home.

Unfortunately, this is the first and last example of unusual editing in this film. Similarly, Cocteau uses a single slow-motion sequence for maybe six seconds of screen-time with no follow-up. It occurs after Tony dresses Stanislas in Royal costumes from the museum and Felix runs into him. Stanislas asks Felix if he truly resembles the slain King because of the startled look upon Felix's face. This is followed by the shot of Stanislas going through the curtain to the top of the stairs. As he comes through the curtain his actions are recorded in slow-motion but it is so quick that it is almost missed. Repeated watching of this segment gives one reason to wonder what was the point of using slow-motion when it does not seem to have any impact on the scene. For as Stanislas descends the stairs the slow-motion ceases, and he begins a conversation with the Queen. This technique merely highlights a specific moment. Maybe if slow-motion had been used when Stanislas approached Felix prior to coming down the stairs, the floating movement would have suggested an image of the King's ghost and mystified Felix's brief bewilderment. On the other hand, when Cocteau had used slow-motion sequences in *La*

---

[1] *L'Aigle à deux têtes*, 'En ce qui me concerne, je ne peux plus vous envisager comme un homme.

Quoi ? Vous me demandez qui vous êtes ? Mais, cher monsieur, vous êtes ma mort.' (Paris: Gallimard, 1946), 59 (Act I, scene vi).

Belle et la bête, for instance, they added a poetic beauty and mysteriousness to the film.

Cut to the stable scene later in the film when the Count checks up on how the Queen will be travelling. The angles in this scene jump midway through for no apparent reason. It looks as if Cocteau just decided to move the camera from its place behind the 180 degree line to put it behind some of the actors to offer a different view of the scene. This throws off the lines of perception for the viewer, a phenomenon rare to most films.

One of the good things Cocteau did with the camera was to exploit its mobility. *L'Aigle à deux têtes* is not a static film. From the beginning of the film, some type of movement always fills the frame. The opening scene shows a carriage moving along mountains. The processional scene where the Queen is flanked by her soldiers is filmed using an almost full 360 degree turn to capture her full surroundings. The dramatic camera turn offers the viewer a full, sweeping view of the Queen's uniformed entourage as they move into formation. Cocteau utilizes this circular technique again at the ball. The viewer can capture everything happening at the ball: all the eloquent movements within a beautiful decor.

By shooting on an angle, the camera is able to obtain clear shots of the depth of the settings. It is accomplished by shooting through one space to reveal a completely different space further in the background as illustrated in the 'Felix spying scene': the camera shoots down the hall on a slight angle to reveal another room in the background with its door ajar. The ballroom scenes give the cameraman the opportunity to use the depth of the set to portray boundless space. The way the ballroom scene is shot helps to suggest to the viewer that something is happening outside the frame. This suggestion is made through the constant movement of the camera and the characters. By having movement take place in the foreground, the middle ground and the background at specifically choreographed moments, the shots always look busy but not crowded. This effect achieves a totality of spatial reality: that which is staged and choreographed looks natural, yet there is always the suggestion of still more fully furnished space and more active people just beyond the edges of the shifting frame. This shot also shows how news that the Queen would not be at the ball is transferred to the guests. The shot begins by focusing on the President's wife who is told by the Queen's major-domo, Adam, and from there it spreads like wildfire. This is illustrated not only with the slow pan around the room but also with the sound of constant whispering. The whispering is of one line only, over and over again. It sounds as if it was recorded once and played repeatedly until Edith's entrance.

Another specifically filmic feature is the use of the voice-over. Cocteau is able to place himself in the film by inserting voice-overs not found in the original play. The first one occurs when Cocteau says:

> Tony has dressed Stanislas in the royal costumes from the museum. Willenstein, unable to forget the room where the Queen went the night before, returned there secretly. He saw the King..[1]

This voice-over could have been left out by having Stanislas say that Tony dresses him; but, instead, Cocteau chose to jump into the story at this point and explain Stanislas' new outfit himself. The second voice-over is a commentary on the events happening on the screen between the Queen and Stanislas, but from a poetic point of view. The voice-over occurs after the Queen finds out that the Count was aware of Stanislas' presence in the building. The Queen begins to confide in the young man as he lays his head in her lap. During a pause, Cocteau's voice enters:

> They were the dream of a sleeper who is sleeping soundly. That he doesn't even know he is sleeping.[2]

These lines are transposed from Stanislas' lines in the play text:

> Some dreams are too intense. They awake the sleeper. We must take care. For we are the dream of one who sleeps so profoundly that he is not even aware that he is dreaming us..[3]

In the play, Cocteau speaks through Stanislas. For the film, Cocteau skips right over Stanislas and makes the words his own. Cocteau often spoke of the importance of dreams in his explanations of his creative vision; he even claimed that he lived 'intensely only in dreams'.[4] The final time the viewer hears Cocteau's voice occurs at the end of the film after the Queen and Stanislas have died:

---

[1] Film: *'Tony venait d'habiller Stanislas dans le musée des costumes du roi. Willenstein ne pouvait oublier la porte mystérieuse ouverte par la reine le soir du bal. Il retourna en cachette. Brusquement, il vit le roi.'*

[2] Ibid: *'Ils étaient les rêves d'un dormeur qui dort si profondément qu'il ne sait même pas qu'il les rêve.'*

[3] Cocteau, 280. *'Il y a des rêves trop intenses. Ils réveillent ceux qui dorment. Méfions-nous. Nous sommes le rêve d'un dormeur qui dort si profondément qu'il ne sait même pas qu'il nous rêve.* 124 (Act II, scene ix).

[4] *Cocteau on the Film*, 25. *'Je ne commence à vivre intensément que dans le sommeil et le rêve.'* 21.

> In the eyes of the police and of history the Krantz tragedy is a mystery.
> But love laughs at politics. Everything happened just like that.[1]

Cocteau's words poetically close the film with the notion that love
and death are mysterious to all, not just to the characters in his film.
Cocteau's final voice-over offers the viewer a personal address from
the poet summing up the experience of the film.

L'Aigle à deux têtes was a success in Europe because it appealed to a
European sensibility for art films. The film that was born from a play
successfully transformed from one medium to another because Cocteau
knew how to trim the text and focus the story on the main characters.
The use of location shooting, point of view shots and a Hollywood-style
score helped to pull the film together. *L'Aigle à deux têtes* was not successful in the United States for several reasons, but perhaps the main
reason was that Cocteau's film was too sophisticated for most American
post-war audiences. American audiences of the time were accustomed to
movies which conformed to specific Hollywood standards. If American
audiences at the time were confronted with a product that they could
not easily instantly consume, they were dissatisfied and responded by
labelling it 'unclear' or 'a dud,' as one finds in reviews by the *New York
Times* and *Variety* of *L'Aigle à deux têtes* when it was released in New
York. For Cocteau, the American response to his film suggested that
they wanted to put a label on his film and categorize it. Perhaps Cocteau's best response to the American critics occurred when, several years
after making the film, he told an interviewer that: 'A work of art ...
should be made of such a shape that people don't know which way to
hold it, which embarrasses and irritates the critics, incites them to be
rude, but keeps it fresh'.[2] Cocteau's remarks appropriately apply to
L'Aigle à deux têtes. In hindsight, perhaps the American critics should
have given this 'oddly shaped' film another look.

---

[1] Film: '*Aux yeux de la police et de l'histoire le drame de Krantz demeure énigme,
mais l'amour est plus fort que la politique et tout est arrivé comme je l'ai dit.*'

[2] *Cocteau on the Film*, 30. '*Une œuvre doit être un "objet difficile à ramasser". Elle
doit se défendre contre les attouchements vulgaires, les tripotages qui la ternissent
et qui la déforment. Il faut ne pas savoir par quel bout la prendre, ce qui gêne les
critiques, les agace, les pousse à l'insulte, mais préserve sa fraîcheur.*' 24.

Léonie: The Director within Les Parents terribles

Tamara El-Hoss

An analysis of the character Léonie in Jean Cocteau's play *Les Parents terribles* shows that she is, in fact, the central character in the play. Léonie (Léo) controls and manipulates every other character and, in doing so, she acts as the director within the play. Furthermore, this character can be fruitfully analysed within the framework of A.-J. Greimas' *Actantial Model* as presented in his work *Structural Semantics: An Attempt at a Method* (1983). Finally, we will discuss Lydia Crowson's model of triangular relationships proposed in *The Esthetic of Jean Cocteau* and Pierre Dubourg's analysis of Léo in *Dramaturgie de Jean Cocteau*. Unless otherwise stated, all English quotations from the play are from the translation of *Les Parents terribles* published by Hill and Wang (1996) entitled *Intimate Relations.*[1]

* * *

'The play opens in the apartment of George and Yvonne (no last names indicated), who live there together with their son, Michel [sic] ... and Yvonne's unmarried sister, Léonie.'[2] George is a failed inventor while his wife Yvonne is a diabetic who spends her days in her room, in bed, worrying about and trying to control her son's life. Throughout the play, we learn that George was Léonie's fiancé but decided to marry her sister Yvonne instead. Henceforth, 'Léonie thought it her *duty* [empha-

---

[1] Cocteau, *Five Plays*, 70–154.

[2] Raymond Bach, "Cocteau and Vichy: Family Disconnections," *L'Ésprit Créateur* 33, no 1 (Spring 1993), 29.

99

sis added] to sacrifice her own happiness in order to take care of her child-like sister and brother-in-law.'[1]

The curtain rises on a *coup de théâtre*: George is looking for Léo because Yvonne has taken too much insulin and has nearly killed herself. Here we are presented with the first part of the common coctelian theme of double death as illustrated in *L'Aigle à deux têtes* where the queen already 'looks dead' when she meets Stanislas and then dies a physical death later in the play. An insulin overdose indicates Yvonne's first (implicit) death; her second (explicit) death, like the queen's, will occur at the end of the play.

During the insulin crisis, George wants to call a doctor, but Léo orders him to get some sugar. The virtual spectator is, again, faced with a rational clear-headed Léo who saves her sister's life, an image strengthened by George saying, 'If you hadn't been here, Léo, I should just have let her die.'[2] What are we to make of this statement? Why didn't George take the initiative and bring sugar to his wife without Léo telling him to do so? The answer is simple: Léo is *the* adult, she is the only character in this play who is controlled rather than impulsive. 'She represents the existence of an order ... As a detached observer of the rest of her family, she plays a role that hides her emotions. Even her stylish clothing contrasts with the others' lack of concern for appearances ... The distinction between the adults and the children of the play is made in the first act'[3]:

> Léo [*speaking to Yvonne*]: There are two kinds of people in this world: the children and the grownups. I, alas, belong to the grownups; you, George, Mick ... you belong to the children ... [4]

'Léo is the only adult in a child's *roulotte* [caravan], which is Yvonne's pet term for the apartment and which evokes the freedom and independence of gypsies. Such people exist outside of society's laws because they refuse to be part of a larger, more regimented system.

---

[1] Ibid., 30.

[2] *Les Parents terribles*, 72. '*Sans toi, Léo, elle mourait.*' *Les Parents terribles* (Paris: Gallimard, 1938), 17 (Act I, scene i). All subsequent French quotations are taken from this source.

[3] Lydia Crowson, *The Esthetic of Jean Cocteau* (Hanover, N.H.: University of New Hampshire Press, 1978), 144.

[4] *Les Parents terribles*, 75. '*En ce monde il y a les enfants et les grandes personnes. Je me compte, hélas, parmi les grandes personnes. Toi... Georges... Mik, vous êtes de la race des enfants..*', 24 (Act I, scene ii).

Therefore, Georges, Yvonne, and their son lead an unstructured life.'[1] Léo, on the other hand, leads a *structured* life. She lives within society's laws and brings order to the caravan and to its occupants. 'She is the voice of reason who explains the characters to themselves and chides them for their shortcomings.'[2] As before, this emphasizes the adult versus child opposition by placing Léonie in a parental role.

This parental role reoccurs throughout the play as we learn that it is Léo who cleans the apartment and controls the money, though she tells Yvonne 'You know what little money I have is yours.'[3] In fact, the family is dependent upon Léonie due to an inheritance from an uncle who respected her *orderly* way of life. She is, therefore, the one who can and does 'keep them all' (Léo's own words). Even when Léonie decides not to play the role of the adult by refusing to do the housework, the other occupants of the caravan are not willing to assume responsibility for the household chores. As Michael tells Madeleine, 'We wash in the basin, when Léo decides to let us down. But she's much too fond of her comfort; she can't keep it up.'[4] Comfort may be Léonie's motivation, but neither comfort nor discomfort seem to motivate Michael, Yvonne or George — they simply wait until Léo can no longer tolerate their disorder. Léonie, therefore, is the only character in the Caravan that is willing to take action.

*   *   *

Léo *manipulates* and *controls* the caravan's occupants; her love of order seeps into other people's lives. She *dictates* and *controls* her family's actions. Léo is the *puppeteer* while the characters around her (Yvonne, George, Michael and Madeleine) are the puppets. In Act I, Léo, playing on Yvonne's inverted Œdipal complex, suggests that Michael's failure to come home that night was because he was with a woman. She also insinuates that her husband, George, has a mistress. Yvonne is more distraught over the possibility of Michael being 'unfaithful' to her with another woman than the implication that George is having an affair. Léo encourages this when she tells her sister that Michael has '*been* unfaithful to you, he is *being* unfaithful to

---

[1] Crowson., 144–45.

[2] Oxenhandler, 187.

[3] *Les Parents terribles*, 98. 'Mon peu d'argent est le vôtre,' 66 (Act I, scene ix).

[4] Ibid., 103. '*Chez nous, on prend des tubs. De temps en temps Léo nous laisse en panne. Mais elle aime trop ses aises. Elle ne tient pas le coup.*' 77 (Act II, scene i).

you.'[1] It is important to note that at this point Léo is only *speculating* about Mick and George being involved with other women. She is clearly playing mind games with Yvonne.

Léo's suspicions about Mick and George are confirmed, however, when Michael confesses his love for Madeleine to his family and when George confides the following to her:

> I've been a fool and I'm paying dearly for it. Six months ago I needed a shorthand-typist. I was given an address and I found a young woman of twenty-five, unhappy, good-looking, simple, perfect. I was feeling very lonely at home ... I said I was a widower ... She told me she loved me ... that young men bored her, and so on and so forth. After three months her attitude changed. A sister from the country came up to stay with her ... The 'sister' was a young man she'd fallen in love with. And the young man was Michael. He just told me so himself.[2]

Upon finding out that Michael and George are both in love with the *same* woman, Léonie devises her first of three plans in the play: Michael and Madeleine's break-up. She convinces George and Yvonne to accept Mick's invitation to meet Madeleine, and tells George what he must do in order to facilitate the break-up: confront and blackmail Madeleine.

*   *   *

The *Actantial Model* theory by A.-J. Greimas, provides a basis for analysing the interaction involved in Léo's plan. In this theory, Greimas states that the Actantial Model 'is entirely centred on the object of desire aimed at by the subject and situated, as object of communication, between the sender and the receiver — the desire of the subject being, in its part, modulated in projections from the helper and opponent.'[3] He uses the following diagram to illustrate his theory:

---

[1] Ibid., 79. *'Il te trompait. Il te trompe.'* 31 (Act I, scene ii).

[2] Ibid., 95. *'Léo, j'ai fait une folie et je la paie cher. Il y a six mois, je croyais avoir besoin d'une sténo-dactylo; on me donne une adresse. Je tombe chez une jeune personne de vingt-cinq ans, malheureuse, belle, simple, parfaite. Je me sentais très seul à la maison... J'invente que je suis veuf... Elle me dit qu'elle m'aime...que les jeunes sont mufles, etc. Au bout de trois mois, elle change d'attitude. Une sœur de province habite chez elle... La sœur était un jeune homme qu'elle aime. Et le jeune homme c'est Michel. Je viens de l'apprendre de sa propre bouche.'* 61.

[3] A.-J. Greimas, *Structural Semantics: An Atttempt at a Method* (Lincoln: University of Nebraska Press, 1983), 207. *'[E]st tout entier axé sur l'objet du désir visé par le sujet, et situé, comme objet de communication, entre le destinateur*

sender — | object | ⇒ receiver
⇑
helper ⇒ | subject | ⇐ opponent

Léo's first plan can be illustrated with the following *Actantial Model*:

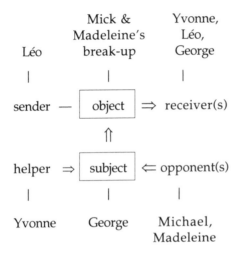

```
              Mick &       Yvonne,
            Madeleine's      Léo,
   Léo        break-up      George

    |            |            |

  sender  — | object | ⇒ receiver(s)
                 ⇑
  helper  ⇒ | subject | ⇐ opponent(s)

    |            |            |

  Yvonne      George      Michael,
                          Madeleine
```

The origin of the *object* in Greimas' *Actantial Model* is the *sender* and not the *subject*. Léo, who orchestrates Michael and Madeleine's break-up (the *object*), is therefore the *sender*. She also acts as the *receiver*, gaining control of George's actions and the young couple's fate. George is the *subject* since he desires the *object*, and he is the *receiver* gaining revenge against Madeleine. Yvonne agrees to meet Madeleine (at Léo's urging); therefore, she is the *helper*. She's also a *receiver* in the sense that her son, having lost Madeleine, will come back to her. Madeleine and Michael are the *opponents*, but not knowingly nor willingly, as they are unaware of Léonie's plan.

In Act II, Léo arrives at Madeleine's apartment before George and Yvonne to set the stage for her plan. She tells Michael: 'I arranged to

---

et le destinataire, le désir du sujet étant, de son côté, modulé en projections d'adju- vant et d'opposant.' A.J. Greimas, *Sémantique structurale, recherche de méthode* (Paris: Larousse, 1966), 180.

get here well ahead of the others,' (110) 'I hate arriving anywhere in a gang ... I wanted to get here first and prepare the ground.'[1] Michael misinterprets the meaning of these words and *assumes* that his aunt came early to help him, an assumption Léonie knew he would make. In fact, Léo has arrived early to 'prepare the ground' for a performance by one of her puppets — George.

She doesn't take Michael's word when he explains that nothing can be heard from the second floor of Madeleine's apartment, a crucial point for the success of her plan. She tests, for herself, the sound effects of the stage she has prepared, indicating, once again, her need for total control. Upon meeting Madeleine, she instructs her to pretend that they had not met in order to give Yvonne the *illusion* of being the first member of the family (aside from Michael) to meet her. If she is to direct this play — and the play within the play — she must, and does, control all of her surroundings and all her players. The stage is set for her plan.

At the end of Act II Léo, who is attracted to Madeleine's personality and sense of order, has a change of heart. '[S]eeing the piteous state to which Madeleine has been reduced by her sacrifice, [Léo] is suddenly filled with regret and decides to turn things around.'[2] 'Damn it all — there are limits' she declares.[3] The beauty of the young lovers seems 'right' to her while the alternative, Michael and Madeleine's break-up, seems deplorable. She tells Madeleine part of the truth, as she always does with those she manipulates: 'I didn't come here as your ally, still less as your accomplice. Now I should like to be both. I am coming over to your side.' 'I've adopted you. From now on you're under my very special protection.'[4] What this means to the rest of the play is that Léo will strive to change the minds of Yvonne, George and Michael. She will set in motion her second plan. Who has such power but the *director* of a play, the one who has complete control over the action of others? Léo's second plan can be illustrated as follows:

---

[1] *Les Parents terribles*, 112. '*Je me suis arrangée pour être très en avance.*' 89 (Act II, scene ii), '*Mais je déteste les arrivées en masse... Je ne vous cache pas que je voulais arriver la première et préparer le terrain.*' 92.

[2] Bach, 30.

[3] *Les Parents terribles*, 129. '*Il y a des limites...*' 130.

[4] Ibid., 129, 131. '*Je ne venais pas comme votre alliée, encore moins votre accomplice. J'ai le désir de l'être. C'est sans doute l'alliance de l'ordre contre le désordre. Toujours est-il que je passe dans votre camp.*' 131. '*Je t'adopte. Ne me reconduisez pas...*' 134.

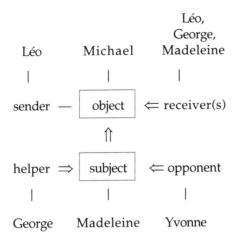

The *subject*, Madeleine, wants to be reunited with Michael (the *object*). Léo is once more the *sender* in the sense that she is the one who *devises* and *initiates* the plan. And, again, she is the *receiver* because she gains *control* (over Yvonne, George, Mick and Madeleine). George is the *helper* since he agrees to speak to Michael on Madeleine's behalf, and he is the *receiver* as he gains his son's happiness. Madeleine is also a *receiver*, gaining her own happiness as well as Mick's. Yvonne, on the other hand, is the unwilling and unknowing *opponent*.

In the third act, Léo's second plan unfolds and her goal is met: Michael and Madeleine are back together. 'But Yvonne, who feels left out and betrayed, reveals in a final *coup de théâtre* that she has poisoned herself.'[1] 'She simply reacts without thinking, as usual, because she understands the inevitability of what is about to take place — Michel's marriage.'[2] While Yvonne is suffering on her death bed, Léo tells Madeleine (who wants to leave): 'Don't be silly. Stay where you are. It's an order. Besides, Michael is going to need you. Just as George is going to need me.'[3] Yvonne can hear what Léonie is saying and realizes that her son's and her husband's life will go on without her. Did Léo make that statement so that Yvonne could hear it? If she is truly the director within this play, then the answer is yes — she *wanted* her

---

[1] Bach, 30.

[2] Crowson, 78.

[3] *Les Parents terribles*, 151. '*Ne soyez pas stupide. Restez. Je vous l'ordonne. Du reste, Michel va avoir besoin de vous, comme Georges aura besoin de moi.*' 173 (Act III, scene vii).

sister to know that her son and her husband will still live and be happy *without* her.

There is, however, a discrepancy between the endings of the English version used in this essay and the original French version of the play. The French version of *Les Parents terribles*, published by Gallimard in 1938, brings a new, more sinister, dimension to the character of Léo. When Michael asks his aunt for something to induce vomiting to help his mother, Léo states that Yvonne did not swallow poison but rather injected it; therefore, giving her something to induce vomiting would have no effect. She adds that even if she had an antidote, she would not administer it. Furthermore, she tells Michael that his mother is better off dead and did not deserve to live. Here is the highlight of this original 1938 scene in English translation:

> *Michael*: You would've killed mother?
> *Léo*: Look at you. You would give anything for her to be alive.... to torture her later. No Michael, we are people of the Street, we are people of mud, we were made to live. Your mother was made to be dead. Where she is now, there is no son, no father, no mistress. There is only love. Now she can live. She can inhabit the house. She can love a shadow.[1]

The answer to Michael's question is yes, Léo *would* have killed her own sister in order to finally be with George, but she does not admit it. The original French version indicates more strongly than the current English version the extent of Léo's power over her family. According to Pierre Dubourg, 'she thinks that the death of her sister is part of a supreme order.'[2] Even though she did not actually *kill* her sister, Léo assumes a god-like attitude when she decides that Yvonne is better off dead. But what if she had *known* —or at least anticipated— that Mick and Madeleine's reunion would push Yvonne into committing suicide? Léo was able to predict every character's reaction throughout the play, so she must have had some idea as to what her sister's reaction would be to the success of her second plan. Keeping this in mind, the following diagram depicts Léonie's *third* plan:

---

[1] Ibid., 246–47. Michel: '*Tu aurais tué maman?*' Léo: '*Le voilà votre milieu. Vous donneriez n'importe quoi pour qu'Yvonne soit vivante...et pour la torturer après. Non, Michel; nous, nous sommes des gens de la rue, des gens de la boue, nous sommes faits pour vivre. Ta mère était faite pour être morte. Là ou elle est il n'existe pas de fils, de père, de maîtresse. Il n'y a que l'amour. A présent, elle peut vivre. Elle peut habiter la maison. Elle peut aimer une ombre.*' (Act III, scene xi) 246–47.

[2] '*Elle croit que la mort de sa sœur est l'expression d'un ordre suprême.*' Pierre Dubourg, *Dramaturgie de Jean Cocteau* (Paris: Bernard Grasset, 1954), 94.

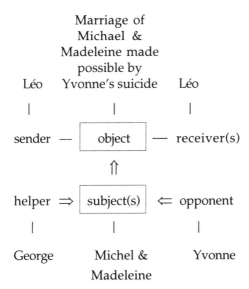

Léo is the *sender* who misleads the *subjects*, the *helper* and the *opponent*. She is also the *receiver* as she stands to 'win' George back after Yvonne's death. The *subjects*, Madeleine and Michael, are misled into thinking that the *object* is their happiness. Léo also misleads George, the *helper*, into thinking that the *object* is Michael and Madeleine's happiness. And finally, Yvonne, as the *opponent*, is manœuvred into attempting suicide before she realizes that that was likely part of her sister's plan.

*   *   *

According to Lydia Crowson, in *The Esthetic of Jean Cocteau*, 'Les Parents terribles is constructed on three triangular relationships.'[1] The first triangle, which generates the play, is that of George, his wife Yvonne and his former fiancée Léo (Yvonne's sister). 'The second triangle is the essentially tragic one composed of Georges, Yvonne and Michel. Yvonne has a *savage, possessive* [emphasis added] love for her child that excludes everyone else,'[2] including her husband. The third triangle, which 'precipitates a crisis in the family' is that of George, Michael and Madeleine: father and son are in love with the same woman. Moreover, George is willing to sacrifice his son's happiness in Act I to gain revenge against Madeleine.

---

[1] Crowson, 75.

[2] Ibid., 75.

Pierre Dubourg states the following: 'Léo is at the same time the victim, the executioner and the saviour of the play's characters.'[1] She is a *victim* of love because George jilted her for Yvonne, and she is victimized by a family that leaches money without giving in return. Furthermore, she is victimized by her own nature, and the apathy of her family, to do all the housework. She is the *executioner* because she devises the plan to sever Michael and Madeleine's relationship in the first act, and, considering her third plan, she practically corners Yvonne into committing suicide. Finally, she is the *saviour* because she is the one who decides that Michael and Madeleine should get married.

Crowson's relationship triangles are explicit, but they fail to capture Léonie's implicit controlling role within the play. Dubourg's statement about Léo's three roles, on the other hand, illustrates how central that character is to the drama. We can take Crowson and Dubourg's analysis a step further: the three triangular relationships can be superimposed onto a fourth, underlying triangle, which represents Léo's three roles (victim, executioner and saviour). Crowson's three triangular relationships form the *inner* triangles, each depicting a different conflict. Each triangle may also be stacked in temporal order: Léo/George/Yvonne represents the most historic conflict, which then generates the trio of Michael/George/Yvonne, upon which the most recent triangle of Michael/ George/Madeleine develops. The following diagram illustrates this:

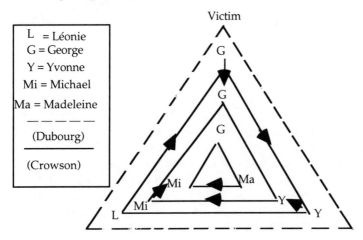

---

[1] 'Léo est en même temps la victime, le bourreau et le sauveteur des personnages de la pièce.' Dubourg, 86.

This diagram reveals the game being played. Léonie forfeited round 1 by sacrificing her potential marriage to George for control over George and Yvonne's household. George and Yvonne advance to the second triangle involving their son, Michael, and Yvonne's unnatural love for him. Having already established control of the household, this situation is to Léonie's benefit because while Yvonne is obsessed with Michael, George is left to her. When George and Michael advance to the next triangle, which introduces Madeleine, Léo sees a potential threat to her possession of George. Plan 1 is enacted to remove the threat. Having accomplished her goal, and reassured that George is safely back in her power, Léo is touched by Madeleine's sadness at losing Michael. Madeleine no longer represents a threat to Léo, and, in fact, they are very alike in their love of order. There is no loss to Léo if Michael and Madeleine get back together, and any upset suffered by Yvonne would be like scoring bonus points.

Now Léo becomes a bit more sinister. The division between Plan 2 and Plan 3 is not explicit and one wonders at what point things turned from reuniting Michael and Madeleine to setting the stage for Yvonne to kill herself. Léo had the opportunity to let Yvonne die of the insulin overdose early in the play, but she didn't. She is not quite cold-blooded enough to commit murder, but after the first plan succeeds, she is cool enough to understand that Madeleine presents an opportunity to rid herself of an opponent without direct involvement. Léo's strategy evolves as follows:

Plan 1. Eliminate Madeleine

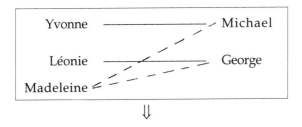

⇓

Plan 2. Reunite Madeleine and Michael

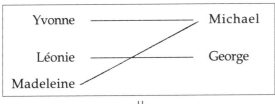

⇓

Plan 3. Eliminate Yvonne, Order Prevails

	Parent/Order	$\Rightarrow$	Child/Disorder
Age	Léonie	————————	George
$\Downarrow$			
Youth	Madeleine	————————	Michael

There are three women and two men, and only two matches are possible; therefore, one of the women must be eliminated to create order. The choice is obvious: since George and Michael are both children, they must be balanced with 'adult' partners like Léo and Madeleine. Yvonne, as a child, has no match, so she is the disposable one.

Léo is the gamesman because she is able to see the broader picture and plan appropriate strategy. She understands the different levels of conflict, and how they affect the interaction between Yvonne, George, Michael and Madeleine. Whether Léo understands her own tripartite role is irrelevant because she is smart enough, and patient enough, to manipulate the others regardless of which role she plays.

*   *   *

Léonie is not only the pivotal character in *Les Parents terribles*, she is also, arguably, the most complex personality ever created by Jean Cocteau. She embodies Dubourg's notion of victim, executioner and saviour, and, in Greimasian terms, she is the *sender* and *receiver* in all three of her plans. She manipulates and controls all three triangular relationships proposed by Crowson. As the director within the play, she manœuvres all of the actions that affect her life. Although others may initiate interaction with other elements without her direction (e.g., Michael started seeing Madeleine), as soon as this interaction disturbs the order (her order) of the Caravan, she will take action. She is the only character who possesses the focus, adaptability and vision necessary to obtain her goals, and in doing so, she is the director within the play.

Les Parents terribles :
A Lacanian Approach

Jacob D. Kruger

Most of our narratives (including the meta-narrative of psychoanalysis) rest on some sort of conflict between the isolated subject and the outside world, the subtle balance and imbalance of a world ruled by prohibition, law and desire, but always the ever-renewing promise of accomplishment, the promise that there would never be an end to the story.[1]

Michel enters at six o'clock shocking the outraged parents into a confrontational skirmish as they press for answers, an excuse for his unqualified absence. 'But it's not my ghost,'[2] he replies, perhaps in jest. He entreats his mother, calling her Sophie. The *narrating instance* witnesses the father's dismay: 'Why call your mother Sophie at your age?'[3] responds Georges. The mother, a split persona — part Yvonne, part Sophie — is momentarily pacified, delighted not only by her son's return, but by the renewed manifestation and activation of her fantasies. Michel's presence encourages her return to the *Imaginary*: 'It's an old joke,'[4] she relents. As the conflict builds, the twenty-three year old

---

[1] Régis Durand in Robert Con Davis (ed), 'On *Aphanisis*: A Note on the Dramaturgy of the Subject in Narrative Analysis,' *Lacan and Narration: The Psychoanalytic Difference in Narrative Theory* (Baltimore: Johns Hopkins University Press, 1983), 869.

[2] *'Ce n'est pas mon spectre...' Les Parents terribles* (Paris: Gallimard, 1938), 76 (Act I, scene iii). All subsequent quotations from the French playtext are taken from this source.

[3] *'D'abord, je trouve indécent, qu'à ton âge, tu t'obstines à appeler ta mère Sophie.'* Ibid., 36.

[4] *'[C]'est une vieille taquinerie...'* Ibid.

child blurts out, 'Ecoutez, mes enfants!'[1] He covers his mouth, realizing his affront to social etiquette, having transgressed the *Name of the Father* by shattering the symbolic language of social convention; a fissure erupts the social discourse, released from the unconscious by Michel's symbolic rendering of his frustrated desire to move beyond the dominating father and obsessive mother. His internal recognition of the equal footing that he shares with his child-like parents is externalized through language. This gap, an open sore in the family discourse, portends the ensuing catastrophe — Michel's Œdipal transgression of a sublimated, symbolic order. Michel covers his mouth, a concretized attempt to heal the would, to restore the situation to its previous, fictional order where he must assume the role of the son. Throughout the ensuing discourse he manages to reformulate the proper names of his father (Papa) and Léonie (Aunt Léo), momentarily patching up the gaping fissure in the symbolic/imaginary matrix. Returning home at six p.m. after a night's unaccounted absence, Michel succumbs to perform the conventions, to meet the expectations, of the Law.

In Cocteau's *Les Parents terribles*, distinction between the individuated, alienated world of adults and the imaginative, coherent world of children is blurred. The call, 'Ecoutez, mes enfants,' is a warning cry to the spectator that the difference between the two worlds may not be easily discerned at first glance. Cocteau considered himself to have maintained the curiosity, imagination and magic of childhood his entire life; he boasted, 'There are poets and grownups,'[2] obviously aligning himself with the former. For Cocteau, childhood was not an age, but a way of being. Yet, the rebirth of child as poet bade Cocteau to suffer as well:

> Children have a magical power to become whatever they want to be. The poets in whom childhood is prolonged suffer greatly from losing this power. That is one of the reasons which impel the poet to take opium.[3]

In becoming a poet, Cocteau claimed to have felt a loss of the infinite potential of childhood, a loss of contact with the unconscious, or preconscious, state — a state which he would continue to contact throughout

---

[1] Ibid., 37.

[2] *Professional Secrets*, 13. From *Essai de critique indirecte* (Paris: Édtions Bernard Grasset, 1932), 148–49.

[3] Ibid., 131. '*Tous les enfants ont un pouvoir féerique de se changer en ce qu'ils veulent. Les poètes en qui l'enfance se prolonge souffrent beaucoup de perdre ce pouvoir. Sans doute est-ce une des raisons qui poussent le poète à employer l'opium.*' *Opium* (Paris: Librairie Stock, 1931), 116.

his life through the many media of art that he practised and through indulging in the lucid embrace of opium; as he claimed, 'Youth drives away our childhood. In the end childhood reasserts its rights.'[1] In spite of his recognition that the enchanted state of childhood was threatened, rendered vulnerable by the chaotic world, Cocteau implored his public, the reader of his poetry and the spectator of his plays and films, to resist the pull of the adult world and maintain the wide-eyed openness of the ideal child:

> I want the kind of readers who remain children at any cost. I can tell them at a glance: loyalty to that first enchantment guards better than any cosmetic, than any diet, against the insults of age. But alas for such readers, who would huddle safe and sound in the asylum of their credulous enchantment as if in the womb — our enervating century offends them by its chaos, its fidgets of light and space, the host of its excuses for dividing, for rending oneself from others and from oneself.[2]

In this passage, Cocteau unwittingly describes the emergence of the subject into the Lacanian *Symbolic* realm — the submergence into language, the social contract with the Other, a culturally engendered system of codified convention — that triggers the schismatic phenomenon of alienation from self and other. Cocteau's visual poetry attempts to integrate and transcend this inherent rift in the subject. *Les Parents terribles* illustrates the externalized split psyche that alienates the child from the Other —by showing the evolution of Michel's rift with the fundamental m/Other— and the internalized split psyche that separates the archetype of child from the archetype of poet — illustrated by the two-headed Yvonne/Sophie.

As a child, Cocteau enjoyed the shelter of family life — the unique perspective that his home offered of the adult world and the brief glimpses of the half buried child that were found to lurk beneath the shell of each adult:

---

1 Ibid., 306. *'La jeunesse chasse notre enfance. À la longue, l'enfance reprend ses droits.' Journal d'un inconnu* (Paris: Éditions Bernard Grasset, 1953), 35.

2 Ibid., 18. *'Je souhaite d'être lu par les personnes qui restent des enfants coûte que coûte. Je les découvre entre mille. Un regard qui donne sur la féerie primitive protège mieux que tous les soins de beauté, tous les régimes, contre les insultes de l'âge. Mais, hélas ! Ces personnes-là, qui veulent vivre chaudement pelotonnés dans le refuge de cette féerie crédule comme dans le ventre maternel, notre époque énervante les blesse par son désordre, par sa bougeotte, ses tics de lumière, ses véhicules, le nombre des prétextes à se diviser, à s'arracher des autres et de soi-même.' Portraits souvenirs* (Paris: Éditions Bernard Grasset, 1935), 49–50.

The child wants a room, in which to collect his toys, his loves. He detests what disperses, is partial to the kind of diseases that cluster and close up tight. I carried this loathing of leave-takings, of places where you cannot visualize those you love, to the point of idolizing thunder. The gentle bowling of an April's thunder, that cooing Sunday thunder which rearranges the furniture in heaven — I still worship it, for such thunder was the signal that there would be no expeditions, that the family would stay home, that my cousins and I would play with my blocks, that the nursemaids would sit sewing in a circle, that I would hear the quartet and then the billiard balls clicking downstairs, testifying to the childishness of grownups.[1]

The uncanny resemblance between the *caravan* family of Michel and Cocteau's characterization of his childhood relationship to the adult world exemplifies Cocteau's tendency to veil autobiographical elements in his *œuvre*:

In an open letter to the Catholic philosopher Jacques Maritain, he [Cocteau] described a religious crisis after the despair over Radiguet's death, thus for the first time directly inviting the public to mix (or, rather, not to separate) his art and his life, to see his published work as a poet-dramatist in historical terms of his private suffering as a bereaved love, and to raise the whole question of what, in the case of a self-mythologizing writer, is to be believed. Cocteau's answer came in one of his best poems: 'I am the lie that always speaks the truth'.[2]

In fact, as Cocteau's *œuvre* and his self-mythologizing anecdotes commingle, it becomes increasingly difficult to separate fact from fantasy. The poet's reconstruction of his past self is filtered through a selective imagination that leaves no raw material unsculpted, forging lies to invoke a deeper apprehension of subjective truths. Like Michel and Yvonne/Sophie, Cocteau and his own mother prolonged the playful element of childhood, entertaining the adult world:

---

[1] Ibid., 18. *'L'enfant veut une chambre, y réunir ses jouets et ses amours. Il déteste ce qui éparpille. Il favorise les maladies qui groupent et qui calfeutrent. Je poussais cette phobie des départs, des endroits où l'on imagine mal ceux qu'on aime, jusqu'à idolâtrer le tonnerre. Le doux bowling du tonnerre d'Avril, ce tonnerre du dimanche qui roucoule, qui range les meubles du ciel, sans doute est-ce à cause de cela que j'en conserve le culte. C'était, ce tonnerre, le signe des projets de promenades à l'eau, l'assurance que la famille resterait à la maison, que mes cousins m'aideraient au jeu de cubes, que les nourrices coudraient en cercle, que j'entendrais le quatuor et ensuite les boules de billiard se heurter en bas et témoigner de l'enfantillage des grandes personnes.'* Ibid., 50.

[2] Ibid., 102.

My mother died in 'childhood.' She did not fall into it: she was a very lively old child. She recognized me, but *her* childhood situated me in *mine*, without, of course, the two childhoods coinciding. An old little girl, surrounded by her little girl's acts, questioned an old little boy about his school, told him to be a good boy the next day. Perhaps I inherit this long childhood, disguised as maturity, from my mother, whom I resemble; it is the cause of all my misfortunes.[1]

Cocteau's early relationship with his mother does seem unusually intimate, exemplified by his own description of gazing at his mother in her preparations for a night at the Opéra or the Comédie-Française.[2]

Cocteau's father died when he was ten years old.[3] The latent guilt attached to an Œdipal complex became a formative, psychically enacted and physically manifest experience. The combination of his father's death with the intimacy he shared with his mother suggests a lived experience that triggers the child's impressionable mind into accepting a personal relationship to the recurrence of suprapersonal, primordial myths such as the Œdipal narrative. As Phelps declares, Cocteau's self-involvement is both narcissistic and cosmologically suprapersonal:

> It looks like narcissism — excessive, obsessive, unrelenting narcissism. In a way, it is. (A poet's strengths are inseparable from his weaknesses.) But it is also something more. For Cocteau believed (or trusted) that his own history was as emblematic as that of Orpheus, his own encounters as fatal as those of Œdipus, his own beloveds as heroic as Eurydice or Hippolytus. And just as we no longer have Orpheus' own poems, only his myth and the meanings we continue to read into it, so Cocteau implies that his personal trajectory of suffering and choice may remain in human memory, and usable to human speculation, longer than his created works of art.[4]

---

[1] Ibid., 306. *'Ma mère est morte en enfance. Et non pas tombée en enfance. Elle était une vieille enfant fort vive. Elle me reconnaissait, mais son enfance me situait dans la mienne, sans que, comme de juste, nos deux enfances concordassent. Une vieille petite fille, assise au centre de ses actes de petite fille, interrogeait un vieux garçon sur son collège, et lui recommandait d'y être sage le lendemain.*

Il est possible que cette longue enfance, qui se déguise en grande personne, me vienne de ma mère, à qui je ressemble, et soit la cause de tous mes malheurs.' *Journal d'un inconnu*, 35–36.

[2] Ibid., 21–22.

[3] Ibid., 29.

[4] Phelps, ibid., xii.

The parallels between Cocteau's biography and *Les Parents terribles*
continue as the artist recounts the unfortunate episode when he intro-
duced his mother to an actress by the name of Madeleine Carlier, with
whom he had fallen in love; this anecdote divulges the inspiration for
the character of Madeleine:

> I was seventeen or eighteen, and Madeleine was thirty, but she passed
> for twenty. There was a family council, and my mother threw up her
> hands, crying, 'Poor Jean — with an old woman!'[1]

This episode in Cocteau's life corresponds to Yvonne/Sophie's numerous
references to the age difference between Michel and Madeleine. The
family life represented in *Les Parents terribles* can easily be discerned
as a loosely veiled allegory of Cocteau's own vision of his filial relationships displaced through the structure of the Œdipus myth.

Before *Les Parents terribles* was conceived, Cocteau had already
treated the Œdipus legend in three separate productions: he composed
the text for Stravinsky's oratorio, performed in 1928, he adapted
Sophocles' original in a 'terse' production and, finally, he used the
thematic and formal logic of the myth in *La Machine infernale*.[2] After
its opening in November 1938, *Les Parents terribles* (the play) was
banned by the City Council because it intimated an incestuous liaison
between mother and son.[3] For Cocteau, however, incest signified more
than a subversion of the symbolic laws of culture; it was an ideal
metaphor for artistic creation:

> Art is born of the coitus between the male and female elements in all of us,
> elements more nearly balanced in the artist than in other men. Art is the
> child of a kind of incest, the lovemaking of self and self, a parthenogene-
> sis. That is why marriage is so dangerous for an artist: it represents a
> pleonasm, the monster's effort toward normality.[4]

In Lacanian analysis, the structural logic of the Œdipal myth —the en-
actment of incest and the cultural codes which it transgresses and there-

---

[1] Ibid., 29. From Jean Cocteau: *Entretien avec Roger Stéphane* (Paris: R.T.F. et Librairie Jules Tallandier, 1964).

[2] Ibid., 140.

[3] *Professional Secrets*, 183.

[4] Ibid., 295. *'L'art naît du coït entre l'élément mâle et l'élément femelle qui nous
composent tous, plus équilibrés chez l'artiste que chez les autres hommes. Il résulte
d'une sorte d'inceste, d'amour de soi avec soi, de parthénogénèse. C'est ce qui rend
le mariage si dangereux chez les artistes, pour lesquels il représente un
pléonasme, un effort de monstre vers la norme.'* Opium, 133–34.

by substitutes— is claimed to be a formative stage in the process of the subject's development.[1] The recognized complex submerges the subject in the transcendental matrix of language —the *code/Name of the Father*— as 'the child realizes that both he and the mother are marked by a lack',[2] divorcing the signifer (m/Other) from the absented signified (Self) and thereby instigating the subject's drive to narrate, to historicize and to fictionalize.

Invoked by the performed Œdipal narrative, the subject is drawn into the sliding chain of signifiers — the *Symbolic* structure — which attempts to suture the Real (being-in-itself, materiality) with the *Imaginary* structure (the ego's identification/alienation with the *specular image* and the Other):

> The drama enacted or reenacted by narrative is the Œdipal myth in which culture, like sexual identity, is founded by an original absence of reality (of the Father), by a break with the I/thou relationship to the mother, and the disguised, guilty, and anxious desire for the death of the Father, in all its anti-mimetic, fictive and narrative dimensions. Narratives as the burying of these primal wishes become in effect the triumph of civilization over the primal, the violent, the instinctual.[3]

The paradigmatic structure of *Les Parents terribles* represents all these structural elements of the Œdipus myth. The absence of Georges (the father) as a complement to Yvonne (the Real mother) is enforced by the desire of Sophie (the Imaginary, all-embracing mother) to forge a complementary couple with Michel (the son); moreover, 'the subject [Michel] seeks to become the object of her desire; he seeks to be the phallus for the mother and fill out her lack'. Michel's break with Sophie, 'when the child's own sexual drives begin to manifest themselves', through his affair with Madeleine —what his mother terms *infidelity*— reflects the 'break with the I/thou relationship to the moth-

---

[1] 'The key function in the Œdipus complex is thus that of the FATHER, the third term which transforms the dual relation between the mother and child into a triadic structure. The Œdipus complex is thus nothing less than the passage from the imaginary order to the symbolic order, "the conquest of the symbolic relation as such." The fact that the passage to the symbolic passes via a complex sexual dialectic means that the subject cannot have access to the symbolic order without confronting the problem of sexual difference.' Dylan Evans, *An Introductory Dictionary of Lacanian Psychoanalysis* (London and New York: Routledge, 1996), 127.

[2] Ibid., 128.

[3] Juliet Flower MacCannell, 'Œdipus Wrecks: Lacan, Stendhal and the Narrative Form of the Real,' in Davis (ed.), *op. cit.*, 911.

er'.[1] Finally the identification with and metaphoric killing of the father is enacted by Michel as he supplants Georges by winning his wife and then mistress, Madeleine. Georges' line that precedes the spectator's first glimpse of Michel, as he opens the door to enter the confrontation with his family, is not surprising; Georges exclaims, 'one day we'll be murdered in our beds.'[2] Throughout the ensuing drama, this unwilling projection is metaphorically actualized.

Lacan declared that 'truth always manifests itself in a structure of fiction'.[3] *Les Parents terribles* reflects this duplicate process of fictionalizing experience that the subject experiences beyond the narcissistic *mirror image* (the stadium 'in which the subject is permanently caught and captivated by his own image') and beyond the symbolic identification with the father (occurring 'in the final stage of the Œdipus Complex' as the subject enter/tains the discourse of the Other).[4] The Œdipal stage, impelling the subject to the act of narration, enables the Real to be contained by Symbolic structure — a structure that is only bound by the rules of the subject's unconscious desires, or fantasies. Sophie's fantasies exist in the Imaginary realm, as does Cocteau's act of artistic creation. Cocteau saw the need for the illusionist to stretch the truth while viewing Barbette's performance, to 'consider the final tour de force: to become a man again, to run the film backward, is not enough. The truth, too, must be translated, must be heightened to keep an equal footing with the lie'.[5] Cocteau cloaks truth in fiction, the empty mask, glorifying the inherent absence of absolute Truth.

Cocteau learned from Picasso that art is self-referential, a mirror reflection of the artist endowing signification upon the object of study, rather than an *objective* rendering of the perceived object in an artistic form:

> Out of everything old he [Picasso] makes the New, which may surprise but which holds you by its *realism*. Let me explain what I mean by the word. Strictly speaking, there is no such thing as abstract painting, for each picture represents an idea of the painter's or, in the long run, the painter himself. Picasso has never claimed to have painted an abstract picture. Savagely he tracks down resemblance and captures it to such ef-

---

[1] Evans, 128. MacCannell, 911.

[2] *'Et un beau jour on s'étonne d'être assassiné!'*, 35 (Act I, scene iii).

[3] Lacan in Durand, 861.

[4] Evans, 115.

[5] *Professional Secrets*, 93–94. From *Le Numéro Barbette* in *Œuvres complètes*, vol. X.

fect that the object or figure at the source of his work often loses power
and character beside its representation.[1]

Like Picasso's formal idealism, Cocteau's *realistic* representation of
the Œdipal narrative in *Les Parents terribles* aimed at the direct
transmission of an ideal form rather than *verisimilitude* of empirical
action. Cocteau justified his *fictions* and *lies* as the expression of deeper
truths which the inimical world had yet to comprehend:

> What happens in a poet's soul is as remote and incredible as the be-
> haviour of the Mongols under the rule of Kublai Khan, grandson of
> Genghis Khan. That is why poets are regarded as liars, just as Marco
> Polo was regarded as a liar till his dying breath.[2]

In *Les Parents terribles*, Cocteau reveals the double nature of fictionalizing experience by contrasting the naive child's inability to comprehend the act of lying with the adult's manipulation of the Other,
through the lie, constructing truth and order.

Michel and his two parents live in a state of disorder, as Cocteau's
stage directions in the playtext and the cluttered bedrooms depicted in
the film make clear. Their actions are ruled by unconscious desires, fantasy and illusion, their psyches closely allied with the pre-conscious,
the Imaginary, the child-like. Previous to the action of the film, the
father and unsuccessful inventor, Georges, has been displaced by his
son's intimacy with his wife; he seeks a supplement, Madeleine, to fulfil his emotional and physical desires through an extra-marital affair.
Yvonne /Sophie has turned a blind eye, satisfying her own desire
through an unusually affectionate and protective relationship to her
son, Michel. Michel has also commenced an affair with Madeleine,
ironically unaware of his father's previous liaison with her. Yvonne's
sister, Léonie, plants the seed in Yvonne's mind that her son has been
lying, hypocritically silent, 'hiding something.' When Yvonne finally
hears of Michel's affair from his own mouth, she accuses him of infi-

---

[1] Ibid., 76. '*Avec tout ce qui est vieux il fait du neuf qui peut surprendre mais qui at-
tache par son réalisme. Entendons-nous sur ce mot réalisme. Il ne saurait y avoir à
proprement parler de peinture abstraite, puisque toute peinture représente soit
une idée de peintre, soit, en fin de compte, le peintre lui-même. Picasso n'a jamais
prétendu faire de la peinture abstraite. Il cherche férocement la ressemblance, et il
arrive de telle sorte que l'objet ou la figure qui soit à l'origine de son travail
perdent souvent relief et force à côté de leur représentation.*' La Corrida du
premier mai (Paris: Éditions Bernard Grasset, 1957), 168–69.

[2] Ibid., 300. From *Démarche d'un poète*, translated from the German text *Der
Lebensweg eines Dichters* by Friedhelm Kemp (München: F. Buckman, 1953), 33.

delity — unfaithfulness to their intimate mother-son bond. Beginning with this initial crisis of the action, Georges, Yvonne and Michel address, and contest, the fantasies which have controlled their lives, while simultaneously displaying to the spectator the fantastic illusions which determine their actions. This is exemplified by Michel's attitude toward his mother as he caters to her unspoken desire: after the others leave the bedroom, he skips the length of the room, jumps onto his mother and bathes her in kisses; he proceeds to cuddle up with Sophie as she feigns that she would prefer him not to; he turns off the bedroom light and whispers, 'Sophie, taisez-vous,' ('Sophie, be quiet') all in the tone of a Don Juan embracing his beloved. Throughout the action, Sophie's sublimated sexual desire for her son competes with the unconscious desire of Yvonne —the complement of Sophie's fractured psyche— the desire for death, in the subject's fatalistic balance between *eros* and *thanatos*.

Meanwhile Georges is coaxed on by Léonie, the ringleader of the Caravan, to accept the adult role of active agency, assuming the function of manipulating the others —Madeleine and Michel— through cunning, deception and lies, for his egoistic ends: Georges desires either to regain Madeleine or to avenge her betrayal of him. At first, Michel retains the naive enchantment of the child who cannot comprehend his lies because, as he claims to Madeleine, they are too complex. However, the lie which Georges concocts through Léonie's aid, that Madeleine has a third lover and is deceiving the young Michel, frustrates Michel's faith in love and authenticity, shattering the mirror —the pure, sutured relationship of self to Other— and fragmenting the narcissistic self, once caught in the vision of ideal spectral unity with the image of his love, Madeleine. Michel is thrust into the endless discourse of the Other through the discovery of deception — the hollowness of the Other — and the recognition of the barred coherent self. Georges, for his part, has momentarily deferred the eternally recurring son's conquest of the father by thwarting Michel's relationship with Madeleine. After the break-up, the spectator views from an ascendant perspective a forlorn Sophie lying on top of her heart-broken son, under a blanket, as Michel cries 'go away!' The rift with Madeleine has hastened the tearing of Michel's relationship with the fundamental m/Other — marked by lack and incompletion. A final lie is needed to return the young lovers to their selfless embrace, restructuring the act of deception as just another rule of the game. Cocteau reveals that the lie —regardless of ethic or intention— constructs the Real; it must be used to reformulate the situation, returning the will to li(v)e to the younger generation. As Georges sacrifices his pride, his status as father, for the son's future, Cocteau negates the negation, using the bona fide lie to speak the truth.

Cocteau was fascinated by the magical power of the mirror, which he regarded as the passage between life and death. In *Orphée*, the 'guardian angel speaks the lines for which, in all his writing, Cocteau became best known':

> I shall tell you the secret of secrets. Mirrors are the doors by which death comes and goes. Don't tell this to anyone. Just watch yourself all your life in a mirror and you will see death at work like bees in a glass hive...[1]

The *mirror stage* occurs through the *Imaginary* confrontation of the self with the hollow image of the self, the self with the possibility of otherness, where the ego is revealed to be 'the product of misunderstanding (*méconnaissance*) and the site where the subject becomes alienated from himself'.[2] According to Schleifer, the 'object in absence is both Greimas' and Lacan's object of desire... with its absence that also carries the possibility of the dialogue, subject to subject, Lacan speaks of';[3] beyond the *mirror stage*, the signifier is hollowed and relativized, intricately linked within a transcendent chain that continues eternally by virtue of the subject's pursuit of an inherently untenable desire for wholeness, completion, the absolute correlation of signifier with signified. Cocteau's anecdote about the public baths sheds light on the relationship between narcissism and the mirror, voyeuristic scopophilia and the unattainable object of desire:

> My only regret was the transparent mirror. You get into a dark booth and shove aside the panel, revealing a metallic sheet through which you can make out a little bathroom. On its other side, the sheet is a mirror so smooth and shiny it is impossible to guess it is full of eyes...
>
> I remember one Narcissus who lovingly brought his mouth to the mirror, pressed his lips against it, and carried to its frenzied conclusion his adventure with himself. Invisible as the Greek gods, I glued my lips to his

---

[1] *Professional Secrets*, 102. '*Je vous livre le secret des secrets. Les miroirs sont les portes par lesquelles la Mort va et vient. Ne le dites à personne. Du reste, regardez-vous toute votre vie dans une glace et vous verrez la Mort travailler comme des abeilles dans une ruche de verre.*' *Orphée* (the play) in *Œuvres complètes*, vol. V, (Geneva Marguerat, 1946), 58 (scene vii).

[2] Evans, 116.

[3] Ronald Schleifer, 'The Space and Dialogue of Desire: Lacan, Greimas and Narrative Temporality,' in Davis (ed.), *op. cit.*, 887.

and imitated his gestures. He never knew that, instead of reflecting, the mirror had acted, had lived, had loved him.[1]

For Cocteau, the bath-house mirror was both a shield from, and a window into, the desiring gaze of the Other; it marked the fractured link between the *barred subject* and his object of desire. As the mirror alienates Cocteau from the exhibitionist, it separates Orphée from Eurydice's descent into the underworld, a fissure that the hero is compelled to traverse in order to re-instate their essential love. Moreover, the mirror separated the admiring gaze of the young Cocteau from the image of his mother, revealed in Cocteau's description of his mother's preparations for the Comédie-Française as he watched the reflection of his mother in the mirrored cabinet of the bathroom:

> [T]he wardrobe mirror showed me my mother, or indeed that madonna encased in velvet, choked by diamonds, beplumed with a dusky aigrette, standing tall and bristling with brilliance, like a glittering horse chestnut, distracted, torn between last-minute instructions to be good and a final glance in the mirror.[2]

Mirrors play a dominant role as objects in *Les Parents terribles*, although certainly in a more subtle manner than in *Le Sang d'un poète* or *Orphée*.

Léonie, the *sender*, the truly active, adult agent in *Les Parents terribles* —having made her sacrifice of abandoning Georges as an object of desire years before— has obviously passed through the mirror stage and entered the Discourse of the Other. Yvonne/Sophie, conversely, is only discovering the crisis of the absented centralizing signifier, Michel; yet, she attempts to defer acknowledging the essential lack of the Other. The two sisters respond quite differently to their environments, specifically to the mirrors present in the rooms. Yvonne/Sophie avoids the reflection of her image in the mirror, while Léonie obvi-

---

[1] *Professional Secrets*, 123–24. 'Un de mes seuls regrets fut la glace transparente. On s'installe dans une cabine obscure et on écarte un volet. Ce volet découvre une toile métallique à travers laquelle l'œil embrasse une petite salle de bains. De l'autre côté, la toile était une glace si réfléchissante et si lisse qu'il était impossible de deviner qu'elle était pleine de regards..

Une fois, un Narcisse qui se plaisait approcha sa bouche de la glace, l'y colla et poussa jusqu'au bout l'aventure avec lui-même. Invisible comme les dieux grecs, j'appuyai mes lèvres contre les siennes et j'imitais ses gestes. Jamais il ne sut qu'au lieu de réfléchir, la glace agissait, qu'elle était vivante et qu'elle l'avait aimé...' *Le Livre blanc* (Paris: Passage du Marais, 1992), 55 & 57.

[2] *Professional Secrets*, 22.

ously basks in her own hollow reflection (if not with the least bit of irony directed towards her own aging). When Yvonne does glance in the mirror, the actions seems barely executed — there is no self-recognition. The first full reflection of Yvonne, in the bathroom mirror, occurs as she is posed beside Léonie. They are both redoubled for the spectator:

> Yvonne: I'm not a woman in his eyes.
> Léonie: In his [Michel's] eyes ... you have become a woman.

The spectator sees the reflection of Yvonne in the mirror, as she pours a glass of water.

> Léonie: And now he is gone.[1]

This moment of self-reflection and self-realization, concretized for the spectator by the redoubled images of the characters, focuses on Yvonne's first stage in the crisis of discovering the impending loss of her son, the object of her desire. She begins to view her age, combined with her lack of the Other, as a sign. Finally, Yvonne applies make-up using her sister's compact, mimicking Léonie's action of applying the inevitable mask.

For the mature Cocteau, 'the true mirror' that entertains the discourse of the Other 'is the screen, on which I can see the physical nature of my dream'.[2] An artist engulfed in fantastic visions of the Imaginary realm, Cocteau positions his medium as the quintessential mirror that concretizes illusions through film images:

> as a 'dual relationship,' and ambiguous redoubling, a 'mirror' reflection, an *immediate* relationship between subject and its other in which each term passes *immediately* into the other and is lost in a never-ending play of reflections. Imagination and desire are the realities of a finite being which can *emerge* from the contradiction between self and other only by the genesis of a third term, a *mediatory* 'concept' [the symbolic signifier] which, by determining each term, orders them into *reversible and progressive* relations which can be *developed* in language.[3]

---

[1] Film: Yvonne: *'Je ne suis pas une femme aux yeux de Mic.'* Léonie: *'Aux yeux de Michel tu es devenue une femme. [...] Michel a quitté la roulotte.'*

[2] *Professional Secrets*, 219. 'La véritable glace, c'est l'écran de la projection, c'est voir la physique de mon rêve.' *La Belle et la bête, journal d'un film* (Monaco: Éditions du Rocher, 1958), 133.

[3] Edmund Ortigues, quoted in Schleifer, 876.

Les Parents terribles : A Family United
(in the foreground: Yvonne de Bray as Yvonne/Sophie)
Courtesy of the Museum of Modern Art Film Stills Archive
© Jean Cocteau/SODRAC (Montréal) 1998

The film language functions as the sign of a sign; the mirror —no longer innocent or authentic in reflecting coherent subjectivity— transcends mortality, enacting through the symbolic matrix the illusory yoking of spectator and object of desire, reflecting and perpetuating the consistent deferral of the satiation of desire.

Lacan built upon Freud's reading of the Œdipus myth by articulating the narrative's function to render 'the structural homology between language and desire'.[1] Through the frustration of articulated desire, a symbolic reaction to the loss of the desired object, the subject performs a positive or negative gesture within the infinitely deferred temporality of desire. For Michel, in *Les Parents terribles*, the mirror phase of identification with the m/Other begins to crack when he decides to value his love for Madeleine above his love for Sophie; this archetypal dilemma engages Michel's psychologically positive reaction that performs the inevitable action of the 'ideal male':

> [who must] come to sacrifice his desire for his mother in order to be constituted as a subject ... the Œdipally based subjectivity must remain unsatisfied: it is the law of the *lack of satisfaction of desire* that is by all accounts necessary for the newly constituted subject to enter in mature, civil life.[2]

Yvonne makes the transitional phase in Michel's development nearly impossible. Once yoked as complementary characters, co-dependants regarding self-identity — illustrated cinematically in the *extreme close-up* as Michel recounts the story of his love for Madeleine and the *narrating instance* crops the spectator's view to include Michel's face from nose down (focusing on his mouth) and Sophie's face from nose up (focusing on her eyes), reflecting the co-dependance of *enunciating subject* (Michel) and the *subject of enunciation* (Sophie), linked as one through visual composition — a schism occurs and the complementary couple is ripped apart by Michel's desire for Madeleine, his movement towards individualism.[3] Michel's growth leads from the Real, cracking through the mirror to the symbolic discourse of the Other; the tragic element of this farce is embedded in Sophie's inability to perform likewise:

---

[1] Richard Macksey, '« Sur un terrain en friche : Liminal Note »,' in Davis (ed.), *op. cit.*, 846.

[2] MacCannell, 917–18.

[3] Raman Selden, Peter Widdowson and Peter Brooker, *A Reader's Guide to Contemporary Literary Theory*, Fourth Edition (London: Prentice Hall/ Harvester Wheatsheaf, 1997), 163.

> For what Lacan demonstrates, as Freud did not, is that the structural ba-
> sis of Œdipus, the source of its symbolic potency, is a simple linguistic
> paradigm, in which a basic dialogic couple, I and thou (mother and
> child/ peer and peer), becomes a grammatical structure capable of gener-
> ating another participant: 'I' and 'you' generate, as Benveniste has so
> convincingly shown us, a third term, 'he,' and 'she,' or most importantly
> 'it,' a third term that not only disrupts the initial dyad, not only comes to
> dominate it as hero or topic, but eventually legislates it... The 'he' — God,
> the father, It — becomes more than 'he'; it expands to become the Sym-
> bolic, and it interrupts the direct exchange of the original dyad to such an
> extent that inter-human interaction *must* henceforth go through its par-
> ticular circuit.[1]

Michel is able to come to accept the generation of the third term, by accepting the *Name of the Father*, whereas Sophie/Yvonne is mired in the evanescence of her own persona. Michel's journey beyond the mirror phase of *imaginary identification* reaches its fruition when he is forced to confront the possibility of Madeleine's insincerity and infidelity. Her love and honesty, once present and existing on the surface, as his Mother's love had always appeared to him, is now challenged, rendered absent, the signifier (Madeleine) hollowed; the object of his desire is placed beyond his reach. Only the final stage of the Œdipal action, *symbolic identification* via the clarification of the father's lie, enables Michel to render his subjectivity meaningful.

Likewise, Yvonne/Sophie experiences a fracture of the self when the object of her desire, her son, becomes the subject of his own desiring impulses; he can no longer be taken-for-granted as the signifier of full presence, wholeness and completion that Sophie requires to feel the illusory coherence of selfhood. According to Jacqueline Rose, 'the truth of the unconscious is only ever that moment of fundamental division through which the subject entered into language and sexuality, and the constant failing of position within both';[2] Sophie's unconscious, sexual longing for Michel positions her failure in the realms of language and sexuality. Lacan's definition of aphanisis as 'the fundamental division of the subject which institutes the dialectic of desire...[and] the disappearance of the subject in the process of alienation'[3] is particularly apt in the world of Yvonne/Sophie. She is unable to overcome the division within her psyche, to embody a signifier: 'the fact of being born with the signifier, the subject is born divided. The subject is this emergence which, just before, as subject, was nothing, but which, having scarcely

---

[1] MacCannell, 915.

[2] Jacqueline Rose quoted by Schleifer in Davis, 855.

[3] Evans, 12.

appeared, solidifies into a signifier.'[1] Yvonne/Sophie is unable to transform herself into a thriving subjectivity as she experiences satisfying relations with her Other, Michel, the principle of her disappearance.[2] Thus, Yvonne/ Sophie's self-alienation exemplifies the Lacanian divided self, whose dialectic shifts between the Imaginary fantasies and the reality to which she must succumb. As Sophie becomes less meaningful to Michel, the fading, disappearance, or aphanisis of her subjectivity ensues: 'Hence the division of the subject — when the subject appears somewhere as meaning, he is manifested elsewhere as "fading," as disappearance.'[3] Sophie acknowledges this principle, but cannot overcome her alienated fading, when she remarks desperately to Léonie, 'what you give to one, you take away from the other.'[4] Thus, Cocteau illustrates that the subject, Sophie/Yvonne, who dwells too long in the mirror phase mode of imaginary identification, experiences alienation and fading of subjectivity; Sophie/Yvonne cannot accept herself as both the hollow subject and object of the discourse of the Otherness. Unable to transcend the fading of her subjectivity, Yvonne/Sophie withdraws from the symbolic game of life, succumbing to the overpowering death force in her situation.

The mother's death submerges Michel in the symbolic matrix of language, as the subject interprets *imaginary identification* as not the end — the *destination* —of the specular gaze, but the beginning— the *sender*. If 'alienation is constitutive of the imaginary order',[5] in the dialectics of identification, then the process of desiring constitutes the symbolic realism, language, narrativity. The action of the film depicts a reconstitution of social order: Michel and Madeleine are drawn together to form a new complementary couple and the death of Sophie/Yvonne intimates the potential re-coupling of Georges and Léonie, a possibility that Léonie acknowledges in observing her sister's final breath. In the tradition of the romance genre, a new order is forged from the old, and Patriarchal Law is passed from father to son, ensuring the continuation of the Discourse of the Other, as Barthes declared in *Le Plaisir du texte* (1973):

---

[1] Lacan quoted in Durand, 860. From Jacques Lacan, *The Four Fundamental Concepts of Psycho-Analysis*, ed. J.A. Miller, translated by Alan Sheridan (New York: Norton, 1978).

[2] Durand, 863.

[3] Lacan quoted in Durand, 866.

[4] Film: Léonie: *'Ce qu'on donne à l'un on enlève à l'autre.'*

[5] Evans, 82.

> Death of the Father would deprive literature of many of its pleasures. If there is no longer a Father, why tell stories? Doesn't every narrative lead back to Œdipus? Isn't storytelling always a way of searching for one's origin, speaking one's conflicts with the Law, entering into the dialectic of tenderness and hatred?[1]

These psychological undercurrents of *Les Parents terribles* invite the spectator —in his tendency towards *Imaginary identification* with the principal subject, Michel— to challenge the very act of identification with the mirror-image, the suturing of the subject and the *spectral image* of the absented object of desire, either in the reflection of a character projected on the film screen or the Other corporeal beings in the subject's own life.

---

[1] Roland Barthes, quoted in MacCannell, 911–12. 'La mort du Père enlèvera à la littérature beaucoup de ses plaisirs. S'il n'y a plus de Père, à quoi bon raconter des histoires? Tout récit ne se ramène-t-il pas à l'Œdipe? Raconter, n'est-ce pas toujours chercher son origine, dire ses démêlés avec la Loi, entrer dans la dialectique de l'attendrissement et de la haine?' *Le Plaisir du texte* (Paris: Éditions du Seuil, 1973), 75–76.

Orphée *and Orphism:*
A Map of Poetic Ascent

Mima Vulović

*It has been said that his voice was so beautiful it could tame Nature
herself: it could quiet down growling bears and lions, wild rivers beneath the Earth and rogue winds above it. His lyre with seven strings
mesmerized the sirens and dragons, so he could take away their golden
fleece. Everywhere he went, peace spread around him in rings. But, he
himself was not peaceful for his beloved one died twice, which is to say
— she was irrevocably gone. The first time this happened, the Gods of
the underworld, pleased by his gift, granted her return on condition
that he did not look back until they reached the light. However, the
excess of his sad longing violated the divine orders and her contours
shattered and faded in the dark. It took a fleeting moment of what was
probably a single sluggish blink of the eyelids, and he was locked in
the ancient curse from the dawn of times, the one that made the whole
world a cheat and a sham. And so the truths of the higher order unfolded. Soul was immortal, his voice let people know, but flesh, made
of ashes, was the soul's grave. Some say he died by a stroke of thunder:
the mighty one burned him back to ashes for initiating the common and
unworthy into the realm of the forbidden. Some say it was the hordes
of drunk women that tore his flesh apart, just as he was making an offering to the God of light and purity. Be that as it may, it is agreed
that the murder could not silence his throat, for his decapitated head
kept on singing. His lyre with seven strings winged itself into the skies,
followed by lions and bears that sit close to listen. We can still see
their constellations among the stars.*

So goes a personal summary of numerous and often conflicting Orphic
legends. In the world of literature, the Universal Poet has given rise to
a wealth of self-appointed heirs, but Jean Cocteau's place amongst
them is unique by virtue of his liberty to stand as a singular self-

appointed *double*. In his account of the myth, Orphée's head proudly exclaims its name: 'C, O, C, T, E, A, U. Cocteau.'[1] This pronouncement is revealing of the position that indeed does set Cocteau apart, at least from most of his contemporaries, the position that concerns the sheer size of the territory he claims — no more and no less than the whole universe! Cocteau, just like Orpheus, travels across it, horizontally and vertically, covering the grounds far beyond the modern edifice of the twentieth century. While, following World War I, most European dramatists remained restricted within its suffocating walls, weighed heavily by the new burden of theatre's *raison d'être*, namely the desire to transform the entire collective consciousness, Cocteau seemed content to only *observe* it as an outsider, through a liberating, self-imposed distance. Pretty sanguine in thinking that the transformation of the mind is not necessarily a subject of our own will, but rather that of mystical and divine forces (given the faith in them), Cocteau also offers something so rarely acknowledged in the analyses of his work — a lesson in poetic humility.

Indeed, it is difficult to debunk such a stance in the world of *Orphée*, where all that is sublime gives way to campy ridicule. The poet of love cares more for his toy than his wife, and the toy is not exactly a lyre. It is a life-size Horse with an annoying hoof-tapping tic. The loving couple bickers over him with neurotic fervour bound to mark each fight with a broken window-pane. Heurtebise, a glass-repair professional, pedantically replaces such a number of those panes that he practically becomes their live-in mate. He happens to be an Angel, in fact, but even Angels need a day-time job. The entrance to Hades is invitingly decorated with silver tinsel, and Death, if judged by fashion, is a party-loving surgeon with clumsy nurses. This sketch would hardly support the loftiness of the common consent that Orphée is 'the seducer at all levels of the cosmos and of the psyche — Heaven, Earth, the ocean and the Underworld; the subconscious, the conscious and the superconscious,' someone who dared to break 'the taboo and dared to gaze at the Invisible.'[2] And yet, it does. Under *Orphée's* surface, endowed with Cocteau's personality, there is a clandestine correspondence with a decidedly Or-

---

[1] Jean Cocteau, 'Orphée', translated by Carl Wildman in *Five Plays* (New York: Hill and Wang, 1996), 44.

[2] Jean Chevalier and Alain Gheerbrant, *Dictionary of Symbols*, translated by John Buchanan-Brown (London: Penguin Books, 1996), 725. '[L]e séducteur, à tous les niveaux du cosmos et du psychisme: le ciel, la terre, les océans, les enfers; le subconscient, la conscience et le surconscient...' *Dictionnaire des symboles*, (Paris: Éditions Robert Laffont et Éditions Jupiter, 1969), 569. All subsequent French quotations are taken from this source.

phic metaphysics of poetry, endowed with profound and humble reverence.

In other words, Cocteau takes up the difficult dichotomy, intrinsic to
the Orphic myth, between the 'life of poetry' and the 'poetry of life.'
He shoots straight for the steep cleavage in which the divine grandeur
of the former collides with the human banality and inferiority of the
latter. A vocal advocate of the notion that poetry is indeed a sublime
entity, Cocteau defends its absolute quality from any plebeian effort to
turn its loftiness into vulgarity, its alluring mechanics of evolving
within a poet into a functional routine of becoming one. In short, according to Cocteau, Orpheus blinks simply because *he wants to!* There is
nothing tragic about it. There is tragedy only from the human point of
view, which is, after all, one-sided. In the final summation, only gods
can account for the proper course and outcome of things. Orpheus' gifts
were not designed to serve Eurydice to begin with, and regardless of
how much he loves her, it is not within his powers to utilize them to
that end. Analogically, regardless of all the flamboyant gestures intended to affirm his star status, Cocteau's own poetic talent could never
be claimed, much less submerged, dimmed or corrupted, by any movement of the day. The poetry of the Dadaists or Surrealists, along with
their overriding manifestos and programs, was too conditional on the
collision with society. Cocteau, despite all evidence of arrogance to the
contrary, simply stayed outside.

To prove the symbolic and conceptual equivalence between Cocteau's
vision and its mythical ancestry, it is necessary to look beyond the Orphic legend into a vast, coherent and organized system of Orphic religion. Substantially different from either Homeric or Mediterranean
traditions and dated as early as fifth century A.D., it is supposed to
have inspired a number of esoteric doctrines: Eleusinian Mysteries,
Pythagoreans or Gnostics (thus by extension also mediæval Al-
chemists), along with main-stream thinkers like Plato or Aristophanes, both of whom in fact considered Orpheus to be the founder of
all mystery-religions.[1] Arguable as this stand may be, it is important
insofar as it points to the *hermetic,* rather than the missionary nature
of Orphism, the idea that doctrines are revealed only to the initiates
and impervious to the rest.

In terms of Cocteau's play, the implication is obvious. *Orphée* could
be observed as a sealed riddle of sorts — as a hermeneutic interpretation of the enigma of poetry that is, at the same time, careful not to be-
tray its secret. The play toys with several decidedly Orphic notions

---

[1] W.K.C. Guthrie, *Orpheus and Greek Religion* (London: Methuen and Co. Ltd.,
1935), 17.

and these, for the most part, resist dramatic analyses of the common sort.

Let us consider the traditional approach for a moment. For instance, the play's unity of time-space-action appears rather linear and ordinary, despite sporadic, stylized improbabilities. An observation through an Orphic prism will prove this unity non-linear and far more complex. Another example: talking heads and horses are distanciating conventions, obvious means of removing the spectators from the automatism of observation, but to what end? Certainly not political in a Brechtian sense. Æsthetic then? Perhaps it is true that Cocteau is suggesting that an artistic picture of the world ought to be a reflection of complete subjectivity. But, at the time, this was hardly news. Distanciating or not, in Orphic terms, the hollow head symbolically represents the body as the shallow grave of the soul. In short, this play guards its golden fleece with secrets that are often disguised as marginalia. Such is the challenge of a true riddle: one has to find a stone that opens a hidden passage.

Since by virtue of allegory, *Orphée* invites the audience of the real world to guess the mystery of a hidden world, then it is this mystery which is truly worth debating. One way of debunking any sort of mystery is through the revelation of the process by which it is born. Thus the lay-out: 1) If the Orphic myth is a mystery, then Orphism is a key to its origins and hidden meanings; 2) If *Orphée* is a riddle, then Cocteau's adherence to its ancestral postulates may reveal a possible answer. This is not to suggest that Cocteau himself was a devout Orphic (the play in fact marks his return to Catholicism), but merely that he was building his drama with the appropriate tools. It is also beyond the scope of this analysis to establish the ways *via* which Cocteau may have been acquainted with Orphic philosophy and religion. Suffice it to say that the sources would have been available in his time as they are now, and that there is no reason why he should not have done the required research.

Also, there is another trap in the above formula that one ought to be aware of. Cocteau's poetic system resembles an Orphic conceptual system, but not necessarily in an analogous manner. While analogies are inescapable in proving this thesis, all conclusions should still rest upon the *present dimension* in Cocteau's drama, for this is the nature of the medium. Again, this goes far beyond matters of form or style, into that residue of individual meditation which is born and bound by one's very own landscape, its space and time. *Orphée* is indeed a *modern* rewrite of the Orphic myth, a verbal account of Cocteau's spiritual correspondence with ancient poetry. Two major tenets of Orphism, paraphrased by Cocteau in *Orphée*, include the belief in the immortality and transmigration of the soul, and the notion that the primary principle of the soul is equivalent with that of the cosmos. The cosmogony and theogeny that situate these postulates will be further qualified in terms of their applicability to *Orphée's* structure and substance. But, before that is accomplished, it is necessary to take a closer look at the protagonists who inhabit this structure and render it substance.

Orphée is a modern archetype of a poet: '[t]he artist is not a person endowed with free will who seeks his own ends, but one who allows art to realize its purposes through him.'[1] The structure of his personality is in fact a twentieth century psychoanalytic composite of id, ego and superego, each in a dialectically reciprocal relationship with other characters in the play. Orphée's id is functional only through the Horse, his ego inexplicable without Eurydice, while his superego is realized through Heurtebise. Cocteau makes these interdependencies so organic that it is almost impossible to fathom Orphée's character as a separate entity.

However, in substance, Orphée is very much an example of a nineteenth century hero, but without the pathos. His search for the perfect poetic correspondence between the human soul and the universe is a probe of a '"disinherited mind" in the ontological sense, of a mind torn between the certainty of man's insignificance in the immensity of a hostile universe, and an urge, born of wounded pride, to endow man with preeminence ... [a mind torn by the] "incessant struggle between arrogance and humiliation ..."'[2] Thus, recognizing the mysterious divinity of creation, Orphée readily 'gives his kingdom for a horse,' but he cannot restrain himself from defying it at the same time by deliberately looking at Eurydice.

In the final outcome —the divine judgment, so to speak— the distinction between deliberation and accident is of no consequence. However, by human standards, it is a detrimental measure of Orphée's morality. This is an important point: by introducing the intent, Cocteau loudly confronts his audience as well. The poet's aim, he exclaims, is simply poetry. There can be no compromises on the path, meaning that the poet will often have to embrace the most terrible immorality which future morality stands for. What people unqualified in poetry make of it should not concern the poet. After all, he does not serve them, but rather is an instrument of a force of nature, revealing the inner necessity which is superhuman.

---

[1] C.G. Jung, *The Spirit in Man, Art, and Literature*, translated by R.F.C. Hull. (New York: Pantheon Books, 1966), 101.

[2] Czesław Miłosz, *The Land of Ulro*, translated by Louis Iribarne (New York: Farrar, Straus and Giroux, 1984), 95.

Eurydice is the epitome of a moralist unqualified in poetry, the only truly human character in the play. Without her, the infantile traits of Orphée's depleted ego, namely his selfishness, ruthlessness and vanity, would hardly matter. She pays dearly for his divine gifts; ultimately, more than he does. But the distinction between Orphée's love for poetry and his love for Eurydice is not quite so crass as it first appears. The two, though often in conflict, are inseparable on every level, human and divine.

Eurydice is the Moon, Orphée is the Sun; she is the female principle of passive, rational and speculative knowledge, acquired by reflection. He is the male principle of active, immediate knowledge. Together, they are spirit and soul, heart and brain, water and fire. The whole realizes itself through these dualities. Further, she is the one who is responsible for Heurtebise's presence, which makes her a chief (though, often unaware) accomplice *en route* to the stars. This suggests that '[t]he creative process has a feminine quality, and the creative work arises from unconscious depths — we might truly say from the realm of the Mothers.'[1]

The Horse and Heurtebise are the stuff that Orphée's poetry is made of, the Primordial and the Sublime. The Horse is the messenger of that unconsciously remembered tongue that all poetry strives to surrender and command; the Angel is the one who relinquishes it from obscurity and cleanses it through distance — the one who deciphers it for the Stars. Orphée is a tangible point of their workings, a mere tool in their photo-lab, a lens that absorbs the primeval opaque glow and a filter that modifies it into a celestial spectrum. This does not make Orphée a lesser hero, for it is in the nature of a true hero to be devoured.

Plato believed that 'poets cannot have knowledge of what they write, in the philosophical sense of being able to explain their own meaning and teach others what they themselves can do. The poet is simply the mouthpiece of the god ... and writes, as it were, a dictation.'[2] Translating this phenomenon into modern psychology, Jung labels it an 'autonomous complex' where a poet, while producing what he consciously intends, nonetheless is so carried away by the creative impulse that he is no longer aware of an 'alien' will.[3] By his own admission, Orphée is only a mouthpiece of the Horse; the Horse is indeed his 'alien' will:

---

[1] Jung, 103.

[2] Guthrie, 241.

[3] Jung, 75.

... The sun and the moon are all the same to me. There remains night. But
not the night of others! My night. This horse plunges into my night and
reappears like a diver. He brings back sentences. Don't you feel that the
least of these sentences is more remarkable than all the poems? I would
give my complete works for one of those little sentences in which I listen
to myself as you listen to the sea in the shell ... I am discovering a new
world, I am living again, I am stalking the unknown.[1]

As a diver, the Horse swims in and out of the murky waters of Orphée's
collective unconscious, carrying the memory of its authentic speech over
the threshold into consciousness. This, however, does not provide for
synthesis: Orphée can only perceive, but not assimilate the Horse. His
dictation cannot be voluntarily induced nor inhibited, and '[t]herein
lies the autonomy of the complex: it appears and disappears in accordance with its own inherent tendencies, independently of the conscious
will.'[2]

Once the Horse has delivered his oracle, he, like all messengers,
must die. At this point Orphée is only human, and therefore, can not be
simultaneously asleep and awake. On the other hand, to recognize
Heurtebise as a truly divine inspiration is not a matter of instantaneous
revelation, but of initiation through self-deluding stages. Like all
awakening, this one has its hazy duration, heavy eye-lids protecting
the torpor of dreams and amnesia. Stumbling points of will, literally
depicted here, are the cause of fall and rise:

> *Heurtebise*: ... You lost your balance, and you turned your head inadver-
> tently; I saw you.
> *Orphée*: I lost my balance on purpose. I turned my head deliberately, and I
> forbid anyone to contradict me ... I congratulate myself for having
> turned my head deliberately toward my wife.[3]

---

[1] Cocteau, 13. '*Je mets le soleil et la lune dans le même sac. Il me reste la nuit. Et pas
la nuit des autres! Ma nuit. Ce cheval entre dans ma nuit et il en sort comme un
plongeur. Il en rapporte des phrases. Ne sens-tu pas que la moindre de ces phrases
est plus étonnante que tous les poèmes? Je donnerais mes œuvres complètes pour
une seule de ces petites phrases où je m'écoute comme on écoute la mer dans un co-
quillage[...] Je découvre un monde. Je retourne ma peau. Je traque l'inconnu.*' Œuvres complètes*, vol. V (Geneva: Marguerat, 1946), 24 (scene i). All subsequent
French quotations from the play are taken from this source.

[2] Jung, 78.

[3] Cocteau, 35. '*Heurtebise:...Vous avez perdu l'équilibre. Vous avez tourné la tête
par distraction; je vous ai vu. Orphée: J'ai perdu l'équilibre exprès. J'ai tourné la
tête exprès, et je défends qu'on me contredise[...] Je me félicite, moi, d'avoir tourné
la tête exprès vers ma femme.*' 72.

Notwithstanding the sheer comedy of the act, this is nonetheless the trying moment of the play. Orphée has just killed his dead wife 'just because' he suspected her 'womanly' ways with Heurtebise, the pure spirit, and, anyway, who wants that which is *allowed*?! It was not an accident, Orphée childishly insists, he did it *on purpose, simply because he wanted to!* But, by doing so, he *questions* both his gods and his audience: is poetic licence absolute, and, if not, who establishes its limits? While the answer may not be clear, this is certain: it is not free, and the price is the one thing most difficult to shed — Ego. Thus the trials of death.

Death, for its part, arrives in a vision of a gorgeous woman of medicine, aided by two male nurses, Azrael and Rafael, who are, according to mythology, responsible for respectively separating the soul from the body and assisting the surgeons. Regardless of this inversion of social power roles, probably far more striking in the late twenties, the idea that death is represented by a woman has often been labelled 'misogynous.' Of course, this would stand correct providing we endow the notion of death with exclusively *negative* attributes. *Nota bene*, the scene is more revealing of our cold, indifferent and reductive views towards inner human values in the Age of Science than it is of Cocteau's misogyny. But, such is the parcel of French magic: hypnotized into seeing the gloves politely laid out for Orphée to find, we suddenly feel them thrown straight into our own faces, the silky texture not quite smoothing our losses in this duel. Incidentally, the female imagery is also faithfully adherent to its mythological precedents: Goddess religions pictured Death as a crone cutting the thread of life; and, yes, originally, it would have been a woman —the beautiful and kind Persephone— to greet Eurydice at the entrance of the Underworld.

Besides claiming Orphée's wife, Death initiates a yet more complex *peripetia*; she takes away the Horse too. It is a castrating act in more ways than one; all of Orphée's rising potentialities, poetic and pelvic, go with the animal. Notwithstanding the obvious cruelty, this will prove beneficial in the long run. *Free from* the Horse, Orphée is *free to* search loftier zones of love. And, if dead himself, he can obtain the loftiest one of all. Once again, Orphée's death will remain a mystery and subject of ominous speculations, including that of Bacchantes being involved in the crime. But, given the final outcome, even if they killed him, they did him a favour. The implications are clear: in purging evil from good, in an overall context of cosmic restoration, it is a woman that is assigned the central role. A far less modern theodicy of Plato (*The Symposium, 179d*) would differently qualify the divine justice: since the poet of love 'lacked the courage to die as Alcestis did for love, choosing rather to scheme his way, living, into Hades. And it was for this that the gods doomed him, and doomed him justly, to meet his death at the hands of women.'[1]

The ground-plan of *Orphée* resembles that of a temple insofar as it reflects the territory of the whole Universe, bound from nadir to zenith, built in the image which Cocteau creates of the Holy. If scrupulously read, the play is unmistakably a model of symbolic geometry that carries meanings of immense consequences in terms of the Orphic religion, particularly its cosmogony and theodicy. The redrafting of its blueprint will require the assistance of Pythagorean theories for the following reason. Since the latter have 'considered him [Orpheus] the author of their fate,'[2] the translation of their mathematical terms into Orphic philosophical postulates will result in an organic and complementary parallelism, which would not be possible with, say, Christian symbolic numerology. This is not to claim that Cocteau did not involve a few arithmetic double-entendres of his own, aimed exclusively at the Christian imagination of his audience. Once again, in reviewing what is to come, it would be helpful to keep in mind that while mirroring the divine exterior, temples are also intended to reflect the human interior.

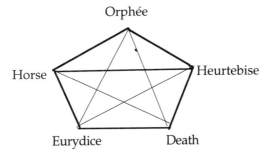

Major characters, Orphée, Eurydice, Horse, Angel and Death, form a self contained quinx — the cryptic symbol of Higher Knowledge or fulfilment in Classical Antiquity. In full compliance with Pythagorean theory of the pentagram, Cocteau unites the three (Orphée, Horse and Angel) and the two (Eurydice and Death), the male and female principles, suggesting the idea that perfection is in essence genderless, or at least androgynous. In other words, *Orphée* expresses a life force as the fruitful marriage of complementary powers: action and submission, order and anarchy, self-sacrifice and egotism, sun and moon, heaven and hell.

---

[1] Mircea Eliade, *A History of Religious Ideas*, Volume 2, translated by Willard R. Trask. (Chicago: The University of Chicago Press, 1982), 181, note 3.

[2] Guthrie, 220.

The quinx is also an integral part of the play's architecture. The geometry of Orphée's two journeys (above and under ground) is outlined by parallel pentagrams. The first level of Orphée's consciousness, the lower incarnation of his soul, is contained within the beginning five scenes of the play's episodic lay-out. It is marked not only by Orphée's leap from ignorance to the capacity to perceive divine forces, but also by his determination to defend such perception, which will, according to the intrinsic dualisms of a pentacle, account for both his fall and subsequent rise. The second level of Orphée's consciousness, undoubtedly an incarnation of a higher order (for now he not only perceives, but *interacts* with the divinities), is similarly divided into five scenes (VII-XI). Again, the synthesis of opposites is at work; Orphée must descend into the heart of darkness in order to obtain his place in the light. In short, on each of the horizontal planes of the soul's transformation, higher knowledge is obtained through five motions, alluding possibly to the Pythagorean notion that the pentagram is the key to 'the door to what was secret.'[1]

The two levels relate as if mirrored, through the spatial and semiotic symmetry where left becomes right, ground sinks into the underground, life evaporates into death, Chronos (time measured by heart-beats) dissolves into Chairos (time between the heart-beats), or where the guiding principles of the Devil (Horse) give way to those of Angels (Heurtebise) — to mention only the obvious inversions. Nonetheless, it is impossible to ignore that each center of the two horizontal pentagrams is penetrated by the same vertical axis. Thus, their hearts are of the same matter; essentially, Cocteau's mythical hero ends up experiencing a similar process on both planes. He is forced *twice* to make a full inventory of his feelings, to document an experience which throws the whole range of his past experiences into relief, and to re-examine himself in the light of these new revelations. The parallelism of the journeys is further emphasized by the identicity of rhythm structures in the two five-scene units. Namely, they both propose the visual pattern of the following tempo:

--------- --- --------- --- ---------

The long passages (scenes I, III, V and VII, IX, XI) are connected by short intervals (scenes II, IV and VIII, X). Perhaps, like his Horse, Cocteau was proposing a riddle by means of tapping, rather than words? If Orphée's head consciously reveals Cocteau's name and address as his own, then it follows that the Horse could be Cocteau himself too,

---

[1] Chevalier and Gheerbrant, 747. '*Il est une des clefs de la Haute-Science: il ouvre la voie au secret.*' 591.

obliged to subliminally add an image which was always a part of his proper signature: five points of a Blazing Star, the Masonic 'emblem of the Genius which raises the soul to great deeds.'[1]

Going from complex to simpler shapes, the pentagon is reducible to its elemental compositions — triangles, considered by Platonic geometrical theories to be primary plane surfaces.[2] And, indeed, a simple line, connecting any two points, drawn through the inside of the original quinx will reveal a number of symbolic fully functioning triads. For example: Orphée-Eurydice-Horse bears an inverted weight of Orphée-Eurydice-Heurtebise in terms of the relationship between love and jealousy, love and subconsciousness or superconsciousness, as well as love and heaven or hell. Death (a triad on its own with Azrael and Rafael) lends air to Orphée's Sun fire and Eurydice's Moon water, to create a mist, the symbol of the indeterminate phase in the soul's transmigration when its old shapes and longings evaporate, while the new ones are not quite formed. Even though he dresses her *chique* and endows her with the precision of a surgeon, Cocteau still implies, at least formally, that Death is a twilight zone, a precipice where Heurtebise's blinding light and the Equestrian icy darkness permanently struggle. With an exception of the Holy Trinity (Orphée-Eurydice-Heurtebise), born in the very finale of the play, the other triads are not of an equilateral nature. They do not represent harmony or proportion, but a division of sorts, where one angle is forcing the other two into imbalance. This too bears resemblance to the Orphic eschatological vision which was one of the first to bound up the soul's destiny with the motions of heavens, and which represented the soul as a charioteer driving his chariot, who found it difficult to control the two horses, due to the antagonism between them.[3]

The fact that the soul's voyage takes place on the vertical *axis mundi* does not only reaffirm the Orphic assertion that '[t]he first principle of the cosmos is found to be identical with the first principle of the soul,'[4] but also brings about another crucial trinity: Underworld-Earth-Skies, one of the most persistent universal archetypes.

On the one hand, Cocteau defines exact spatial coordinates of such a cosmological division by showing where the axis hides a secret passage, by exposing the secret of the mirror. When gone behind it, Orphée is not on Earth, the spectator is certain of that much. On the other

---

[1] Ibid., 748. '[L]'*emblème du* Génie *qui élève l'âme à de grandes choses.*' 591.

[2] Ibid., 1034.

[3] Eliade, 201.

[4] Ibid., 201.

hand, given that time is insolubly linked with space, Cocteau blurs the cosmic planes with the non-linear treatment of time. First, both Death and Heurtebise provide literal accounts for the fact that the time of gods and time of humans are not one and the same. Secondly, even human time is subject to doubt, for gods enjoy playing tricks. The play practically opens with the line 'Orphée hunts Eurydice's lost life,'[1] which according to Orphée is not merely a sentence but '... a poem of vision, a flower deep-rooted in death.'[2] So, the Underworld is inhabiting the Earth as we speak, while the present tense is mingling with future, providing that is what 'vision' implies. Moments later, he also claims: 'Without noticing it, we *were* dead.'[3] All of a sudden, past penetrates

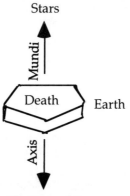

into 'now' and 'here' as well! In short, the principle of time-bound causality is disturbed: Orphée's walk through the dark is not the consequence of Eurydice's death but, rather, the other way around. Or is it quite so? The circles close, not only in place, but in time, making it impossible to pin either the beginning or the end. 'We are knocking against each other in the dark ... We are playing hide-and-seek with the gods,'[4] warns the Poet.

What makes it clear that Cocteau had to be aware of the religious teachings beyond the mythical fabula is not only the fact that his twofold nature of time fully corresponds to the Orphic representation of 'normal' and 'grotesque' time, nor the fact that the triad of the Past-Present-Future is in dual bound (again conditionally inverted) with

---

[1] Cocteau, 14. 'Madame Eurydice reviendra des enfers...' 24.

[2] Ibid., 14. '[U]n poème, un poème du rêve, une fleur du fond de la mort.' 25.

[3] Ibid., 15. 'Nous étions morts sans nous en apercevoir.' 26.

[4] Ibid., 14. 'Nous nous cognons dans le noir[...] Nous jouons à cache-cache avec les dieux...' 25.

that of Below-Here-Above, but the concept of the *time and memory* in the transmigration of the soul. Even though, without noticing it, he was already dead and his recollection of the underground is vague, like '... recovering from an operation,'[1] on the whole, Orphée is in full possession of his faculty of remembering, at all times and on all planes. Most official or esoteric eschatologies presume that each incarnation simply carries its own separate consciousness, but that is not so with the Orphics. They believed that the retaining of memory is a key to timeless consciousness, a means of achieving the ultimate incarnation — the union with the Divine Whole. To this end, the Orphic gold plate from Petelia, South Italy, fourth-third century B.C. offers precise instructions for the after-life, all inclusive with a detailed geography of the resort:

> Thou shalt find to the left of the House of Hades a spring,
> And by the side thereof standing a white cypress.
> To this spring approach not near.
> But thou shalt find another, from the Lake of Memory
> Cold water flowing forth, and there are guardians before it.
> Say, 'I am a child of Earth and starry Heaven;
> But my race is of Heaven (alone). This ye know yourselves.
> But I am parched with thirst and I perish. Give me quickly
> The cold water flowing forth from the Lake of Memory ...[2]

Is it a mere coincidence or a witty little clue that upon his return from the underworld, Orphée exclaims: 'I am thirsty?'[3]

Of course, there is an entire gallery of witty little clues left in the labyrinthine garden of *Orphée*, which (wisely, as they are supposed to) open the high hedges — not to paths, but to cross-roads. Suffice it to glance only at ones that lead back to the riddles of numbers. Why does the entire journey of Orphée's soul constitute the sum total of thirteen scenes? Are there eleven or thirteen characters? Is death as ambivalent as the number six? Is the Divine Incarnation as unlucky as thirteen?

The two five-scene units previously described as pentagonal constructions of *Orphée's* linear structure are followed by accounts of catharses, in the Orphic sense — the rituals of purgation. The first is temporary — death of the body; the second is permanent — a state of bliss. For this alone, they ought to contrast more than they do in Cocteau's version of the myth. Death comes in scene VI, originally the number of ambivalence with as 'strong a tendency towards evil as to-

---

[1] Ibid., 32. '[I]l me semble que je sors d'une opération.' 66.
[2] Guthrie, 172-73.
[3] Cocteau, 33. 'J'ai soif!' 60.

wards good, towards rebellion against God as towards union with him.'[1] And indeed the appearances would suggest so: there is a strange ambivalent harmony between the Surgeon and her two helpers, the mood of calmness and kindness not so essentially different from that of the blissful trio above. On the other hand, Cocteau must have been aware that in the Christian imagination (which most of his spectators would share), six is inexorably linked to the false prophet, the Anti-Christ — this devilish note further emphasized by names of archangels: Azrael and Rafael.

In turn, the final incarnation of Orphée-Eurydice-Angel, as happy and enlightened as it may appear, happens in scene XIII, the number unmistakably considered (by both Classical antiquity and Christianity) as unlucky and 'separated from the normal order and rhythm of the universe.'[2] Moreover, if yet another incarnation of Orphée —this time in the shape of his plaster bust— is observed as a separate character in the play (as statues in Cocteau's other works often are), then the sum total of personages is really twelve. Twelve apostles and Christ celebrated the Last Supper, the occasion which not only proved unfortunate for Jesus, but also proved the fact that even Gods do not escape the bad luck of thirteen.

This of course brings about the central question — is God a character in Orphée? Does God (in the form of Beauty or Love) exist as an invisible, but omnipresent cause of all action in this drama, like He does in Ibsen's Brand? If so, then there are thirteen members of the cast roaming in the fortuitous cloister of thirteen scenes, threatening the momentary aberration of this Divine Architecture.

Mircea Eliade says that Orphic religion 'somber and tragic as it seems to be, paradoxically contains an element of hope that is absent not only from the Mesopotamian Weltanschauung but also from the Homeric conception.'[3] Inversely, it could be said in conclusion that Cocteau's Orphée, as witty and hopeful as it seems to be, paradoxically contains an element of tragedy. Perhaps it is only fitting that a mirror between Cocteau and Orpheus should reflect the inverted likeness, for their respective planes of incarnation are about twenty-five centuries apart.

On the other hand, the cosmos has hardly changed in the meantime, inside or out. Cocteau's architecture of it is the same as the Orphic.

---

[1] Chevalier and Gheerbrant, 885. 'Il peut pencher vers le bien, mais aussi vers le mal, vers l'union à Dieu, mais aussi vers la révolte.' 798.

[2] Ibid., 988. "[C]'est une unité secouant l'équilibre des rapports variés dans le monde.' 766.

[3] Eliade, 190.

Analogous to Kot's description of Prometheus' world, at the bottom there is a primordial sea, on the top there is an ocean of paradise, and in between, there is the dry disk of planet Earth.[1] They all revolve around the *axis mundi*, the river of death, for it is only through death that other bodies of water could be reached. Orphée inhabits the Earth with Eurydice, his other half. They have a Horse and an Angel. The Horse swims below the disk, presumably searching for the Orphic Egg with Zeus inside. He is both Orphée's and the collective subconscious. He could easily represent libido too, not only by means of obvious allegory, but because Orphic cosmogony is, in its essence, monistic and sexual at once. According to their teachings, Zeus did not will the world with the motion of his head, but with motion of his abdomen. The Earth, therefore, is the prison where a primordial crime is punished and where 'the soul is shut up in the body (*soma*) as in a tomb (*sema*).'[2] By the end of the play, the hollow casket of a plaster head is all that is left of Orphée. 'Hence, incarnate existence is more like a death and the death of the body is therefore the beginning of true life. However, this "true life" is not obtained automatically; the soul is judged according to its faults or its merits, and after a certain time is incarnated again.'[3] For all that the passage offers, there could be two thousand disks stacked in the planet's juke-box. Cocteau talks of two only. Therefore, they represent them all. The road from one to the other 'is neither straightforward not single ...; there are many forkings and crossroads.'[4] Jacob's Ladder reveals many faces of the same riddle, confusing the directions of descent and ascent. Salvation is obtained primarily through cosmological and theosophical revelations, discoveries of secrets that are designed by gods, but carried down by angels in disguise. Orphée's own repairs and washes windows, no doubt, those of the soul. In comparison with the Horse, Heurtebise is the superconsciousness. But he too is separate from Orphée, so separate that it takes the Poet a whole lifetime to recognize the Angel as his Guardian. In retrospect, Heurtebise is the one who sifts the minuscule particles of virtue through the sieve of Orphée's egotism and the one who reminds him to listen to the time between his heart-beats in order not to lose them all in an eye blink ... When all is seen and learned, the poet is invited to join his race in starry Heaven.

---

[1] Jan Kot, *Jedenje Bogova* (Beograd: Nolit, 1974), 14.

[2] Eliade, 186.

[3] Ibid., 186.

[4] Ibid., 190.

In essence, Cocteau is more removed from the Orphic myth than he is from the complex Orphic theogeny. For one thing, his hero is less prone to saccharine love and far more grumpy and pragmatic than we fancy the original; but again, in two-thousand five-hundred years his landscape has drastically altered. Stifling urban walls are erected where the trees used to be; poisonous serpents cannot dwell there, whereas poisonous people do; and poetry is no longer revered by wild beasts, but by both official and alternative police commissioners of the social order. However, the sentimental considerations still oblige the Moon to eclipse the Sun.

Finally, it should be stated once again in conclusion that such broad analogies in matters of poetry and faith are only one means of interpretation, and are true only up to the point of the most obvious resemblance, for afterwards they inexorably stumble on form. But, Death is Death, whether dressed in a snake's skin or an evening gown. Besides, since their purpose is to be revealing, the analogies just may be in poor taste when coupling Cocteau's play with Orphism, an essentially hermetic doctrine. There is a good reason for respecting the precious mystic sense of both: the secrecy is a guardian of treasures. Such is one of the lessons of *Orphée*. Thus, it would be an impropriety to attribute a missionary message to it. Cocteau often claimed that his work contains no symbols either, and considering that symbol is an 'intimation of a meaning beyond the level of our present powers of comprehension,'[1] he probably had a point there too. For lack of any better choice of synonyms, this present writing is shamelessly guilty of this 'impropriety.'

What Cocteau offers us are only the signs by the road: a levitating angel, thread cut from the bobbin, a spectator's wrist-watch, a confession of thirst, Black Sun, pentagons, triads and whatever else is lost through translation or our inadvertence. These signs are *within* our powers of comprehension. They are both the guiding principles and a promise of future reconciliation with the place where poetry is the language heeded by animals and stones.[2] What gives the voyage focus, of course, is the poet's —Cocteau's— abiding faith in beauty.

---

[1] Jung, 76.
[2] Milosz, 212.

Servicing Orpheus: Death, Love and Female Subjectivity in the Film Orphée

Rebecca Conolly

'You mustn't try too hard to understand what's happening, my dear Sir. It's a very serious mistake'.[1] These words, spoken by the Princess in Jean Cocteau's 1950 film *Orphée*, though directed at the poet Orpheus, also subtly reveal the *auteur's* personal resistance to the over-analysis, symbolic interpretation and deconstruction of his work. In his notes to the screenplay, Cocteau states explicitly that '[t]here are no symbols or messages in this film ... It is a realistic film, which expresses cinematically that which is truer than truth itself — a superior realism, the truth that Goethe opposes to reality, the truth that is the greatest conquest of the poets of our era'.[2]

The transcendent form of truth that informs Cocteau's *Orphée* pushes the boundaries of conventional cinematic representation, resulting in a thematically and æsthetically challenging film. However, obscured under the layers of artistic innovation lies one of the few entirely (and uncomfortably) conventional aspects of Cocteau's film — his representation of women. Although Cocteau recontextualized or contemporized several elements of the myth of Orpheus for his film, he left intact a sizeable amount of the myth's inherent misogyny — privi-

---

[1] *Orphée. Three Screenplays*. Trans. Carol Martin-Sperry (New York: Grossman Publishers, 1972), 116. All subsequent quotations in English are taken from this source. *'Vous cherchez trop à comprendre ce qui se passe, cher Monsieur. C'est un grave défaut.' Orphée* (film). Photographies de Roger Corbeau (Paris: La Parade, 1950), 18–19. All subsequent quotations from the French screenplay are taken from this source.

[2] Ibid., 188. *'Il n'y a dans ce film ni symbole, ni thèse... C'est un film réaliste et qui met cinématographiquement en œuvre le plus vrai que le vrai, ce réalisme supérieur, cette vérité que Gœthe oppose à la réaliste et qui sont la grande conquête.' Orphée*, i.

leging other thematic or artistic considerations over issues of female subjectivity. As will be shown, each of the three female characters in *Orphée*, although seemingly vital players in the film's action, are ultimately restricted to the role of dramatic device — serving solely to forward and ensure the completion of Orpheus' heroic quest for artistic immortality. Not only are they limited in this capacity, but also, in their rigidly defined characterization — Eurydice, Aglaonice and the Princess are little more than somewhat embellished versions of the rigidly archetypical female roles of the virgin, the bitch and the whore, respectively. Each of them exists to fulfil a specific need of the poet, which, once satisfied, necessitates their disappearance (both literal and metaphorical) or destruction.

In order to better understand how female subjectivity functions in *Orphée*, I will first of all examine briefly the mythological roots of the characters in conjunction with Cocteau's thematic and structural choices for the film. I will then consider the ramifications of such choices on the construction and development of female characters with particular reference to Laura Mulvey's germinal article 'Visual Pleasure and Narrative Cinema.' Lastly, as a means to emphasize the rigidity of Cocteau's female characterization, I will attempt a concise masochistic reading of the Princess, employing as a framework Gaylyn Studlar's article 'Masochism and the Perverse Pleasures of the Cinema,' which draws upon the work of Gilles Deleuze as a means to offer an alternative to more sadistic interpretations (such as Mulvey's) of visual pleasure. Ultimately, it should be seen that even such a seemingly powerful and assertive character as the Princess falls victim to the paternalistic mode of representation at work in *Orphée*.

My perspective on Cocteau's film takes as its starting point Jill Dolan's assertion that '[o]ne of the basic assumptions of feminist criticism is that all representation is inherently ideological'.[1] With all due respect to Cocteau's insistence on the transcendent and untouchable qualities of *Orphée*, I hope not to impose an interpretation upon his text, but uncover some of the ideological determinants behind his creation of that which he claims is 'truer than truth itself.'

Perhaps somewhat ironically, Cocteau's quest for a supreme truth originates in his fascination with a myth. This is a myth, however, with which Cocteau takes great liberties, interweaving, as he explains in his notes to the screenplay, the Orphean theme with other, more contemporary elements. He adds to this that the film is accordingly no

---

[1] Jill Dolan, *The Feminist Spectator as Critic* (Ann Arbor: U. of Michigan Press, 1991), 41.

more than a 'paraphrase of an ancient Greek legend,'[1] arguing that this is a completely logical approach to a legend, which is by definition timeless and therefore not limited to any one interpretation .

Cocteau's modernization and in many ways humanization of the myth of Orpheus effects both his choice and depiction of characters. Mythological precedents are clearly discernible for some of the central figures, but all of the characters are essentially original Cocteau creations. However, with respect to the three female characters in the film, instead of liberating them through his innovative approach from some of the misogynous elements of the myth, Cocteau seems to have restricted them even further through rigidly defined, fairly unsympathetic characterization.

Eurydice, for example, in several of the accounts of the myth, is much more idolized by Orpheus than she is in Cocteau's film. Ovid's account of the myth in *The Metamorphoses* describes how distraught Orpheus became over the untimely death of his wife, and cites him as pleading to the gods of the underworld that 'I wanted to be able to endure [her death] and I admit that I have tried; but Love has conquered'. Orpheus adds to this that '[i]f the Fates refuse this reprieve for my wife, it is sure that I do not wish to return either. Take joy in the death of us both!'.[2] Such husbandly devotion is not nearly as pronounced in Cocteau's version, in which the rather confused Orpheus admits to Heurtebise that he wants to travel to the 'Zone' to see not just Eurydice, but also the Princess for whom he has clearly developed a deep attraction .

Cocteau also twists other aspects of the myth, describing, for example, at the beginning of the film how, in his conception, Orpheus' songs 'distracted him from his wife,' an interpretation that clearly places art above earthly love. Eurydice's second death is accordingly treated with some levity by Cocteau, who makes a casual glance into the rearview mirror of a car the reason for her return to the Zone; whereas in Ovid's version, Orpheus looks at his wife 'through love' as he was 'frightened that she might not be well and yearn[ed] to see her with his own eyes'.[3] In short, the mythical Orpheus is utterly devoted to Eurydice — she is the centre of his world, while in Cocteau's version, he is much more concerned with his poetry and the Princess.

---

[1] *Orphée*, 191. '[L]a paraphrase d'un mythe de l'antiquité grecque...' *Orphée*, xii.

[2] Mark P.O. Morford & Robert J. Lenardon, *Classical Mythology* 3rd ed. (New York: Longman, 1985), 283..

[3] Ibid., 284.

Orphée : The Death of Orpheus (Maria Casarès as the Princess)
Courtesy of the Museum of Modern Art Film Stills Archive
© Jean Cocteau/SODRAC (Montréal) 1998

Cocteau describes the very compelling Princess as the Death of Orpheus —not Death itself— who in a way 'plays the role of a guardian whose job is to watch over someone and who saves him at the price of their own destruction'.[1] Her precedent can perhaps be seen in the mythological character of Persephone, the wife of the lord of the underworld. Ovid paints both Persephone and her husband as sympathetic figures, who could not endure Orpheus' pleas for Eurydice's return and accordingly let her go.[2] Cocteau's panel of judges and his unrelenting Princess take over the role of Persephone and Hades in the film. The Princess —far from facilitating in the return of Eurydice to the land of the living— is quite conversely charged with her wrongful death.

The last of the three female characters in Cocteau's film is Aglaonice, who, as the leader of a league of women called the Bacchantes, is clearly Cocteau's modernized version of the mythic Bacchic women (or Mænads) — Dionysian worshippers who in several accounts of the myth are responsible for the death of Orpheus. Eurydice's affiliation with the Bacchantes in the film as one of the club's former waitresses stems from her mythological association with them as a Dryad, or tree nymph.

Orpheus' deep hostility toward Aglaonice and her club can be seen as linked to the mythology which has him killed at the hands of a group of women. According to Morford and Lenardon, '[t]he common tradition (which both Ovid and Virgil reflect) has the women of Thrace [or perhaps the Bacchantes] responsible for his [Orpheus'] death. But the reasons for their hostility vary: they were angry when he neglected them after the death of Eurydice, or refused to initiate them into his mysteries, and enticed their husbands away from them'.[3] Ovid has the Bacchic women drowning out the sound of Orpheus' lyre with their 'shrieks,' stoning him to death and finally tearing him apart with various farm tools.[4] Aglaonice, though Cocteau's invention, is arguably the most mythologically 'accurate' of the three female characters: as the representative of the Bacchantes, her hatred for Orpheus (and his for her) is foregrounded, as is her role in the death of the poet through her association with the avant-garde who confront Orpheus.

Clearly, there are some fairly misogynous elements inherent in the myth of Orpheus, many of which Cocteau retained in his film. Forsak-

---

[1] *Orphée*, 190. 'Elle joue en quelque sorte le rôle d'une espionne chargée de surveiller un homme et qui le sauve en se perdant.' *Orphée*, ix.

[2] Morford and Lenardon, 283.

[3] Ibid., 288.

[4] Ibid., 286.

ing any interest in 'rescuing' the mythologically misaligned female characters, Cocteau instead focuses on more general themes and, more specifically, on the centrality of Orpheus and his heroic quest for artistic immortality. This is a theme that is evolved directly from the myth itself — Orpheus is frequently attributed with having originated the mystery religions, a key feature of which, according to Morford and Lenardon, is 'the belief in man's immortal soul and future life'.[1] Cocteau's personal belief, as Parker Tyler explains, that the artist attains immortality through his work, accordingly led him to incorporate into his film the concept derived from the mystery religions that 'man can attain the birth of his eternal soul in this life'.[2] In order to attain immortality in life, the poet, according to Cocteau, 'must die several times'. Varying notions and incarnations of life and death are accordingly a central feature of *Orphée*.[3]

In his article, 'Cocteau's *Orphée*: From Myth to Drama and Film,' Chester Clayton Long suggests that there are three discernible forms of death in *Orphée* — 'physical death, love-sex death, and the symbolic death of the creative artist' .[4] However, it is not just the second of these forms of death —love-sex death— that is linked with the notion of love. As Raymond Durgnat explains, love is inextricably intertwined with death in the film, both thematically and in terms of characterization: 'Orphée, who is alive,' he writes, 'loves his death; his death, because she loves him, kills his wife, and later, when he is killed, undoes his death'. Adhering to Cocteau's penchant for oppositional, often contradictory themes, death, in a general way, as Durgnat acknowledges, '... is the opposite of love ...'.[5] Each of the characters at one time or another flirts with this opposition — even Eurydice, as Durgnat points out, in her 'suicide' attempt just after returning to the land of the living, is for a brief time aligned with death, while at the same time embodying (in her pregnancy and unrelenting optimism) life and love. Durgnat goes on to underline the fact, however, that in Cocteau's universe, there is no hierarchy of life over death or vice-versa: 'The living are morally no superior to the dead ... Death is the work of the living,

[1] Ibid., 242.

[2] Parker Tyler, *Classics of the Foreign Film*. (New York: Citadel Press, 1962), 188.

[3] *Orphée*, 188. '[O]n endort les néophytes du Thibet afin de les faire voyager dans le temps, peut-être prise pour la mort infligée à un mort, donc qui le fait revivre.' *Orphée*, iv.

[4] Chester Clayton Long, 'Cocteau's *Orphée*: From Myth to Drama and Film,' *Quarterly Journal of Speech* 50 (February 1965), 320.

[5] Raymond Durgnat, *Films and Feelings* (London: Faber & Faber Ltd., 1967), 244.

as well as of the dead'.[1] The characters are accordingly described by
Durgnat as 'wobblers' — 'torn between opposing principles'.[2]

As the central 'wobbler' in the film, it is Orpheus' primary task, as
Durgnat explains, to resolve the two contradictory principles, master-
ing them by paradoxically remaining obedient to them.[3] The successful
resolution of life and death is that which provides the poet with the
inspiration that will ensure his artistic immortality. 'Inspiration,' according to Arthur B. Evans, 'stands as the outcome of a process in which
the poet passes through a number of deaths to finally culminate his art
in life'.[4] Evans adds to this the crucial point that '[i]t is only in life
that the poet's death-produced inspiration can come to true fruition and
become immortal through artistic representation'.[5] Inspiration then, as
Cocteau cleverly points out in his screenplay notes, is utterly contingent
upon 'expiration'.[6]

The primacy of the heroic quest for inspiration and artistic immortality has interesting ramifications on the film's dramatic structure
and the place of female subjectivity therein. Cocteau's almost exclusive
focus on Orpheus' journey carves out very specific, if somewhat contradictory roles for each of the characters. As will be seen, all three of the
female characters in particular are defined solely through Orpheus —
acting as facilitators more than individuals in his heroic quest. As
such, the dramatic structure of the film relies heavily upon their respective role-fulfilments. They are the satellites orbiting around Orpheus; he is their *raison d'être*, without whom they have no role. As an
aside, I should acknowledge that to a certain extent, Heurtebise can
also be considered from this perspective, with the exception that he
firmly asserts his free will in his devotion to one other than Orpheus
—Eurydice— and as such remains somewhat on the periphery of Orpheus' quest, and rather inadvertently advances the heroic plot. His
split-focus therefore places him in a slightly different category than
the singly-focused females.

For a better understanding of the way in which character roles are
determined by the centrality of the heroic quest theme, one need only
attempt to apply A.J. Greimas' actantial model to the film. Keir Elam

[1] Ibid., 245.

[2] Ibid., 246.

[3] Ibid., 245–46.

[4] Arthur B. Evans, *Jean Cocteau and his Films of Orphic Identity* (Philadelphia:
The Art Alliance Press, 1977), 120.

[5] Ibid., 120–21.

[6] *Orphée*, 188.

describes the actantial model as a method used for uncovering the 'deep structure' inherent in any given narrative, which is responsible for generating the surface structure of events.[1] The actantial roles provided by this structure, as Elam explains, refer to the 'universal (oppositional) functions analogous to (and indeed, supposedly derived from) the syntactic functions of language'.[2] Greimas' theory posits that a single actantial model can be derived for any narrative structure, regardless of number of characters or other differentials, because the underlying actants are constants.[3]

According to Greimas, there are six actantial roles or functions: Subject, Object, Sender, Receiver, Helper, and Opponent.[4] Elaine Aston provides an example of an actantial model as derived from a traditional love narrative: '... the hero (Subject), under the influence of love (Sender), seeks the heroine (Object), as a result of his own desire (Receiver), and is aided by friends (Helper/s), or opposed by his adversaries ... (Opponent/s)'.[5]

In attempting to apply an actantial model to *Orphée*, it becomes readily apparent that as a result of Cocteau's ubiquitous use of contradictions, oppositions and dichotomies, the only consistent actantial roles are those filled by the Subject (Orpheus/poet) and the Object (inspiration/artistic immortality). The other characters paradoxically often fulfil two seemingly contradictory actantial roles. Heurtebise, for example, is both Orpheus' Helper, in that he facilitates the poet's entry into the 'Zone,' and his Opponent, in that he initially attempts to save Eurydice, which, had he been successful, would have collapsed the entire heroic quest. Similarly, Aglaonice, in being pitted against Orpheus as his long-term enemy, may initially appear to be his Opponent, yet her role in his physical death ironically helps him in his heroic quest.

Ultimately, however, it becomes clear that despite his manipulation of a traditional narrative structure, Cocteau, in his re-telling of the myth of Orpheus unquestionably adheres to the primacy of the hero and his quest. This agrees with Aston's contention with the inherent gender bias of the actantial model — she argues from the perspective of feminist methodology that '[t]he "quest," the "desire," the

[1] Keir Elam, *The Semiotics of Drama and Theatre* (London: Routledge, 1980), 126.

[2] Ibid., 127.

[3] Ibid., 126.

[4] Ibid., 130.

[5] Elaine Aston, *An Introduction to Feminism and Theatre* (London: Routledge, 1995), 39.

"action" are all male-determined and male-centred, and are privileged at the expense of the female'.[1]

The centrality of Orpheus and his heroic quest has important ramifications on the film's (under)development of female subjectivity. The way in which each of the female roles is positioned in relation to both Orpheus, and, by extension, the spectator, can be illuminated by considering some of the central issues of female subjectivity as they are articulated in Laura Mulvey's article 'Visual Pleasure and Narrative Cinema.'

Employing psychoanalysis as a 'political weapon' to demonstrate how 'the unconscious of patriarchal society has structured film form,' Mulvey takes as her starting point 'the way film reflects, reveals and even plays on the straight, socially established interpretation of sexual difference which controls images, erotic ways of looking and spectacle'.[2] One of the central premises on which Mulvey builds her argument is that 'Woman ... stands in patriarchal culture as signifier for the male other, bound by a symbolic order in which man can live out his phantasies and obsessions through linguistic command by imposing them on the silent image of woman still tied to her place as bearer of meaning, not maker of meaning'.[3] In linking this viewpoint to narrative theory, Mulvey quotes Budd Boetticher's summary of the role of the film heroine: 'What counts is what the heroine provokes, or rather what she represents. She is the one, or rather the love or fear she inspires in the hero, or else the concern he feels for her, who makes him act the way he does. In herself the woman has not the slightest importance'.[4]

As has already been discussed, it is difficult at best to isolate either Eurydice or the Princess as the sole 'heroine' of *Orphée* — rather, they each share the qualities and responsibilities of this role in their respective relationships with Orpheus. As such, each of them embodies some of the elements outlined by Boetticher. Eurydice, for example, is the quintessential 'wife' figure in the film. According to Lydia Crowson, the prototype for Eurydice is the Virgin Mary — a character in a one-act play Cocteau wrote about Jesus that subsequently evolved into

---

[1] Ibid., 40.

[2] Laura Mulvey, 'Visual Pleasure and Narrative Cinema.' *Film Theory and Criticism.* 4th ed. Eds. Gerald Mast, Marshall Cohen & Leo Braudy (New York: Oxford U.P., 1992), 746.

[3] Ibid., 747.

[4] Ibid., 750.

Orphée.[1] The few similarities between Eurydice and the Virgin Mary are fairly transparent — Cocteau himself describes Eurydice in his screenplay notes as an exceedingly pure, devoted wife (and mother-to-be). However, Eurydice's characterization is not nearly as rich as that of the Holy Mother; unlike the Virgin, she is described by Cocteau as 'quite impervious to the mystery' of her situation. He adds to this she is 'a very straightforward woman, a housewife who cannot be touched by anything that does not concern her home'. Her sole objective throughout the course of the entire 'legend' is also stated unequivocally by Cocteau as 'her love for her husband'.[2]

These features of Eurydice's character are readily apparent in the film — within seconds of our introduction to her (weeping over the 'disappearance' of her husband) we see evidence of her complete preoccupation with Orpheus. She herself openly declares to Heurtebise that she is a 'simple woman' with much to fear from 'certain people' whose backgrounds differ from her own, and that it is 'a miracle' that Orpheus is faithful to her. This self-deprecation is punctuated by her cry of 'I am stupid' at allowing the water to boil over on the stove. That Orpheus shares this opinion of her is demonstrated later in the film as they sit together in the car listening to the incomprehensible phrases on the radio and Eurydice comments that sentences alone will not feed their child, to which Orpheus replies, '[j]ust like a woman, Heurtebise. You discover the world and they talk to you about taxes and baby clothes'.[3] As much as he feels that she inhibits his creative drive, however, Eurydice ironically instigates, through her death, Orpheus' journey toward artistic greatness. Her key role then, in accordance with Boetticher's model, is to elicit some concern from Orpheus so that he will commence his journey.

It is not altogether coincidental that Eurydice is initially killed on her way to seek advice from Aglaonice. This is simply one of the two instances of Aglaonice also being instrumental in the advancement of Orpheus' quest. Her implicit lesbianism ('It's quite natural, Orpheus, when you abandon your wife for her to appeal for help to those who love her' (123)) and affiliation with the avant-garde situate Aglao-

---

[1] Lydia Crowson, *The Esthetic of Jean Cocteau* (Hanover: U.P. of New Hampshire, 1978), 29.

[2] *Orphée*, 190. 'Elle est imperméable au mystère.' *Orphée*, vii–viii; '[U]ne femme très simple, une femme d'intérieur (rien d'extérieur à cet intérieur ne saurait l'atteindre). Ibid., vii; '[L]'amour que'elle porte à son mari.' Ibid., viii.

[3] Ibid., 132. 'Voilà les femmes, Heurtebise. On découvre un monde, elles vous parlent layette et impôts.' Ibid., 40.

nice in direct opposition to Orpheus.[1] Her attitude of repugnance toward both Orpheus and men in general is made clear at the beginning of
the film as she comforts Eurydice by saying '[c]ome now, keep calm. Men
always come back, they're so absurd'.[2] Although Aglaonice's role in
the death of Orpheus is not as involved as it is in the play *Orphée*, she
is nonetheless there at the scene of the crime, egging on Orpheus' adversaries. In this respect, she can be seen as little more than another of
Cocteau's *trucs*, ensuring the instigation and fulfilment of the heroic
quest. Ironically, all of Aglaonice's acts of hatred toward Orpheus ultimately do him more *good* than *harm*.

A somewhat more complex role is played by the Princess in the film.
She is much more individualized than either Eurydice or Aglaonice,
who at times tend to slip into abstraction. She is also a much more sexualized character, both in terms of her appearance and behaviour. According to Margaret Crosland, Christian Bérard 'had said that she
must be an elegant woman because she has no one else in the world to
think about except herself'. Crosland adds to this that the role of
death in much of Cocteau's work is 'strongly decorative' — an assess-
ment that agrees with Parker Tyler's description of the Princess as 'the
eternal, intangible "vamp" ... [who] seduces by her immutable repose,
her elusiveness'.[3] Orpheus himself comments upon first seeing the
Princess that she 'is the most beautiful and the most elegant ... ,' trail-
ing off his words in stunned admiration.[4]

This seems an appropriate juncture to return to Mulvey and her description of the way in which female characters in cinematic representation are constructed to be looked at:

> In a world ordered by sexual imbalance, pleasure in looking has been
> split between active/male and passive/female. The determining male
> gaze projects its phantasy on to the female figure which is styled accord-
> ingly. In their traditional exhibitionist role women are simultaneously
> looked at and displayed, with their appearance coded for strong visual
> and erotic impact so that they can be said to connote *to-be-looked-at-
> ness*.[5]

---

[1] Ibid. '*Il est normal, Orphée, quand vous abandonnez votre femme, qu'elle fasse
appel à ceux qui l'aiment.*' Ibid., 29.

[2] Ibid., 120. '*Allons...allons...du calme. Les hommes reviennent toujours. Ils sont
tellement absurdes.*' Ibid., 24.

[3] Tyler, 189.

[4] *Orphée*, 105. '*Cette princesse est fort belle et fort élégante...*' *Orphée*, 5.

[5] Mulvey, 750.

The controlling male gaze that infiltrates *Orphée* determines that each of the three female characters are visually coded to look their respective parts. Eurydice, for example, is dressed in a rather demure dressing gown for a significant portion of the film — fitting in very well with her domestic surroundings. In fact, Eurydice almost becomes one with her domestic environment — on the single occasion she attempts to leave this realm, she is killed.

Aglaonice, by contrast, makes quite a different statement with her long dark hair and black dress — a rather bohemian appearance that underlines her difference from the fair, fragile Eurydice. She is clearly constructed to give off an air of unconventionality — lending credence to Eurydice's description of her as a 'dangerous' member of a 'very powerful' Women's League.[1]

Extending beyond mere visual encoding, the 'to-be-looked-at-ness' factor operative in *Orphée* is also quite literally demonstrated on several occasions in the film. The most notable, and ironic, of these instances is that of the condition imposed upon Orpheus that he may never again look at Eurydice if she is to be returned to the land of the living. Cocteau describes the ensuing farcical scenes as 'an illustration of what men say when they love another woman: "I can't bear to look at my wife," or "I can't stand the sight of her"'.[2] Describing the situation as such, Cocteau points to the significance of the gaze as a means of indicating both desire for and ownership of women. Significantly, during the tribunal scene when Orpheus is told of this 'not looking' condition, he is entirely preoccupied with staring at the Princess — even shifting his position to maintain his view of her. He goes so far as to ask, after the judgement has been made that he cannot look at his wife, if he is still permitted to look at the Princess.

Ironically, as shall be dealt with shortly, it is the Princess herself who spends a great deal of her time gazing at Orpheus through the cinematically impressive 'eyes of death,' a feature which does not, however, undermine her own aspect of 'to-be-looked-at-ness.' Rather, as an extension of Orpheus' artistic ego, in that she is *his* death, the Princess is almost necessarily constructed to be desirous. It is Orpheus' destiny to attain artistic immortality, which means that he must be seduced to and by death. That this is indeed what will come to pass is anticipated early in the film when Orpheus is at the Princess' chalet after the death of Cégeste. Seated in front of her mirror, the Princess and Or-

---

[1] *Orphée*, 123–24.

[2] Ibid., 165. '*La scène bouffe de retour à la maison illustre la phrase des hommes qui aiment une autre femme que la leur et disent: "Je ne peux plus regarder ma femme" ou: "Je ne peux pas la voir en peinture."*' Ibid., iv.

pheus both gaze into it as the radio repeatedly broadcasts, '[i]t would be better if mirrors reflected more' — at which point the mirror shatters.[1] As Heurtebise reminds us later in the film, mirrors, in Cocteau's universe 'are the doors through which Death comes and goes'[2] — but this segment takes on even greater significance when examined from a Lacanian perspective.

Mulvey draws upon Lacan's conception of the mirror phase as a means to elucidate what she describes as the narcissistic aspect of scopophilia, or an objectifying gaze. She writes of how the mirror phase, occurring at a time 'when the child's physical ambitions outstrip his motor capacity,' provides him with an image that he imagines 'to be more complete, more perfect than he experiences his own body'. His recognition of this image, she continues, is therefore 'overlaid with misrecognition: the image recognised is conceived as the reflected body of the self, but its misrecognition as superior projects this body outside itself as an ideal ego'..[3] Mulvey then goes on to associate this mirror moment with a larger framework of image, self-image and joy of recognition in conventional representation; but of particular interest in her discussion are the links that can be drawn between the child's perception of an ideal self and Orpheus' quest (through death, as represented by the mirror) for his own poetic ideal. Whereas the Lacanian child initially incorrectly perceives himself as 'other' in the mirror, but is subsequently 're-united' as it were with his ego ideal, thus facilitating his entry from the imaginary into the symbolic realm, Orpheus actually *becomes* his ideal ego. This is the ultimate fantasy of artistic immortality that is realized in the film.

The fulfilment of the poetic fantasy is, however, the exclusive property of Orpheus, despite the fact that his entry into a different kind of symbolic realm is only made possible by the Princess. This distinction between the abilities of the hero and his female counter-part stems from the film's contention with issues of destiny versus free will. Although the Princess undoubtedly exercises her free will in killing Eurydice, falling in love with, killing and resurrecting Orpheus, in so doing, she transgresses certain codes of behaviour and is accordingly punished. Cocteau describes her 'flaw' in one of his conversations with André Fraigneau: '... the Princess dares to substitute herself for destiny, to de-

---

[1] Ibid., 115. *'Les miroirs feraient bien de réfléchir davantage.'* 18.

[2] Ibid., 150. *'Les miroirs sont les portes par lesquelles la mort vient et va.'* Ibid., 67.

[3] Mulvey, 749.

cide that a thing *may be*, instead of being ...',[1] or, as her judges put it at the tribunal, she shows 'initiative'.[2] Accordingly punished for her actions, the Princess becomes a self-sacrificing victim for the sake of Orpheus' destiny of artistic immortality. This is a necessary step in the realization of the heroic quest, as Cocteau's voice informs us near the end of the film: 'The Death of the Poet must sacrifice herself to make him immortal'.[3]

Although Cocteau explains in seemingly legitimate terms the necessity of this sacrificial act, it is hard to ignore the ideological ramifications of the castigation of the Princess. As Dolan explains in *The Feminist Spectator as Critic*, '[a] woman is never "a woman is a woman is a woman," particularly when she is part of a representational frame ... Placing women in a representation always connotes an underlying ideology and presents a narrative driven by male desire that effectively denies women's subjectivity'.[4] Indeed, it is not only the Princess whose subjectivity is denied in *Orphée* — through other, more covert means, both Aglaonice and Eurydice effectively remain on the margins of the male-driven narrative.

Establishing, through Mulvey's methodology, that the female characters in Cocteau's film are marginalized subjects arguably denies the possibility of salvaging their potential for greater agency. In her article, 'Masochism and the Perverse Pleasures of the Cinema,' Gaylyn Studlar describes critical models such as Mulvey's which draw upon the links between sadism, the male gaze and visual pleasure as a 'dead end for feminist-psychoanalytic theory'.[5] She accordingly offers an alternative model of a masochistic reading of visual pleasure as derived from Gilles Deleuze's *Masochism: An Interpretation of Coldness and Cruelty*. Masochistic theory, as Studlar explains, 'questions the pre-eminence of a pleasure based on a position of control rather than

1 *Cocteau on the Film* (New York: Dover Publications, 1972), 129 '[L]a princesse ose se substituer au destin, décider qu'une chose pourrait être au lieu qu'elle soit...'. *Orphée*, 86.

2 Ibid., 157.

3 *Orphée*, 182. 'La Mort d'un poète doit se sacrifier pour le rendre immortel.' *Orphée*, 109.

4 Dolan, 57.

5 Gaylyn Studlar, 'Masochism and the Perverse Pleasures of the Cinema,' *Film Theory and Criticism*, 4th ed. Eds. Gerald Mast, Marshall Cohen & Leo Braudy (New York: Oxford U.P., 1992), 775.

submission').[1] As such, her reading offers new possibilities for female subjectivity and spectatorship.

Of particular interest in Studlar's treatment of masochistic theory is the pre-eminence of the female, who in sadistic discourse is negated in favour of the almighty father figure. According to Studlar, Masoch's fictive world is ultimately centred around 'the idealizing, mystical exaltation of love for the punishing woman'. Studlar describes this woman as follows: 'In her ideal form as representative of the powerful oral mother, the female in the masochistic scenario is not sadistic, but must inflict cruelty in love in order to fulfil her role in the mutually agreed upon masochistic scheme'.[2] This is a description that bears striking parallels to the role of the Princess in *Orphée*. Considering the Princess from a masochistic perspective, as a potential means to attribute her with greater subjectivity, is accordingly a very useful, and telling exercise.

The centrality of the female in the masochistic scenario stems from a shift of focus from the Freudian phallic stage of development to the pre-genital phase in which the mother, according to Deleuze, is the 'primary determinant in the structure of masochistic fantasy and in the etiology of the perversion'.[3] Whereas in a sadistic scenario, the 'heroine,' if there is one, is inevitably demystified, objectified and destroyed, the masochistic female is an 'idealized, powerful figure, both dangerous and comforting'.[4] This too seems a fitting description of the Princess, who, through her affiliation with Death, is clearly powerful and dangerous, yet also a source of comfort for Orpheus, who is apparently at ease only when in her company. Indeed, according to Studlar, 'Deleuze associates the good oral mother of masochism with the "ideal of coldness, solicitude, and death," the mythic extremes that crystallize her ambivalence'.[5]

The inherent power of the masochistic female creates a hierarchy between herself and the male subject, one that is akin to the relationship between mother and son. Deleuze's model, as Studlar explains, '... may be viewed as a situation in which the subject (male or female) assumes the position of the child who desires to be controlled *within* the dynamics of the fantasy'.[6] Blatant evidence of this kind of relation-

---

[1] Ibid., 778.

[2] Ibid., 774.

[3] Ibid., 776.

[4] Ibid., 775.

[5] Ibid., 780.

[6] Ibid., 778.

ship between Orpheus and the Princess is found near the end of the film
when the Princess asks Orpheus if he will obey her, whatever she does,
even if she condemns or tortures him. He answers, 'I will obey you ...
Whatever you may ask ... I belong to you and I'll never leave you'.[1] Interestingly, the child-like nature of Orpheus is described in a larger
context by Lydia Crowson who writes of how, in Cocteau's mythology,
the poet figure is a kind of 'child-anarchist' who becomes 'an ideal, an
object of awe'.[2]

A further example of the inversion of the traditional power dynamic between male and female is also demonstrated by the Princess'
perpetual gazing at Orpheus. Visiting him every night as he sleeps,
the Princess stares at Orpheus from the foot of the bed with her mas-
sive painted-on eyes. In so doing, the Princess effectively appropriates
the traditionally male-owned power of the gaze. Her actions are particularly relevant to a masochistic reading, as Studlar explains: 'The
female in the masochistic æsthetic is more than the passive object of
the male's desire for possession. She is also a figure of identification,
the mother of plenitude whose gaze meets the infant's as it asserts her
presence and power'. Using Von Sternberg's films as an example, Studlar goes on to describe how this process essentially turns the male into
an object of 'to-be-looked-at-ness,' while the woman, though still the
object of the look, also projects an 'asserting gaze'.[3]

At the heart of the masochistic scenario, according to Studlar, is the
subject's pleasure in suspense and distance from the mother: 'To close the
gap, to overcome separation from the mother, to fulfil desire, to
achieve orgasm means death. The contracted, mutual alliance of the
masochistic relationship guarantees distance/separation'.[4] The 'final
gratification' of death is accordingly suspended. This is clearly a mode
of interplay that bears striking parallels to the end of *Orphée*, when,
as Cocteau explains, '[t]he poet's death is cancelled in order to make
him immortal'.[5] Orpheus is accordingly separated from death/the
Princess/ the mother.

However, it is at this point that a masochistic reading of the relationship between the Princess and Orpheus becomes problematic. After
returning Orpheus to the land of the living, thereby helping him

---

[1] *Orphée*, 181–82. '*Je t'obéirai... Quoi que tu me demandes... Je t'appartiens et je ne te quitterai plus.*' 108–09.

[2] Crowson, 150.

[3] Studlar, 782.

[4] Ibid., 785.

[5] *Orphée*, 190. '*La mort du poète s'annule afin de le rendre immortel.*' *Orphée*, viii.

achieve his heroic quest, the Princess is escorted away by her former attendants to face a punishment that is beyond description. The condemnation of the Princess effectively strips her of all her power, thereby inverting the masochistic relationship — she is no longer the controller, but the controlled. By exercising her free will, the Princess exhausts the limits of her power and becomes answerable to the elusive force (designated as a 'he' in the screenplay) that gives her her orders. Once again, she is framed, or constrained, within the male gaze as we watch her in the closing shot, hair flowing down her back, walk toward her doom.

The Princess' unhappy fate is juxtaposed with the image of the happy reunion of Orpheus and Eurydice. Although Heurtebise comments rather cynically that the couple have merely been returned to 'their muddy waters',[1] which Cocteau clarifies as referring not to a state of earthly love, but simply 'back to the world'[2], any sense of foreboding seems somehow undermined by the shot of the couple smiling in (albeit) ignorant bliss. Furthermore, even if we are to consider that Orpheus and Eurydice are in the 'mire' of the real world, the heroic quest has nonetheless been realized —Orpheus has attained artistic immortality— which necessarily brings a satisfying sense of closure to the film. The icing on the cake for Orpheus is the fact that he is to be rewarded with a child, which he feels certain is a boy. His immortality thus ensured through his male progeny, the cycle continues.

The final indication that male dominance has been reinstated in the film comes when Orpheus returns to his bedroom and watches Eurydice sleep. This action signifies a complete transfer of the power of the gaze — Orpheus, previously watched in his sleep by the Princess, now gazes at his own wife, thereby re-establishing both his desire and control.

By way of conclusion, I would like to consider briefly the issue of where such an exclusively male-driven narrative potentially situates the film spectator, who, according to Jill Dolan, is implicitly constructed to receive the ideological meanings of representation.[3] Laura Mulvey's analysis of spectatorship helps to demonstrate that the intended film spectator for *Orphée* is undoubtedly male. Mulvey argues that by structuring a film around a main controlling figure (who in this, and many other cases, is male), the spectator is provided with a protagonist with whom to identify.[4] During this process of identification,

---

[1] '*Il fallait les remettre dans leur eau sale.*' Ibid., 116.

[2] '*"sur la terre"*' Ibid., vii.

[3] Dolan, 41.

[4] Mulvey, 751.

she continues, the spectator 'projects his look on to that of his like, his screen surrogate, so that the power of the male protagonist as he controls events coincides with the active power of the erotic look, both giving a satisfying sense of omnipotence'. In this respect, as Mulvey explains, the filmic hero becomes the spectator's ideal ego — but an even more powerful and complete ideal ego than is conceived of in the mirror phase.

The supposition that the female spectator is able to identify with the hero in such a sadistic narrative framework assumes, as Elaine Aston points out in relation to an equally male-driven text, *Death of a Salesman*, that she appear in 'male drag'[1] and become complicit in the denigration and objectification of her own gender. Conversely, if she attempts to identify with any of the rigidly-defined female characters in *Orphée*, she must reproduce herself as either a submissive virgin, a man-hating bitch, or a self-sacrificing whore. Perhaps little more could be expected of a film that projects not just the male spectator's ideal ego, but more significantly, the director's. As Cocteau himself stated outwardly in a letter, '[*Orphée*] is much less a film than it is myself — a kind of projection of the things that are important to me'.[2] It is made very apparent, through the magnificent cinematography, clever dialogue and magical film trickery, what those things are, just as it is lamentably obvious what those things are not.

---

[1] Aston, 44.

[2] Francis Steegmuller, *Cocteau: A Biography* (Boston: Little, Brown & Co., 1970), 479.

Melville's Version of
Les Enfants terribles : *What's in A Look?*

Roxanne Chee

No doubt, films within Jean Cocteau's *œuvre* may be pressured from various methodological and ideological positions — the thematic, mythological, romantic, literary, melodramatic among them. Continuing on in the feminist-psychoanalytic veins, I wish to further the debate on gazes, spectator positions, and desire by positing *Les Enfants terribles* (Melville, 1950) within, first, the feminist discourse of Laura Mulvey who theorizes the spectator as a sadistic male, then that of Gaylyn Studlar who provides an oppositional alternative with the masochistic male gaze, and finally that of Elizabeth Cowie whose notion of fantasy unfixes fixed spectator positions. As each of these feminists mines the field of psychoanalysis, I will be (re)articulating their (re)interpretations of Freud's notions of castration and the Œdipus complex, of Deleuze's application of the pre-Œdipal, and finally of Laplanche and Pontalis' concept of fantasy as a *mise-en-scène* of desire respectively.

It has been remarked that Cocteau is a misogynist. As such, within a feminist politics which bases itself on a theory of an oppressive patriarchy, it can be inferred that the coctelian text, filmic, prosaic and poetic, is erected, consciously or unconsciously, on a misogynist foundation and thus is endowed with a certain sadistic thrust.[1] Following from the misogynist inscription, within a feminist discourse then, it can be claimed that 'scopophilia' or 'pleasure in looking at another person as

---

[1] Connecting author and text presupposes that author and text are one, inextricably intertwined somehow so that textual meaning/fantasy and authorial intention/fantasy are inseparable. Since the film version of *Les Enfants terribles* has been filtered through the directorial lens of Melville, and Cocteau is named only as screenwriter, the term 'author' is used in a more literal sense.

an erotic object'[1] privileges male gaze and male desire, thus supporting Laura Mulvey's formulation of a sadistic, implicitly heterosexual, (white) male voyeur whose controlling gaze serves only to objectify woman as an erotic or fetish thing. In psychoanalytic terms, the male voyeur's active fetishization of woman is explained as an unconscious desire to disavow the threat of castration which he sees conveyed by the 'lack' of the imaginary phallus on the woman's body. Thereby, the male spectator is able to gain possession of both the on-screen woman and women in general.

In *Les Enfants terribles*, Mulvey's contention quickly breaks down, however, because the fetishization she attributes as being marked onto the female body does not materialize. Instead of a passive, eroticized woman, in *Les Enfants terribles* woman's image is equated with Death. Elisabeth is portrayed as a cold murderess of blossoming (male) poets, as a siren whose hypnotic voice lulls men into a perpetual somnambulism or drives them to madness, if not to death. As Death or deadly statue, Elisabeth's association is confirmed by the *mise-en-scène* which pairs her always with the moustached bust, itself a symbol of death and phallicized power. These latter identifications are informed by an earlier statue which orders the poet to his death, notably the one in *Le Sang d'un poète*.

Stylistically, Cocteau's/Melville's cinematic language also affords no fetishization of women, hence an absence of seductive looks of or from Elisabeth, Agathe, Mariette and the mother. All the classical stylistic devices used to eroticize the female form and turn her into a desirable object —for instance, the extreme close-ups of or travelling shots over female body parts, simulating caresses by the phallic recorder, the camera,— get subverted so that what is 'negotiated' within the frame meets with cold derision, even shock, rather than erotic pleasure or desire. It is 'unpleasure'.[2] An example is the close-up of the dead mother's grotesque face. Another is Elisabeth's androgynous face complete with thick unplucked eyebrows, square jaw and chin, and Roman profile more suited to a man than a movie star. Rather than a Hollywood construction of glamorous 'to-be-looked-at-ness', Elisabeth is a case of to-be-looked-at-*mess*.[3]

In the one instance where male fetishization of the female body is most possible, at the Dior fashion house where Agathe is pictured

---

[1] Laura Mulvey, 'Visual Pleasure and Narrative Cinema' in *Film Theory and Criticism*, Fourth Edition, Gerald Mast, Marshall Cohen, and Leo Braudy (eds.) (Oxford: Oxford University Press, 1992), 756.

[2] Ibid., 753.

[3] Ibid., 750.

semi-nude and dressing before new-comer model Elisabeth, the camera impotentiates the image by remaining at a distance, thereby effecting the untitillating coldness that characterizes coctelian women. That coldness is further articulated by Agathe's instruction to return a buyer's/consumer's gaze with a deliberate look of 'scorn.' The acting out of this instruction both demonstrates and situates the heterosexual woman's gaze in *Les Enfants terribles*. Instead of parading as passive exhibitionists enticing male or female/lesbian fantasy (note the entrance of the masculine-appearing woman, in pants, watching Elisabeth perform her catwalk), Agathe's and Elisabeth's overt return of the gaze fixes woman's look as an active, conscious, self-possessed stare aimed at piercing and deflating the voyeuristic fantasies of the visual consumer. It is an act which defines woman, Elisabeth moreso than Agathe, as the (sadistic) power figures within coctelian film structure, capable of punishing and castrating as well as reclaiming and repossessing lost, imaginary phalluses.

If 'to-be-looked-at-ness,' seductive intrigue, and scopophilic pleasure do not rest on the woman's body, then where is it located? Filmic evidences show that the site of male fantasy and desire has been transferred or displaced onto the male body, Paul's body. No one is more eroticized and conferred the status of a movie star than Paul. He is the brilliant star around whom all the satellites orbit. No one is more caressed and loved by the camera than Paul. Consider how beautifully photographed he is, especially in the close-ups, like the one of him being fed crayfish in bed. All the stylistic strategies, —the soft-focus, the composition of the face, slightly inclined, alluring and evoking frailty, femininity, orality and sickness usually inscribed onto the passive masochistic female of melodramas and women's films,— all, reinforce Paul as the site of male fantasy and desire, thereby fixing him as the emasculated feminine object of lack to be fetishized by a male gaze.

That male gaze, has been 'renegotiated' as a homosexual one rather than heterosexual, and is made apparent by the male-male exchanges that pass from Gérard to Paul in the taxi and from Paul to Dargelos. Outside the diegesis of the film, the homosexual gaze is complicit with the author's own sexuality, as well as his autobiography. To elaborate, Cocteau has written extensively about his childhood experience of group masturbation, linking it to sexual feelings for Dargelos: 'Everyone had a hole in his pocket, a damp handkerchief. Art classes especially inspired us, concealed behind the rampart of our drawing boards ... The classroom reeked of gas, chalk and sperm.'[1] Re-played in the snowy

1 Marjorie Keller, *The Untutored Eye: Childhood in the Films of Cocteau, Cornell, and Brakhage* (London and Toronto: Associated University Press, 1986), 26.

schoolyard, of course, is Cocteau's homosexual fantasy of Dargelos and group masturbation confirmed in the image of the brick wall flecked by so many impacted snowballs leaving traces like so many male ejaculations. In this orgasmic male space, woman's presence in the film then seems intrusive, and is thus coded as such by the colder than ice reception Paul gets from Elisabeth when he enters the woman-dominated space of the room for the first time.

To complicate matters, Paul's 'to-be-looked-at-ness' is not only constructed for the homosexual spectator, but also for the sadistic female, Elisabeth. That is confirmed in the crayfish feeding shot which is taken from Elisabeth's point of view, thereby suggesting that she, like the homosexual male, also desires and sees Paul in a sexually fetishized light.

How then, within a feminist psychoanalytic reading, are we to explain all these new perverse systems of seeing that arise which do not ascribe to the standard of the active male and passive female? To do so, we must look to the unconscious primal and repressed mechanism at work in the individual which drives the individual to be as he or she is, thereby determining a particular system of gazes. That is, we must look to an individual's way of *being* to understand his or her way of *seeing*. I am, of course, presuming there is a correlation between the two. In the brother-sister relationship, the structure of gazes between Paul and Elisabeth, the passive male and active female can be situated within a developmental trajectory, that of Freud's Œdipal complex. This appears to be the most likely trajectory since there is much role-playing at being adults within the film: the young boys play military-like games; Elisabeth plays nurse-maid; and Paul demands to be recognized as the 'boss' of the house.

The Œdipal complex is a decisive moment in the child's emergence into 'sexed selfhood.'[1] Roughly summarized, it states that a child has sexualized feelings for the parent of the opposite sex which being taboo are accompanied by great guilt and anxiety.[2] To overcome that, the child rejects the opposite sex parent by identifying (rather over-identifying) with the same sex parent. The goal of the Œdipal is for the

---

Quoted in *Le Secret professionnel*, 24. *'Ce n'étaient que poches trouées et mouchoirs sales. La classe de dessin surtout enhardissait les élèves, dissimulés par la muraille des cartons... La classe sentait le gaz, la craie, le sperme.'* From *Le Livre blanc* (Paris: Éditions Persona, 1981), 33–34.

[1] Sandy Flitterman-Lewis, 'Psychoanalysis, Film and Television' in *Channels of Discourse*, Robert Allen (ed.) (North Carolina: University of North Carolina Press, 1987), 174.

[2] Flitterman-Lewis, 174–75.

child to be *properly normalized*, that is, *heterosexualized* so that he/she can assume his/her roles in culture where rules are dictated by a heterosexual patriarchy.[1] Sandy Flitterman-Lewis provides a more detailed summary:

> In the pre-Œdipal stages, both male and female child are in a dyadic rela-
> tion with the mother [as Paul and Elisabeth are at the beginning of the
> film]; with the Œdipal moment, this two-term relation becomes three, and
> a triangle is formed by the child and both parents. The parent of the same
> sex becomes a rival in the child's desire for the parent of the opposite sex.
> The boy gives up his incestuous desire for the mother because of the
> threat of punishment by castration perceived to come from the father; in
> so doing, he *identifies* with his father (symbolically becomes him) and
> prepares to take his position of a masculine role in society. The forbid-
> den desire for the mother is driven into the unconscious, and the boy will
> accept substitutes for the mother/desired object in his future as an adult
> male. For the female, the Œdipal moment [otherwise known as the Electra
> complex] is not one of threat, but of realization — she recognizes that she
> has *already* been castrated, and, disillusioned in the desire for the father,
> reluctantly identifies with the mother. In addition, the Œdipal complex is
> far more complicated for the girl, who must change her love object from
> mother (the first object for both sexes) to father, whereas the boy can
> simply continue loving the mother.[2]

With the father already dead, all that remains for Elisabeth to fulfil the Œdipal contract is the realization that she is and has been symbolically 'castrated,' and thereby, identify with the mother. But, the mother being an invalid and soon to be dead, is someone Elisabeth adamantly refuses to identify with. Her disavowal of her castrated status is demonstrated by her active pursuit and occupation of roles and spaces traditionally reserved for the father/phallus figure, such as be-ing provider and ruler of the houses she inhabits. As she is always in possession of the imaginary phallus, signalled in the mise-en-scène by a pairing with the moustached statue, Elisabeth's gaze remains as cold and manipulative, searching and penetrating as the masculine, phalli-cized gaze is construed to be. This is exhibited when Elisabeth realizes Paul's photographs are all versions of Dargelos and Agathe; the cam-

---

[1] Flitterman-Lewis, 175, acknowledges that a (normally) developed child enters into patriarchy when he or she enters into a cultural system represented by law, morality, conscience, authority, etc. Freud designates anything outside of male/ female union as 'deviations' or 'inversions' (46), then actual 'perversion' 74–76. Sigmund Freud *On Sexuality* (London: Penguin Books, 1991), 46–76.

[2] Ibid, 174–75.

era holds its position as she slowly turns and intently examines the pictures on the off-screen wall.

Like his sister, Paul is also being processed through the Œdipal. Within the Œdipal model, it can be said that as a result of (over) identification with an invalid, symbolically castrated mother, Paul becomes similarly weak and emasculated — so much so that he cannot even withstand the blow of a snowball. Thus the reason for the inscription of passive gazes he effects from the beginning. When Elisabeth becomes the substitute mother figure after the mother's death, Paul's 'incestuous desires for the mother' get transferred to Elisabeth and are coded in the bonding he desires from playing 'the game.' To fulfil the Œdipal fantasy, then, and become normalized, Paul must reject Elisabeth at some point by identifying with a masculine phallus figure. It comes in the form of Agathe who represents a kind of repressed paternity in that she resembles Dargelos and her name is a reminder of male hardness. Momentarily toughened by this identification, Paul manages to take control of his life and even commit (traditionally masculine) abuses such as ruthlessly tormenting and victimizing Agathe.

By identifying with masculine principles, then, he is able to cast off taboo feelings by rejecting Elisabeth and eventually transferring sexualized feelings to Agathe, who, by then, is miraculously transformed into a desired object substitute of the mother. That moment when Paul rejects the incestuous mother figure is also the moment when Paul is shown in possession of the phallicized bust which had always been associated with Elisabeth, the ultimate ruler of this coctelian kingdom. For once, Paul's voice and gazes assume an authority that was not present before and which is confirmed by the formal suit he wears instead of the usual bathrobe or juvenile child's uniform of shorts and shirt. Unfortunately, Paul's efforts to become masculinized or 'normalized' are frustrated because of Elisabeth's interference and insistence on keeping them in a perpetual state of childhood, hence the quick fall back into passivity. In fact, outright masochism and hystericism as can be perceived by a hyperbolic crying fit reminiscent of melodramatic heroines'!

Unable to complete the Œdipal trajectory by the end of the film, neither child is able to pass into society outside the pre-Œdipal space of the room as properly heterosexed adults. This idea is reinforced by the fact that the children rarely leave the two womb-rooms, the 'zones' where their sexualities have been incubating throughout the film. Nor do they ever inherit a last name, the name of the father, which is the definitive signifier of belonging to a patriarchal order. Since they do not develop into ideal Freudian adults, Elisabeth's masculine gaze and Paul's effeminate one, deemed to be perversions of

Les Enfants terribles : Coctelian Siblings
(Nicole Stéphane and Edouard Dermit)
Courtesy of the Film Reference Library, Toronto, Canada

the ideal, do not and cannot change by the film's end. Rather, they remain inscribed on the subjects as one may see from the shots of Elisabeth pulling Paul into her hypnotic orbit and Paul rising up in response, thereby re-inscribing the positions of active female and passive male.

Within feminism, the Freudian Œdipal explanation can be unsatisfying because the Œdipal agenda is ultimately complicit with a patriarchy whose moral centre insists on a particular structure of being that does not view deviations favourably. A radically alternative rationale for the perverse gaze can be found within Deleuze's text on masochism which revolves around a contract between a masochistic male and an all-powerful punishing mother. As articulated by Gaylyn Studlar in 'Masochism and the Perverse Pleasures of the Cinema,' and by Daniel Gercke in 'Ruin, Style and Fetish: The Corpus of Jean Cocteau,' the Deleuzian phantasy of the non-castrated maternal body attempts to open up a space in feminist-psychoanalytic theory that goes beyond Freudian Œdipal phallocentricism, and reinvent a place for the omnipotent mother of the pre-Œdipal oral stage.[1] This mother is all-powerful and is defined not by what she lacks, but by what she rightfully possesses — 'the breast and the womb.'[2] Roughly stated, the Deleuzian model rotates its axis around the matriarchal instead of the patriarchal. As alternative, when subjected to a discourse on cinematic gazes, the masochistic agenda demands that images, spaces and gazes be reinterpreted and 'renegotiated' so that the terms of pleasure and desire account for a masochistic tendency/sensibility also perceived in cinema.

Deleuze's theory is neatly summed up by Naomi Greene in 'Deadly Statues: Eros in the Films of Jean Cocteau.' Greene writes:

> Long and complex, the story that Deleuze perceives in masochism revolves about his contention that the punishing women of masochism are forms of the powerful, pre-Œdipal, oral mother. The masochist relives the child's attitude toward this powerful mother who, in the absence of the father from the symbolic order, embodies law. The attitude of the child (and later the masochist) is profoundly ambivalent since his desire to be blissfully reincorporated into the mother's body is also threatening for it would entail the destruction of his own self, his own ego. Bound to the mother, the child/masochist must suffer in order to expiate/ expunge the

---

[1] Daniel Gercke, 'Ruin, Style and Fetish: The Corpus of Jean Cocteau' in *Nottingham French Studies*, Vol. 32, No. 1, (Spring 1993), 15–16.

[2] Gaylyn Studlar, 'Masochism and the Perverse Pleasures of the Cinema' in *Film Theory and Criticism*, Fourth Edition, Gerald Mast, Marshall Cohen, and Leo Braudy (eds.) (Oxford: Oxford University Press, 1992), 780.

punishing super-ego and genital sexuality that he embodies through his resemblance to the father. He must, in fact, undergo a process not only of de-sexualization but even of death so that a 'new self,' free of the super-ego and sexuality, can be born uniquely of the mother who, through disavowal, magically possesses a phallus.[1]

Since the desire or fantasy of the masochist is to be 'reincorporated' into the mother's body, figuratively speaking, or restored to the breast and womb, in *Les Enfants terribles*, Paul's trajectory must be toward the powerful, pregenital, oral mother rather than away from her as the Œdipal text demands. Certainly, it is Paul's desire to be bound to the mother, hence, the rationale for his passivity toward an icy, authoritative mother-figure, Elisabeth, his somnambulistic oral desires and regressive infantilism. Further evidence includes his complaint that Elisabeth, now a working mother figure, no longer plays 'the game' with him, 'the game' from which pleasure is derived through a bonding both mental and physical as can be seen from the overhead shot of the two in bed together with bodies overlapping as if they are joined at the hip like Siamese twins floating in a symbiotic fluid.

The purpose of joining with the mother is 'to reformulate a masculinity from which the image and legacy of the father have been ejected, to be reborn as a "new, sexless man"'.[2] Being reborn with a new masculinity is Paul's desire and is indicated in his wish for a 'plaster sphinx,' a creature of animal and human female forms. One of the implications of becoming de-sexualized or re-sexualized (rather than heterosexualized), is that there no longer arises a fear of castration or of castration anxiety.[3] Castration itself becomes a necessary and desired process in helping the masochist arrive at his destination of sexlessness and re-fusion with the mother. Since this is the case, emphasis on possessing the phallus and owning gazes gets deflated and images encrusted with any degree of phallicization get reconstituted into (an)other order of seeing/being. That other order is one which revolves around phallocentricism's oppositional axis, castration. Consequently, a masochistic æsthetic privileges elements such as collapse, reversal, regression, powerlessness, degradation, delay, infantilism, submission, narcissism, orality, passivity, etc. — all the negative spaces out of which transformation is made possible.[4] These spaces are well-imprinted onto Cocteau's

---

[1] Naomi Greene, 'Deadly Statues: Eros in the Films of Jean Cocteau' in *The French Review*, Vol. 61, No. 6, (May 1988), 892.

[2] Gercke, 16.

[3] Studlar, 782.

[4] Studlar has elaborated on some of these points in her article.

signature style and have provided access into a system of seeing/gazing that forces one to re-evaluate purely Mulvian and Freudian assumptions.

In *Les Enfants terribles*, there are many images deemed 'castrating' which within Mulvian and Freudian sensibility underscore only a disconcerting or shameful 'lack' on the part of the subject. An example is Paul's crying fit over Agathe's (supposed) lack of love for him. Crying being a sign of a lack of control over one's self usually associated with women, the Mulvian/Freudian assumption is that Paul is 'lacking' and not in possession of the much prized phallus. Within a Studlerian/Deleuzian way of seeing, the question of possessing the phallus is not at issue. Rather, the relinquishing of the phallus is preferred since sexless identity is an aim. So being, 'lack' and its connotations of powerlessness are transformed to mean power. Since meaning and perception get turned head over heels, the spectator is forced to re-orient his/her scope of seeing. Thereby, instead of 'lacking,' the spectator comes to see Paul's tears as liberating, liberating because tears are cleansing[1] and because the outward spectacle of his inner turmoil provides an opportunity in the narrative to disclose his secret love for Agathe to Elisabeth, who, in turn, is given the impetus to initiate the trajectory to death — and in death, sexless rebirth to fulfil Paul's masochistic fantasy. Since a primary goal is to become de-sexed, this, in turn, opens up a space where bisexuality, androgyny and homosexuality can be articulated, (but not lesbianism, it seems, because we are still dealing with a male subjectivity). Thus the justification for Paul's unapologetic effeminacy and homosexual gaze, and unashamedly fetishized 'to-be-looked-at-ness.'

Given the desire for sexless symbiosis with the mother, the masochist is driven by a powerful 'Death Instinct'[2] which is enacted throughout *Les Enfants terribles* by Paul's fatalism and culminates in the taking of the poison. As with castration, rather than seeing Paul's trajectory towards death as an embarrassing loss of the phallus from within a masochistic construction, Paul's path is viewed as empowering; for, in the imagination and fantasy of the masochist, only through death is he able to expiate the father and restore a 'symbiotic union with the idealized maternal rule'. That is, only through death can he finally and symbolically escape the terrors of sexual difference and blissfully re-fuse with the mother figures, Elisabeth and Agathe.

---

[1] Steve Neale, 'Melodrama and Tears.' Steve Neale has written in depth on tears within melodramas as liberating and cleansing within a masochistic subjectivity.

[2] Studlar, 776.

Death, then, promises a renewal of sorts which is imagined to be 'the final triumph of a parthenogenetic rebirth from the mother'.[1]

An important implication of masochism's order of being with respect to spectatorship in *Les Enfants terribles* is that we, the spectator, must reinterpret and renegotiate what we see in the film image and in the gazes elicited and elided by the sadistic female, Elisabeth, and the masochistic male, Paul. We must re-read the terms of signification expressed on the screen and recognize that the 'lack,' traditionally construed as powerlessness by Mulvey and Freud, has been transformed to signify power and completeness. The problem with the masochistic model is that, on the one hand, it provides a viable alternative to counter the patriarchal Œdipal standard: after all, it celebrates a matriarchal pre-Œdipal intervention, thereby offering up a masochistic male scopophilia instead of a purely sadistic one. Yet on the other hand, it degrades the patriarchal norm which also has a meaningful place and value within our structures of seeing. Without supplanting one over the other, is there a place where both models of seeing/being can come together so that we, the spectator, can experience and identify with the gazes in *Les Enfants terribles* from more than one side and gain scopophilic pleasure and desire from everywhere? Yes, there is. That place is in fantasy.

Through the definitions and articulations of French post-Freudians Jean Laplanche and Jean-Baptiste Pontalis, in her article 'Fantasia,' Elizabeth Cowie explores the meaning of fantasy and its many implications on being and seeing. Reaching beyond isolated structures of seeing and being, what Cowie, Laplanche and Pontalis recognize is that there is no single, mutually exclusive spectator position, but many. By extension, there is not one identification, or one gaze, or one desire, or one model of being, but many. Every one is valid and potentially accessible to the spectator. The key to unwrapping Cowie's, Laplanche and Pontalis' conclusion is in understanding fantasy itself and its operation within individuals.

Cowie side-steps into a discourse on fantasy with Pat Califia's recognition that sado-masochist or S/M subculture provides 'a theatre in which sexual dramas can be acted out.'[2] In recognizing the theatrical, make-believe, or play element of sado-masochistic dramas and by extension, the necessity of polar positions in facilitating the sexual narrative, Cowie and Califia open up a space where both active and passive binaries may co-exist without the one privileging the other. Cali-

---

[1] Ibid., 780.

[2] Elizabeth Cowie, 'Fantasia' in *Representing the Woman: Cinema and Psychoanalysis* (Minneapolis: University of Minnesota Press, 1997), 126.

fia's insight recalls Laplanche and Pontalis' definition of fantasy as 'imaginary scenarios to which the instinct becomes fixated and which may be conceived of as true *mises-en-scène* [stagings/performances] of desire'.[1] Seizing on the equation of S/M play as 'theatre' and fantasy as 'imaginary scenarios,' Cowie impresses on us the idea that film too is theatre and fantasy, 'a veritable *mise-en-scène* of desire' where characters role-play and make visible or present what is not there or what can never *directly* be seen.[2] That is, through role-playing and *mises-en-scène*, conscious wishes of the imagination such as daydreams or reveries, or products of the unconscious such as dreams, repressed thoughts or behaviour are revealed.[3] For instance, in *Les Enfants terribles*, the dire consequences of Elisabeth's manipulations and control in the final 'game' of love are made visible to her (and to us) through a dream and its *mise-en-scène*. While she is being reborn into something tidier, (coded by the donning of a new blue dressing gown entirely different from the shabby ones she wears throughout), Paul is pictured dying on a billiard table named 'Gloom,' the billiard table being a visible symbol for the 'game' at which he is being check-mated.

As fantasy, all of *Les Enfants terribles* is about making visible conscious and unconscious desires through *mises-en-scène*. For instance, the children's desires to be grown-up and assume adult roles are expressed through and supported by their performances and the many scenarios constructed for their play, their games of pretend and make-believe. The snowball fight, for one, is a make-believe scenario for a battle field satisfying young boys' fantasies of becoming soldiers, or, given Gérard's gallantry and Paul's noticeably pale, frail comportment, a romantic hero and a casualty of war respectively; Elisabeth's nursing duties inform her wish to be a (failed) nurturer; and Paul and Elisabeth's imitation of seasoned tourists with much baggage on their first seaside excursion announces their yearning to enter into the outside world of the adult where posing and proper decorum are in order. Or at least they fancy putting on adult airs and playing at being adult. The children's desire to leave the realm of childhood is further signified by the various invasions of settings which reflect and embody the realm of the grown-up, specifically, the exchange of naïve spaces like the playground and messy bedroom for the fashionable Dior house and cosmopolitan interiors of Michael's mansion. The exception, however, is the gallery, in that it gets transformed into a fantasy setting all its

---

[1] Flitterman-Lewis, 180.

[2] Cowie, 133, 127–28.

[3] Ibid., 127–28.

own; for, within its irregular contours and shifting planes, all the wishes of the children converge, collide and tragically collapse.

There are as many fantasies as there are individuals who can fantasize. Some fantasies are conscious. Others are not. In *Les Enfants terribles*, there is the fantasy of living forever in an ideal state of childhood closely related to the state of the artist;[1] a fantasy of death associated with snow, snowballs and statues;[2] of collecting objects associated with an eventful moment; of having separate rooms and being grown up; of union with another; and many more. Some fantasies appear to exist alone within the wisher, like Paul's wish for 'a chandelier dipped in enamel paint' or Elisabeth's wish that Paul be 'all fire and ice' like herself.[3] Many are shared. For example, within the diegesis of the film, the fantasy of union with another is imagined by everyone, not just by the siblings for each other: Gérard desires Paul then Elisabeth; Paul desires Dargelos then Agathe; and Michael desires Elisabeth. These fantasies of union carry strong sexual undertones which are absent from the fantasy of union conceived by the Doctor and Mariette with the children. What differentiates the Doctor's and Mariette's fantasy of union with the children is sexless love rather than sexual love. Theirs is really the wish of a (surrogate) mother and father to keep a family united through basic provisions like unconditional love and unconditional money respectively.

Outside the diegesis of the film, all or most of the fantasies can be traced back to the authors, Cocteau and Melville; for, after all, they are ultimately the dreamers of the text and the origins of the film fantasy itself. In acknowledging the auteur as the original fantasist, within a discourse on gazes, one may mistakenly conclude that the system of gazes constructed satisfies only the auteur's/dreamer's pleasure. Although the creator's gaze is unquestioningly inscribed, the existence of many 'imaginary scenarios' for a given fantasy, such as the example of the wish for union described above, shows there can be many other

---

[1] See Keller's, *The Untutored Eye* for a detailed discourse on childhood and Cocteau's view that it is the state of artists.

[2] See Jennifer Hatte, 'Jean Cocteau's Snow' in *The Modern Language Review*, vol. 89, part 2 (April 1994), for a full discussion on the relationship of snow to death.

[3] Film: '*[U]n lustre Louis XIV au ripolin [...] Cette nature toute de feu et de glace ne pouvait admettre le tiède. Bête de race elle était, bête de race elle voulait Paul, et cette petite fille qui roule en express pour la première fois, au lieu d'écouter le tam-tam des machines, dévore le visage de son frère, sous les cris de folle, la chevelure de folle, l'émouvante chevelure de cris flottant par instants sur le sommeil des voyageurs.*'

positions of fantasizing besides that of the auteur/voyeur. Albeit, these positions branch out from and find voice and presence through the auteur. Given the variety of positions, there are indeed many different 'theatres,' '*mises-en-scène,*' or settings where the dreams, wishes and stuff of human desire and experience can be played and replayed. Perhaps Cocteau intuitively understood this when he moved the drama unfolding in the space of the womb-room to the dead-end gallery, a gallery being a kind of theatre where art is exhibited. In this instance, the art displayed is the final unfolding of the children's 'game' of love and union itself.

Essentially, these 'theatres' of desire are repetitions of a common theme 're-worked through the material of everyday, that-day, experiences'.[1] Therefore, held together by a common thread, the story is always the same but different. Another, more reductive way of understanding fantasy as *mise-en-scène* or setting is to realize that woven into the fabric of every story of human experience lies an archetypal fantasy which is masked behind the narrative itself. In *Les Enfants terribles*, the Œdipal fantasy is one such archetype masked behind the narrative of Paul and Elisabeth's struggle for union and growth. Roland Barthes reminds us of this archetype when he writes: 'Doesn't every narrative lead back to Œdipus? Isn't storytelling always a way of searching for one's origins, speaking one's conflicts with the Law, entering into a dialectic of tenderness and hatred?'[2]

If Barthes is correct in asserting that all narrative can be reduced to archetypes such as the Œdipal story, then by inference, we, the coctelian spectator, are able (both consciously and unconsciously) to access, recognize, and find identification with the fantasy (or fantasies) at work within the narrative of *Les Enfants terribles* despite all the fluffy, external, contingent or digressive material within the narrative. This inference is supported by the nature of an archetype itself. In Jungian psychology, an archetype is 'a primitive mental image inherited from man's earliest ancestors, and supposed to be present in the collective unconscious.'[3] Being part of our primitive inheritance, our prehistory, and existing in our collected memory, an archetype is innately accessible and understood by us consciously or unconsciously. Accord-

---

[1] Cowie, 137.

[2] Roland Barthes in Cowie, 138. '*Tout récit ne se ramène-t-il pas à l'Œdipe? Raconter, n'est-ce-pas toujours chercher son origine, dire ses démêlés avec la Loi, entrer dans la dialectique de l'attendrissement et de la haine?*' From *Le Plaisir du texte* (Paris: Éditions du Seuil, 1973), 75–76.

[3] Joyce M. Hawkins and Robert Allen (eds.), *The Oxford Encyclopedic English Dictionary* (Oxford: Clarendon Press, 1991), 69.

ingly, since the fantasies enacted by the children, Paul, Elisabeth, Agathe and Gérard, can be stripped down to archetypal situations, the imaginary scenarios presented by Cocteau necessarily recast and replay fantasies and fantasy positions which can be intuitively understood by all and which all may identify with regardless of difference, sexual and otherwise.

Archetypal fantasies include original fantasies. Since 'all fantasy involves original fantasies',[1] universal access and identification are further granted through these unconscious fantasies of origins or primal fantasies. Laplanche and Pontalis explain that primal fantasies — primal scene, castration, seduction — operate 'like myths' (the Œdipal or Orpheus myths for examples), for 'they claim to provide a representation of, and a solution to, the major enigmas which confront the child'.[2] Essentially, originary or primal fantasies explain the beginnings of the child through constructed scenarios and can be understood as a prestructure in the subject's prehistory. That is, they pre-exist the child.[3] The implication following is that primal fantasies, like archetypes, are inborn and their significances are comprehended intuitively by everyone. Thus, the idea that fantasy or wish is about the desire for something already present in the subject, auteur and spectator is justified, and the spectator's potential for appreciating the whole spectrum of fantasies, fantasy positions and ways of being in *Les Enfants terribles* and in Cocteau's cinema overall is ratified.

If fantasy and wishful desire are intrinsic to us, and we are able to identify instinctively and innately with Cocteau's cinema and the variety of gazes exhibited, is the pleasure in fantasy then found in identification or recognition alone? Since film is fantasy and fantasy is about wish fulfilment), scopophilic pleasure in fantasy is found 'in the setting out, not in the having of the objects'. In a restatement of Laplanche and Pontalis, Cowie writes, 'fantasy is not the object of desire, but its setting'.[4] It is about the 'arranging' of the objects in the setting of desire or the *mise-en-scène*, not the 'achievement' of the objects, for once the achievement is made, the pleasure is over. As such, the emphasis is on process and setting out, more than on achievement. Taken within this configuration, in *Les Enfants terribles*, it does not matter if any of the children's fantasies of union, death, being grown up or permanently immature come true, if Paul and Elisabeth complete the Œdipal trajectory

---

[1] Cowie, 137.
[2] Ibid., 130.
[3] Ibid., 131.
[4] Ibid, 133.

assigned by Freud, or if Paul is incorporated into the body of the symbolic mother, Elisabeth, as is required by Deleuze's masochist. It only matters that there was the wish for the new phase. By extension, it does not matter if our gazes are fetishistic, sadistic, masochistic, or other, only that we, the spectator, can 'enter the fantasy-structure and identify *as if* it were our own'.[1]

Within feminism, the idea of a spectator finding his or her identification inscribed as sadist or masochist is problematic, inasmuch as it raises a moral question of dehumanization. To counter this charge, Cowie notes Califia's study of sado-masochistic relationships as 'egalitarian' because each partner recognizes he/she is clearly role-playing within a theatre of his/her own making and consequently each partner has the freedom to choose which role he/she will play in order to obtain the greatest sexual pleasure.[2] In short, in the S/M 'theatre' of active/passive play, Califia insists there is 'free will and ... choice'.[3]

If Califia's assumptions are correct, then the spectator is encouraged to view the gazes inscribed in the theatres of sexual drama between Paul and Agathe, Elisabeth and Gérard, and Elisabeth and Paul (all essentially sado-masochistic relationships with an incestuous twist) as 'egalitarian' due to an inscription of wilful role interchange and the recognition that it is all just play and make-believe. And indeed all have displayed traits and behaviour divergent from their general characters. For instance, both Gérard and Agathe, who initially appear self-possessed, lose control of themselves when they enter into the space of the room; Paul steps out of a masochistic orbit when he victimizes Agathe with abusive taunts; and Elisabeth betrays a tenderness and vulnerability when she admits to Paul she feels 'lost' and 'lonely' in her new room without him. Thereby, all reflect reversals of active/passive, sadist/masochist expectations. Since these screen subjects occasionally switch temperaments, the spectator realizes that assigned subject/object positions can shift so that the terms of viewer identification become unglued. As a result, there is no one clear place of being, and pleasure, then, becomes negotiable for the spectator/subject depending on where he/she finds his/her place of desire and desiring. This capability to shift gears by negotiating a place of desire is what accounts for

---

[1] Ibid., 140.
[2] Ibid., 125–26.
[3] Ibid., 127.

positions within Cocteau's film fantasy and *Les Enfants terribles* as being equal and equally valid.[1]

Another way to account for the validity of polarized fantasy positions is in relating the fantasy process to dream. In dream as in play, where fantasy scenarios get acted out, the positions we assume constantly devolve depending on our position of desire: active or passive, feminine or masculine, mother or son, father or daughter.[2] Thus, we have 'multiple points of entry which are also mutually exclusive positions'.[3] These points, however, are not taken up sequentially but simultaneously, making it possible for us to identify with many characters at the same time, with Paul, Elisabeth, Gérard, Agathe, Michael, Dargelos, even the Doctor and Mariette, and gain meaning from everywhere. Consequently, our position is never fixed but will shift depending on our desire at the moment. This being the case, in fantasy, we can be each subject and every subject, each object and every object, depending on what we wish as the story unravels before us. We are, after all, 'the only place in which all the terms of the fantasy come to rest'.[4]

From all the interpretations of theories put forth by Mulvey, Studlar and Cowie, it is clear that there is no single fixed spectral position but, rather, there are many shifting positions depending on interpretation. It is my wish or fantasy that a consideration of the theories touched upon has brought us to a space where we can see Cocteau's films, specifically *Les Enfants terribles*, not from *a* single mutually exclusive position —that of Mulvey's sadistic spectator or of Studlar's masochistic male, for instance— but from *many* juxtaposed side by side, existing in conjunction with each other within us. And, within this space or 'setting,' all positions are possible and desirable. Cowie's contribution of applying fantasy to film, in the case of Cocteau's films, is significant inasmuch as it expands our scopic horizon, taking us beyond single, isolated models of being and seeing. Like Cocteau, she reminds us of one most important thing: that all art is play and make-believe. It is not real life but provides a chance to live out a life or lives possible only in the imagination. Thus, like Paul and Elisabeth who are playing at being adults, through fantasy scenarios enacted in film we get to play out different roles, different dreams, different desires. And, as in

---

[1] The idea of a wilfully shifting subject identification with a shifting theatre of desire is further supported by Freud's analysis of fantasy in 'A Child is Beaten' where subject/object positions shift according to what is at stake in the fantasy.

[2] Cowie, 141.

[3] Ibid., 135.

[4] Ibid., 149.

the clicking of a camera awakening a host of memories within the listener, the value of Cocteau's cinematic fantasy is in the triggering of wishes and desires deep within us which, in the end, serves only to illuminate something of our lives.

'Stranded Bodies, Found Objects':[1] The Masochistic Æsthetic in Le Testament d'Orphée

Iain Arthur Hill

The vast majority of Cocteau's film work tends toward a varied narcissism but this, in and of itself, is an over-simplification. The parodic and playful style that Cocteau deploys in Le Testament d'Orphée elicits a far more provocative reading of his work. The following is an examination of Cocteau's masochistic æsthetic with particular attention paid to the male body and the activities of that body. My project will illustrate the masochistic æsthetic as a point of resistance against the primacy of spectatorial identification. While Laura Mulvey's article, 'Visual Pleasure and Narrative Cinema,' has had a profound impact on our understanding of spectatorship and cinematic scopophilia, her insistence on the essential nature of Freud and the phallocentric order eclipses the desire for identification outside the functions of voyeurism and/ or narcissism.[2] I will variously cite the work of Gilles Deleuze, Gaylyn Studlar and Kaja Silverman as it relates specifically to the figure of the poet in Le Testament, along with supplementary criticism by Daniel Gercke and Naomi Greene. The emerging binary of Mulvey's argument serves as the departure point for Deleuze, Studlar and Silverman among others. As Gaylyn Studlar has written:

> The formal structures of the masochistic æsthetic —fantasy, disavowal, fetishism, and suspense— overlap with the primary structures that en-

---

[1] Title inspired by Eric L. Santner's book Stranded Objects: Mourning, Memory, and Film in Postwar Germany (New York: Cornell University Press, 1990).

[2] Laura Mulvey, 'Visual Pleasure and Narrative Cinema,' Film Theory and Criticism, edited by Gerald Mast, Marshall Cohen, Leo Braudy (Oxford: Oxford University Press, 1992), 746–57.

able classic narrative cinema to produce visual pleasure. These similarities raise fundamental questions about the relationship of cinematic pleasure to masochism, sexual differentiation, processes of identification, the representation of the female in film, and other issues in which a model derived from Deleuze's theory offers a radical alternative to those Freudian assumptions that have been adopted by most of psychoanalytic film theory.[1]

Le Testament d'Orphée, as a cinematic text, excavates the mechanics of filmic desire principally because desire is left abject; it exists in the coctelian *zone*, somewhere between here and there, home and away, the self and the other, this world and the next, etc. For Cocteau, the male body and its object(s) of desire are transmogrified into a phantastical realm which simultaneously resists the inscription of the male body into classical subject and object relations. This inscription of the male body can variously be described as a form of ideological coding, a situation that is constantly frustrated in *Le Testament d'Orphée*. The self (specifically the Poet in *Le Testament*) is never reflected back onto the individual as a unified image; instead, it becomes a hall of mirrors, an anxious moment in a carnival of the soul. This fractured mirror demonstrates how the masochistic æsthetic in *Le Testament* frustrates the drive toward primary identification, laying naked the cultural and ideological imperatives that code conventional desire.[2]

Gilles Deleuze, according to Gaylyn Studlar and others, has broken up the exclusive relationship between Sadism and Masochism, arguing that the two appear in different stages of development. The masochistic drive, for Deleuze, is a product of the oral stage as it acknowledges the supreme authority of the mother and is pre-genital in character, which, in turn, prefigures the influence of the father. Sadism, however, appears in the genital stage and becomes the site of an over-determined identification with the phallus (the father) resulting in the formal negation of the mother. Studlar writes:

> In the masochistic æsthetic, dramatic suspense replaced Sadian accelerating repetition of action, intimacy between mutually chosen partners re-

---

[1] Gaylyn Studlar, 'Masochism and the Perverse Pleasures of the Cinema,' *Film Theory and Criticism*, edited by Gerald Mast, Marshall Cohen, Leo Braudy (Oxford: Oxford University Press, 1985), 775.

[2] 'The very fact that something is posited as primary should make us instantly suspicious. To say something is primary is simply to locate it back farther in the psychic apparatus. It does not, or should not, invite any conclusions about its efficacy.' Geoffrey Nowell-Smith, 'A Note on History/Discourse,' *Edinburgh '76 Magazine*, No. 1 (1976), 31.

places the impersonality of masses of libertines and victims, idealized eroticism replaces the obscenity that threatens to burst the limits of conventional language in an attempt to match the unattainable, destructive Idea of Evil.[1]

As the masochistic impulse is generated in the oral stage, it necessarily calls into question the efficacy of the phallic order.

The current debate surrounding a masochistic æsthetic for the cinema hinges on whether or not it is a desire for a return to the oral mother, as Studlar argues, or whether it is an æsthetic predicated on the desire to rebel against the law of the father.[2] Cocteau's masochistic æsthetic is neither the ideality of mother-longing, as put forward by Studlar, nor is it the *fort/da* game that Silverman insists upon.[3] The coctelian masochistic æsthetic is the *zone* itself; the nexus of a metaphorical before and after. As the poet states at the tribunal in *Le Testament*, 'I would like to say that if I deserve punishment I cannot imagine any more painful one than being forced to live between two worlds, or to use your own words, between two realms. A filmmaker would say "through a coloured filter." I'd give anything to be able to walk on solid ground again, and not be lost in the shadows of a strange universe.'[4] As Deleuze contends, the masochistic impulse is:

---

[1] Studlar, *Film Theory and Criticism*, 775.

[2] 'Gaylyn Studlar conflates Deleuze's oral mother with the pre-Œdipal mother of object relations psychoanalysis, and extrapolates from that conflation a highly dubious argument about the origin of masochism. According to Studlar, that perversion has its basis in the (male) child's relationship with the actual mother prior to the advent of the father, a relationship predicated upon his helpless subordination to her, and the insatiability of his desire for her. Masochistic suffering consequently derives from the pain of separation from the mother, and the impossible desire to fuse with her again, rather than from the categorical imperatives of the Œdipus complex and symbolic law.' Kaja Silverman, *Male Subjectivity at the Margins* (New York and London: Routledge, 1992), 417, note 50.

[3] Silverman's position on the appearance of masochism is essentially akin to Deleuze's theory. The anal stage is not privileged over the phallic. For Silverman the phallic (symbolic) stage is inevitable.

[4] Jean Cocteau, 'Le Testament d'Orphée,' *Two Screenplays*, translated by Carol Martin-Sperry (New York: The Orion Press, 1968), 114. *'J'ai à dire que, si je mérite une peine, je n'en saurais subir de plus pénible que celle qui m'oblige à vivre entre deux eaux, ou, pour employer votre propre langage: entre deux règnes. Un cinéaste dirait "en fausse teinte". Je donnerais n'importe quoi pour fouler de nouveau le vieux plancher des vaches et ne pas me perdre dans la pénombre d'un drôle d'univers.'* From *Le Testament d'Orphée/Le Sang d'un poète* (Monaco: Éditions

> A contract ... established between the hero and the woman, whereby at a
> precise point in time and for a determinate period she is given every right
> over him. By this means the masochist tries to exorcise the danger of the
> father and to ensure that the temporal order of reality and experience
> will be in conformity with the symbolic order, in which the father has
> been abolished for all time. Through the contract ... the masochist reaches
> towards the most mythical and most timeless realms, where [the mother]
> dwells. Finally, he ensures that he will be beaten ... what is beaten, hu-
> miliated and ridiculed in him is the image and likeness of the father, and
> the possibility of the father's aggressive return ... The masochist thus lib-
> erates himself in preparation for a rebirth in which the father will have
> no part.[1]

What pre-tends this rebirth is the necessity for a symbolic death. In *Le
Testament d'Orphée* the Orphic tradition variously provides Cocteau
with a cyclical pattern of death and rebirth. The Poet's entry into the
underworld rests on his ability to transmigrate through the realms of
being and non-being, life and death, but this is done at a high cost to
the cinematic body. Kaja Silverman writes:

> Masculinity is particularly vulnerable to the unbinding effects of the
> death drive because of its ideological alignment with mastery. The nor-
> mative male ego is necessarily fortified against any knowledge of the
> void upon which it rests, and —as its insistence upon an unimpaired
> bodily 'envelope' would suggest— fiercely protective of its coherence.[2]

Cocteau's Poet in *Le Testament* has abandoned the safety of that
'envelope' because it is the void that must be consciously traversed. The
body of Cocteau's poet is distended with conflicting desires. Cocteau
narrates the beginning of *Le Testament* by stating: 'My film is nothing

---

du Rocher, 1983), 89. All subsequent quotations from the original French
screenplay are taken from this source.

[1] Gilles Deleuze as quoted in Silverman, *Male Subjectivity at the Margins*, 211.
'[C]'est le contrat fait avec la femme qui, à un moment précis et pour un temps
déterminé, confère à celle-ci tous les droits. C'est par le contrat que le masochiste
conjure le danger du père, et tente d'assurer l'adéquation de l'ordre réel et vécu
temporel avec l'ordre symbolique, où le père est annulé de tous temps. Par le contrat...le masochiste rejoint les régions les plus mythiques et les plus éternelles —
celles où règnent les trois images de la mère. Par le contrat, le masochiste se fait
battre; mais ce qu'il fait battre en lui, humilier et ridiculer, c'est l'image du père, la
ressemblance du père, la possibilité du retour offensif du père...le masochiste se
rend libre pour une nouvelle naissance où le père n'a aucun rôle.' Gilles Deleuze,
Présentation de Sacher-Masoch: le froid et le cruel (Paris: Éditions de Minuit,
1967), 59.

[2] Kaja Silverman, *Male Subjectivity at the Margins*, 61.

other than a striptease show, consisting of removing my body bit by bit and revealing my soul quite naked.'[1]

There is little argument that Le Testament d'Orphée is Cocteau's most autobiographical film — in a literal and figurative sense. There are numerous persons in the film who impacted on his personal and creative life, along with the oblique historical references that he shoulders throughout the film. As author, narrator and interpreter of Le Testament Cocteau succeeds in occupying a number of spaces and places all at once. We are never really sure where the fictive Cocteau begins and ends. What haunts Le Testament are the visual frustrations endured by the male body. Often harrowing, occasionally comedic, the male body runs the cinematic gauntlet of a fractured and episodic narrative. As predicated earlier, the masochistic æsthetic is best illustrated in Le Testament in the spaces between here and there, life and death. Daniel Gercke states that:

> Where Cocteau finds himself most entangled in the questions of psychoanalysis is in the shadowy domain of the body. Cocteau's cinema is deeply marked by a preoccupation with the male body, both as specular object and metaphorical source of the film work. On the one hand, there is the body on the screen — haunted, castrated, hysteric, and often rather dazzling in its pathos. On the other hand there is the insistent shadow of the authorial body, masked and enigmatic, whose position 'behind' the images is actively hypothesized by the films themselves. Two bodies then, yet the two are twinned and intertwined in such a way that it becomes impossible to say where one body ends and the other begins; corps and corpus are pierced with strange relation.[2]

Ironically, Cocteau is playfully aware of what his hero must endure. In the initial scenes of Le Testament the Poet attempts to navigate his way back into the present time so that he may introduce himself to the Professor whose invention (in the form of a bullet) will release him from his bondage to the past and the future. In cavalier Louis XV dress, Cocteau, as the Poet, explains his circumstances to the Professor and soon after the scene becomes a mock firing squad, with the Poet, cigarette in hand, administering his own execution. The Professor's invention offers up a curative that will realign the space-time continuum so that the Poet can be reborn into the present timeline. As the Poet

---

[1] Cocteau, Two Screenplays, 83. 'Mon film n'est pas autre chose qu'une séance de strip-tease, consistant à ôter peu à peu mon corps et à montrer mon âme toute nue.' 58.

[2] Daniel Gercke, 'Ruin, Style and Fetish: The Corpus of Jean Cocteau,' Nottingham French Studies, Vol. 32, No. 1 (Spring 1993), 10.

Le Testament d'Orphée : The Poet and the Sphinx
(Jean Cocteau as Orpheus)
Courtesy of the Museum of Modern Art Film Stills Archive
© Jean Cocteau/SODRAC (Montréal) 1998

says, 'It's because of your bullets that I am looking for you through this frightful muddle of time and space. If I am not mistaken, they travel faster than light. Professor, I would like to be your guinea pig. It's my last hope. The only way I can go home.'[1] Curiously, the bullets take on a heightened eroticism with the Poet fondling them in close-up. The bullets become a fetish object that hold the magical ability to simultaneously grant the Poet what he desperately needs, death, and what he desires most, rebirth. The fetish object takes on an important role in the two-fold process of what Cocteau has termed *Phoenixology*. Gercke writes:

> The fetish is a utopian figure. The mother's castration is disavowed by means of an object which comes to stand for the mother's penis. She becomes impossibly complete ... the phantasy of the non-castrated maternal body represents an attempt to open a horizon beyond the Œdipal, phallic standard, and reinvent a durable linkage to the omnipotent mother of the oral stage.[2]

The magic bullets become the Poet's source of agency. With them he can return to the *zone* and resume his (mis)adventures. The tribunal scenes illustrate the transgressive nature of Cocteau's Poet. During the tribunal the fetish is not displaced onto an object but is corporeal in the form of the Princess, whose authority cannot be contested. The Princess appears as the principal judge of the Poet's claim to the mythic world but it is a world in which he cannot remain. He receives visitation privileges because of his poetic gifts, albeit grudgingly. The Princess and Heurtebise act as the border police of the *zone*. The Poet is interrogated about the extent of his knowledge of the mythic realm. The validity of his claim to the *zone* is his very presence. Heurtebise openly acknowledges the quality of the poet's passage into the mythic realm. It is the range of being/non-being that he sympathizes with, a place of dreams. Heurtebise states that: '... you are a nocturnal amalgamation of caves, forests, marshes, red rivers, populated with huge and fabulous beasts who devour each other. It's nothing to show off about.'[3] The

---

[1] Cocteau, *Two Screenplays*, 90. '*C'est à cause de vos balles que je suis à votre recherche dans cet épouvantable capharnaüm de l'espace-temps. Si je ne m'abuse, elles se déplacent plus vite que la lumière. Professeur, je compte être votre cobaye. C'est ma seule planche de salut. Le seul moyen de rentrer chez moi.*' 60.

[2] Gercke, *Nottingham French Studies*, no. 32, 15–16.

[3] Cocteau, *Two Screenplays*, 108. '*N'oubliez pas que vous êtes un amalgame nocturne de cavernes, de forêts, de marécages, de fleuves rouges, amalgame peuplé par des bêtes gigantesques et fabuleuses qui s'entre-dévorent. Il n'y a pas de quoi faire le mariole.*' 68.

Princess represents the law of the *zone*. Heurtebise extols its compassion but he is powerless to give down the law. These qualities are noted in Heurtebise's comment: 'You should be glad of the incredible leniency that the preventive tribunal has shown you.'[1] As Naomi Greene writes:

> ... [The masochist] is profoundly ambivalent since his desire to be bliss-fully reincorporated into the mother's body is also threatening for it would entail the destruction of his own self, his own ego. Bound to the mother, the child/masochist must suffer in order to expiate/expunge the punishing super-ego and genital sexuality that he embodies through his resemblance to the father. He must, in fact, undergo a process not only of desexualization but even of death so that a 'new self,' free of the super-ego and sexuality, can be born uniquely of the mother who, through dis-avowal, magically possesses a phallus.[2]

This ambivalence is clearly apparent when reading the transcript of the tribunal. The poet's discourse clearly demonstrates a resistance to the authority of the Princess but the manner in which it is delivered is extraordinarily passive. This contradicted position in the presence of the oral mother (figuratively the Princess) augurs the Poet's submission to the Princess and ultimately the renunciation of the self. Later, during the reading of the charges the Princess comments:

> I am aware that the detours on your road are a sort of labyrinth —quite different from ours although they intermingle— and that although you were able to find the only person who could correct your mistakes and your disobedience of terrestrial laws, this was not because of absent-mindedness on the part of the unknown, but because of a kind of supreme indulgence that you abuse, dear Sir, and that could well betray you one day.[3]

The tribunal's sentence for the Poet is to live, to which Heurtebise comments, 'That's the minimum, especially at your age.'[4] Disoriented, the

---

[1] Cocteau, *Two Screenplays*, 113. '*Vous devriez vous féliciter de la mansuétude in-croyable dont le tribunal préventif fait preuve à votre égard.*' 88.

[2] Naomi Greene. 'Deadly Statues: Eros in the Films of Jean Cocteau,' *The French Review*, Vol. 61, No. 6 (May 1988), 892.

[3] Cocteau, *Two Screenplays*, 112. '*Je n'ignore pas que les détours de votre itinéraire sont une sorte de labyrinthe fort éloigné du nôtre, bien qu'il s'y mélange et que, s'il vous a été possible de découvrir la seule personne apte à corriger vos erreurs et votre désobéissance aux lois terrestres cet acte ne bénéficiait pas d'une distraction de l'inconnu, mais d'une sorte d'indulgence suprême dont il vous arrive, cher Monsieur, d'abuser, et qui pourrait bien vous manquer un jour.*' 88.

[4] Cocteau, *Two Screenplays*, 115. '*Le minimum. Surtout à votre âge.*' 89.

Poet makes his way further into the netherworld of the *zone*. Having crossed the borderland between life and death, the Poet becomes a creature of fate. The *zone* takes on a double set of meanings and becomes a double-bind for the poet. Deleuze states:

> Disavowal should perhaps be understood as the point of departure of an operation that consists neither in negating nor even destroying, but rather in radically contesting the validity of that which is: it suspends belief in and neutralizes the given in such a way that a new horizon opens up beyond the given and in place of it ... fetishism is first of a all a disavowal ('No, the woman does not lack a penis'); secondly it is a defensive neutralization (since, contrary to what happens with negation, the knowledge of the situation as it is persists, but in a suspended, neutralized form); in the third place it is a protective and idealizing neutralization (for the belief in a female phallus is itself experienced as a protest of the ideal against the real; it remains suspended or neutralized in the ideal, the better to shield itself against the painful awareness of reality).[1]

The Poet is released into the hands of Cégeste (played by Edouard Dermit) who will guide him farther down into the underworld to his meeting with Minerva. Cégeste's powers as a guide are limited. His presence during the tribunal indicates that he is also a trespasser in the zone but he has lingered in the realm of non-being for too long. The Poet remarks as they leave the tribunal: 'Our works dream only of killing both father and mother —in the person of ourselves— and of being free. But the creatures of our mind remain curious about their origins ...'[2] Cégeste and

---

[1] Gilles Deleuze as quoted in Silverman, *Male Subjectivity at the Margins*, 212. *'Peut-être faut il comprendre la dénégation comme le point de départ d'une opération qui ne consiste pas à nier ni même à détruire, mais bien plutôt à contenter le bien-fondé de ce qui est, à affecter ce qui est d'une sorte de suspension, de neutralisation propre à nous ouvrir au-delà du donné un nouvel horizon non-donné...le fétishisme est d'abord dénégation (non, la femme ne manque pas de pénis); en second lieu, neutralisation défensive (car, contrairement à ce qui se passerait dans une négation, la connaissance de la situation réelle subsiste, mais est en quelque sorte suspendue, neutralisée); en troisième lieu, neutralisation protectrice, idéalisante (car, de son côté, la croyance à un phallus féminin s'éprouve elle-même comme faisant vouloir les droits de l'idéal contre le réel, se neutralise ou se suspend dans l'idéal, pour mieux annuler les atteintes que la connaissance de la réalité pourrait lui porter).' Présentation de Sacher-Masoch: le froid et le cruel.* (Paris: Les Éditions de Minuit, 1967), 28–29.

[2] Cocteau, *Two Screenplays*, 116. *'Nos œuvres ne songent qu'à tuer père et mère en notre personne et à prendre le large. Mais les créatures de notre esprit restent curieuses de leurs origines...'* 89.

the Poet are linked together because they inhabit the *zone;* they speak the same language and are privy to the same dangers. There is an interesting inversion of roles here, Cégeste as guide but also as neophyte and the Poet, who is the 'blind' seer. Their journey together is laden with homoerotic desire but it is in mutual recognition of, and desire for, the fetish object (i.e. the hibiscus flower, the death mask).

After the Poet's first resurrection in the presence of the Professor, he (Cocteau) makes his way at twilight toward the heart of the *zone.* Along the road he crosses the path of a man/horse who draws him into a camp of Catalan singers. There he rescues a torn picture of Cégeste that has been taken from the fire by one of the Catalonian women. As he leaves, Cocteau (the Poet) narrates: 'I recognized from afar the photo of Cegestius, one of the last shots from my film *Orpheus.* I did not like that man-horse. I guessed that he was drawing me into a trap, and that I would have been wiser not to follow him.'[1] There is a foreboding feeling as the Poet retreats from the camp and turns to leave with Cégeste's image in his hands. From there he throws it into the sea from which Cégeste is born up out of water. The transgressive nature of the Poet's power is evident here. Even Cégeste witnesses the Poet's transgressive power by stating after the tribunal:

> Sometimes I blame you for abandoning me in the zone of shadows. Sometimes I am pleased to live outside the absurd world that I used to live in. In spite of my revolts, I would like to rescue you from the dilemma you are in. However, although the zone ignores yesterday, today and tomorrow, your human state is subject to them, and in order to reach my goal, I must guide you, or rather follow you through unavoidable trials ...[2]

These comments are prophetic as the two descend for a second time into the heart of the *zone.* The male body has suffered much and will ultimately suffer more. As Cégeste leaves, the Poet is left to wait in a vaulting antechamber at the threshold of the *zone.* The Usher to the *zone* asks for the Poet's indulgence in a series of remarks that heighten the suspense and ultimate deferral of the Poet's meeting with male au-

---

[1] Cocteau, *Two Screenplays,* 94. 'J'avais reconnu de loin la photographie de Cégeste, une des dernières de mon film Orphée. Cet homme cheval m'avait déplu. Je devinais qu'il m'attirait dans un piège et que j'aurais mieux fait de ne pas le suivre.' 62–63.

[2] Cocteau, *Two Screenplays,* 116. 'Parfois je me félicite de vivre en dehors du monde absurde où j'ai vécu. Malgré mes révoltes, j'aimerais vous sauver de l'impasse où vous êtes. Seulement, si la zone ignore l'hier, l'aujourd'hui, le lendemain, votre condition humaine y est soumise et, pour atteindre mon but, je dois vous guider ou plutôt vous suivre à travers des épreuves inévitables...' 89–90.

thority. Instead, he is met with the goddess Minerva. Naomi Greene relevantly writes:

> Embodiments of law in this world without fathers, these implacable women inhabit a universe of persecution and tribunals ... Cocteau reveals the arbitrary and unfathomable nature of the laws the poet has 'broken' ... The poet's indictment ... reveals that poet is at once guilty of everything and nothing.[1]

The poet is the transgressor; against time, against the laws of physics; against the rule of the father. If the masochistic æsthetic has any currency in the imagination, it does so at a high cost to the body. As the Poet approaches Minerva he witnesses the goddess's statuesque disapproval of his resurrection and he mutters: 'Lazarus didn't smell too good either. There is even a painting where Martha and Mary are holding their noses with a cloth ... I'm sorry ... I ... I'm sorry ...'[2] As he turns from her he is impaled through the back with Minerva's spear, his passage complete. As he is laid to rest in a ritualized procession by the horse-men of the underworld, the Poet leaves behind him his two signatures: his blood and the hibiscus flower. The flower would seem to represent the poet's regenerative power, his blood, the price he pays for that power. The psychic violence that subtends *Le Testament d'Orphée* is to postpone the installment of the law of the father and to refuse the regulation of normative desire. As Deleuze writes:

> To become a man is to be reborn from the woman alone, to undergo a second birth. This is why castration ... cease[s] to be an obstacle to or a punishment of incest, and become[s] instead a precondition of its success with the mother, since it is then equated with a second, autonomous and parthenogenic rebirth.[3]

What is not wholly acknowledged in Deleuze's analysis, but becomes critically apparent, is how this rebirth is achieved in the cinema. As a discussion of the fetish object in *Le Testament* demonstrates, rebirth can be achieved anthropomorphically, but the body itself will eventually undergo tremendous strain. 'Vanishing is not easy ...'[4] says the Poet,

---

[1] Greene, *The French Review*, 893–94.

[2] Cocteau, *Two Screenplays*, 131. '*Lazare non plus ne sentait pas très bon... Il y a même un tableau où Marthe et Marie se bouchent le nez avec des étoffes... Je m'excuse... Je... m'excuse...*'95.

[3] Gilles Deleuze as quoted in Daniel Gercke, *Nottingham French Studies*, vol. 32, no. 1, 16.

[4] Cocteau, *Two Screenplays*, 106. '*Disparaître n'est cependant pas commode.*' 68.

and we must acknowledge, as spectator, the unreal truth of what we cannot see; but the male body, having disavowed the phallic order and the law of the father, will ultimately find a reconstituted law in the realm of the mother. The price for this reconstituted law means to negate the self, and as a consequence the gendered body. This can only be achieved through a literal or symbolic death, the male body as its ultimate sacrifice.

Le Testament d'Orphée in its visual construction offers many options for reading against the grain of what Silverman has called 'the dominant fiction.'[1] While a masochistic æsthetic does not necessarily negate the existence of the phallic order or Mulvey's assertion of 'Visual Pleasure,' *Le Testament* clearly demonstrates that there are different positions of seeing and being, and that these subject positions can happen simultaneously. They are not limited to one container, one body. The frustrations endured by the male body in *Le Testament* show us the multiplicity of the male subject in cinema. For Cocteau, the broken mirror will always reveal our greatest hopes, fears, and ultimately our dreams.

---

[1] See Kaja Silverman's *Male Subjectivity at the Margins*, Chapter 1.

The Cinema of Jean Cocteau:
A Select Bibliography

I. BASIC PRINTED TEXTS BY COCTEAU

Cocteau, Jean. *The Art of Cinema.* Compiled and edited by André Bernard and Claude Gauteur. Translated by Robin Buss. London: M. Boyars, 1992. A translation of *Du cinématographe.* Paris: Belfond, 1988.

_____. *Beauty and the Beast: The Shooting Script.* Edited by Robert M. Hammond. New York: NYU Press, 1970. A translation of *La Belle et la bête.* Moulins: Éditions Impomée, 1988.

_____. *Les Chevaliers de la Table Ronde,* in Jean Cocteau, *Théâtre 1.* Paris: Gallimard, 1948.

_____ *Cocteau on the Film.* Conversation recorded by André Fraigneau. Translated by Vera Traill. New York: Dover Publications, 1972. A translation of *Entretiens autour du cinématographe.* Paris: Éditions André Bonne, 1951.

_____. *La Corrida du premier mai.* Paris: Grasset, 1957.

_____. *Diary of a Film: 'Beauty and the Beast.'* Translated from the French by Ronald Duncan. London: D. Dobson, 1950. A translation of *La Belle et la bête, journal d'un film.* Monaco: Éditions du Rocher, 1958.

_____. *Diary of an Unknown.* London: St. Edmundsbury Press Ltd., 1985. A translation of *Journal d'un inconnu.* Paris: Bernard Grasset, 1953.

_____. *The Difficulty of Being.* Translated by Elizabeth Sprigge. New York: Coward-McCann, Inc., 1996. A translation of *La Difficulté d'être.* Monaco: Éditions du Rocher, 1989.

_____. *The Eagle has Two Heads.* Adapted by Ronald Duncan. London: Vision Press, 1947. An adaptation of *L'Aigle à deux têtes* in Cocteau, *Théâtre,* vol. 1. Paris: Gallimard: 1948.

_____. *Les Enfants terribles* (a.k.a. *Children of the Game*). Translated by Rosamond Lehmann. London: Penguin, 1996. A translation of *Les Enfants terribles.* Paris: Bernard Grasset, 1929.

_____. *Five Plays.* Translations of *Orphée, Antigone, Les Parents terribles, Les Monstres sacrés, L'Aigle à deux têtes.* New York: Hill and Wang, 1996.

____. *The Journals of Jean Cocteau*. Edited and translated by Wallace Fowlie. Bloomington: Indiana University Press, 1956.

____. *Œuvres complètes*. Geneva: Marguerat, 1946 et 1948.

____. *Opium: The Diary of a Cure*. Translated by Margaret Crosland and Sinclair Road. London: Peter Owen Ltd., 1947. A translation of *Opium*. Paris: Librairie Stock, 1931.

____. *'Orphée': The Play and the Film*. Oxford: Blackwell, 1976. A translation of *Orphée* (the play) in *Œuvres complètes*, vol. V. Geneva: Marguerat, 1946. Also of *Orphée* (the film script with photography by Roger Corbeau). Paris: La Parade, 1950.

____. *Les Parents terribles* (the play). Paris: Gallimard, 1938.

____. *Past Tense: The Cocteau Diaries*. Translated by Richard Howard. Two Volumes. New York: Harcourt Brace Jovanovich, 1987, 1988. A translation of *Le Passé défini*. Paris: Gallimard, 1983, 1985.

____. *Three Screenplays: 'L'Eternel Retour,' 'Orphée,' and 'La Belle et la bête.'* Translated from the French by Carol Martin-Sperry. New York: Grossman Publishers, 1972.

____. *Two Screenplays: 'Blood of a Poet' and 'The Testament of Orpheus.'* London and New York: Marion Boyars, 1993. Translations of *Le Sang d'un poète*. Paris: Robert Martin, 1948 and *Le Testament d'Orphée*. Monaco: Éditions du Rocher, 1983.

____. *The White Book*. A translation by Margaret Crosland. San Francisco: City Lights Books, 1989. A translation of *Le Livre blanc*. Paris: Éditions Persona, 1981.

II. PRINCIPAL BOOKS ON COCTEAU IN ENGLISH

Brown, Frederick. *An Impersonation of Angels: A Biography of Jean Cocteau*. New York: Viking, 1968.

Crosland, Margaret. *Jean Cocteau: A Biography*. New York: Knopf, 1956

Crowson, Lydia. *The Esthetic of Jean Cocteau*. Hanover, N.H.: University Press of New Hampshire, 1978.

Evans, Arthur B. *Jean Cocteau and his Films of Orphic Identity*. Philadelphia: Art Alliance Press,1977.

Fowlie, Wallace. *Jean Cocteau: The History of a Poet's Age*. Bloomington: Indiana University Press, 1966.

Fraigneau, André. *Cocteau*. New York: Grove Press, 1961. A translation of Fraigneau, *Cocteau par lui-même*. Paris: Éditions du Seuil, 1963.

Gilson, René. *Jean Cocteau*. Translated by Citra Vaughan. New York: Crown Publishers, 1969. A translation of *Jean Cocteau*. Paris: Seghers, 1964.

Keller, Marjorie. *The Untutored Eye: Childhood in the Films of Cocteau, Cornell and Brakhage*, London and Toronto: Associated University Presses, 1986.

Knapp, Bettina. *Jean Cocteau*. Boston: Twayne, 1989.

Michalczyk, John J. *The French Literary Filmmakers*. Philadelphia: Art Alliance Press, 1980.

Oxenhandler, Neal. *Scandal and Parade: The Theater of Jean Cocteau*. New Brunswick, N.J.: Rutgers University Press, 1957.

Peters, Arthur King (ed.). *Jean Cocteau and the French Scene*. New York: Abbeville Press, 1984.

____. *Jean Cocteau and his World*. London: Thames and Hudson, 1987.

Phelps, Robert (ed.). *Professional Secrets: An Autobiography of Jean Cocteau Drawn from His Lifetime Writings*. Translated by Richard Howard. New York: Farrar, Straus and Giroux, 1970.

Sprigge, Elizabeth and Jean-Jacques Kihm. *Jean Cocteau: The Man and the Mirror*. London: Victor Gollancz, 1968.

Steegmuller, Francis. *Cocteau: A Biography*. Boston: Little Brown, 1970.

III. SOME PERTINENT BOOKS ON COCTEAU IN FRENCH

Dubourg, Pierre. *Dramaturgie de Jean Cocteau*. Paris: Bernard Grasset, 1954.

Lannes, Roger. *Jean Cocteau*. Paris: Éditions Seghers, 1945 et 1989.

Marais, Jean. *Histoires de ma vie*. Paris: Albin Michel, 1975.

____ *Jean Cocteau*. Paris: Albin Michel, 1987.

Marny, Dominique. *Les Belles de Cocteau*. Paris: Éditions Jean-Claude Lattès, 1995.

Meunier, Micheline. *Jean Cocteau et Nietzsche ou Philosophie du matin*. Paris: Jean Grassin, 1971.

Millecam, Jean-Pierre. *L'Étoile de Jean Cocteau*. Paris: Éditions Criterion, 1991.

Philippe, Claude-Jean. *Jean Cocteau*. Paris: Seghers, 1989.

IV. BOOKS ON FRENCH CULTURE OF THE PERIOD IN ENGLISH

Flanner, Janet. *Paris Was Yesterday, 1925–1939*. Edited by Irving Drutman. New York: Viking, 1972.

Glassco, John. *Memories of Montparnasse*. Toronto: Oxford University Press, 1970.

Hemingway, Ernest. *A Moveable Feast*. New York: Scribner, 1964.

Shattuck, Roger. *The Banquet Years: The Origins of the Avant-garde in France 1885 to World War I*. New York: Doubleday Anchor, 1961.

V. HISTORIES AND STUDIES OF FRENCH CINEMA OF COCTEAU'S PERIOD IN ENGLISH

Abel, Richard. *French Cinema: The First Wave (1915–1929)*. Princeton, N.J.: Princeton University Press, 1984.

Andrew, Dudley. *Mists of Regret: Culture and Sensibility in Classic French Film.* Princeton, N.J.: Princeton University Press, 1995.

Armes, Roy. *French Cinema.* New York: Oxford University Press, 1985.

Bandy, Mary Lea (ed.). *Rediscovering French Film.* Boston: Little Brown, 1983.

Buss, Robin. *The French Through Their Films.* London: Batsford, 1988.

Crisp, Colin. *The Classic French Cinema, 1930–1960.* Bloomington: Indiana University Press, 1993.

Hayward, Susan. *French National Cinema.* London and New York: Routledge, 1993.

Hayward, Susan and Ginette Vincendeau (eds.). *French Film: Texts and Contexts.* London: Routledge, 1990.

Martin, John W. *The Golden Age of French Cinema 1929–1939.* Boston: Twayne, 1983.

Paris, James Reid. *The Great French Films.* Secaucus, N.J.: The Citadel Press, 1983.

Slide, Anthony. *Fifty Classic French Films 1912–1982.* New York: Dover, 1987.

Tyler, Parker. *Classics of the Foreign Film.* New York: The Citadel Press, 1962.

Vincendeau, Ginette. *The Companion to French Cinema.* London: Cassell and BFI, 1996.

Williams, Alan. *Republic of Images: A History of French Filmmaking.* Cambridge, MA: Harvard University Press, 1992.

VI. THEORETICAL AND PHILOSOPHICAL WORKS

Andrew, Dudley. 'The Neglected Tradition of Phenomenology in Film Theory'. *Movies and Methods*, vol. II. Edited by Bill Nichols. Berkeley: University of California Press, 1985, 625–32.

Aston, Elaine. *An Introduction to Feminism and Theatre.* London: Routledge, 1995.

Barthes, Roland. *Le Plaisir du texte.* Paris: Éditions du Seuil, 1973.

Baudry, Jean-Louis. 'Ideological Effects of the Basic Cinematographic Apparatus', and 'The Apparatus: Metapsychological Approaches to the Impression of Reality in Cinema'. *Narrative, Apparatus, Ideology: A Film Theory Reader*, ed. Philip Rosen. New York: Columbia University Press, 1986, 286–318. A translation *L'Effet cinéma*. Paris: Éditions Albatros, 1978, 13–49.

Bell, Clive, *Art*. London: Chatto and Windus, 1949.

Cowie, Elizabeth. *Representing the Woman: Cinema and Psychoanalysis.* Minneapolis: University of Minnesota Press, 1997.

Davis, Robert Con (ed.). *Lacan and Narration: The Psychoanalytic Difference in Narrative Theory.* Baltimore: Johns Hopkins University Press, 1983.

Deleuze, Gilles. *Présentation de Sacher-Masoch: le froid et le cruel.* Paris: Éditions de Minuit, 1967.

Derrida, Jacques. *Dissemination.* Translated by Barbara Johnson. Chicago: The University of Chicago Press, 1981. A translation of *Dissémination.* Paris: Éditions du Seuil, 1972.

Dolan, Jill. *The Feminist Spectator as Critic.* Ann Arbor: University of Michigan Press, 1991.

Durgnat, Raymond. *Films and Feelings.* London: Faber & Faber Ltd., 1967.

Easthope, Anthony (ed.). *Contemporary Film Theory.* London and New York: Longmans, 1993.

Elam, Keir. *The Semiotics of Drama and Theatre.* London: Routledge, 1980.

Eliade, Mircea. *A History of Religious Ideas.* Volumes 1 & 2. Translated by Willard R. Trask. Chicago: The University of Chicago Press, 1982.

Evans, Dylan, *An Introductory Dictionary of Lacanian Psychoanalysis.* London and New York: Routledge, 1966.

Flitterman-Lewis, Sandy. 'Psychoanalysis, Film and Television' in *Channels of Discourse.* Edited by Robert Allen. North Carolina: University of North Carolina Press, 1987.

Freud, Sigmund. *On Sexuality.* London: Penguin Books, 1991.

Greimas, Algirdas-Julien. *Structural Semantics: An Attempt at a Method,* translated by D. McDowell, R. Schleifer and A. Velie. Lincoln: University of Nebraska Press, 1983. A translation of *Sémantique structurale, recherche de méthode.* Paris: Larousse, 1966.

Guthrie, W.K.C. *Orpheus and Greek Religion.* London: Methuen & Co. Ltd., 1935.

Janaway, Christopher. 'Plato's Analogy between Painter and Poet.' *British Journal of Æsthetics.* Vol. 31, no. 1 (January 1991), 1–12.

Jung, C.G., *The Spirit in Man, Art and Literature.* Translated by R.F.C. Hull. New York: Pantheon Books, 1966.

Kaplan, E. Ann. *Psychoanalysis and Cinema.* London and New York: Routledge, 1990.

Metz, Christian. *The Imaginary Signifier: Psychoanalysis and the Cinema.* Translated by Celia Britton, Annwyl Williams. Ben Brewster and Alfred Guzzetti. Bloomington: Indiana University Press, 1982. A translation of *Le Signifiant imaginaire: Psychanalyse et cinéma.* Paris: Christian Bourgois, 1984.

Mulvey, Laura. 'Visual Pleasure and Narrative Cinema.' *Film Theory and Criticism*. Fourth edition. Edited by Gerald Mast, Marshall Cohen and Leo Braudy. New York: Oxford University Press, 1992, 746–57.

Nowell-Smith, Geoffrey. 'A Note on History/Discourse.' *Edinburgh '76 Magazine*. No. 1 (1976), 26–32.

Sartre, Jean-Paul. *Being and Nothingness*. Translated by Hazel E. Barnes. New York: Washington Square Press Incorporated, 1953. A translation of *L'Être et le néant*. Paris: Gallimard, 1968.

Selden, Raman, Peter Widdowson and Peter Brooker. *A Reader's Guide to Contemporary Literary Theory*. Fourth Edition. London: Prentice Hall/Harvester Wheatsheaf, 1977.

Silverman, Kaja. *Male Subjectivity at the Margins*. New York and London: Routledge, 1992.

Studlar, Gaylyn. 'Masochism and the Perverse Pleasures of the Cinema.' *Film Theory and Criticism*. Fourth Edition. Edited by Gerald Mast, Marshall Cohen and Leo Braudy. New York: Oxford University Press, 1992, 773–90.

Watmough, J.R. *Orphism*. Cambridge: The University Press, 1934.

VII. MISCELLANEOUS WORKS

Bédier, Joseph. *The Romance of Tristan and Iseult*, translated by Hilaire Belloc & Paul Rosenfeld. New York: Random House, 1965. A translation of *Le Roman de Tristan et Iseult*. Paris: H. Piazza et Cie., 1910.

Chevalier, Jean and Alain Gheerbrant. *Dictionary of Symbols*. Translated by John Buchanan-Brown. London: Penguin Books, 1996. A translation of *Dictionnaire des symboles*. Paris: Éditions Robert Laffont & Éditions Jupiter, 1969.

Feydeau, Alain. *Edwige Feuillère*. Paris: Veyrier, 1991.

Gide, André. *Journal 1889–1939*. Paris: Gallimard, Bibliothèque de la Pléiade, 1939.

Gill, Brendan. *Tallulah*. Toronto: Holt, Rinehart and Winston, 1972.

Graves, Robert (ed.). *New Larousse Encyclopedia of Mythology*. New York: Crescent Books, 1986.

Green, Julien. *Journal 1926–1955*. Paris: Gallimard, Bibliothèque de la Pléiade, 1975.

Greenberger, Howard. *The Off-Broadway Experience*. Englewood Cliffs: Prentice Hall, 1971.

Kael, Pauline. *5001 Nights at the Movies. A Guide from A to Z*. New York: Holt, Rinehart and Winston, 1984.

Little, Stuart W. *Off-Broadway: The Prophetic Theater*. New York: Coward, McCann and Geoghegan, 1972.

Milosz, Czeslaw, *The Land of Ulro*. Translated by Louis Iribarne. New York: Farrar, Straus and Giroux, 1984.

Morford, Mark P.O. and Robert J. Lenardon. *Classical Mythology*. Third edition. New York: Longmans, 1985.

VIII: ARTICLES ON COCTEAU AND THE CINEMA IN ENGLISH

Andrus, Toni W. 'Œdipus Revisited: Cocteau's "Poésie de théâtre."' *The French Review* 48 (1975), 722–28.

Bach, Raymond. 'Cocteau and Vichy: Family Disconnections.' *L'Esprit Créateur* 33, no.1 (Spring 1993), 29–37.

Batts, Michael. 'Tristan and Isolde in Modern Literature: *L'Eternel Retour*.' *Seminar: A Journal of Germanic Studies* 5 (1969), 79–91.

Bryant, Sylvia. 'Re-constructing Œdipus through *Beauty and the Beast*.' *Criticism: A Quarterly for Literature and the Arts* 31, no. 4 (Fall 1989), 439–53.

Christensen, Peter G. 'Three Concealments: Jean Cocteau's Adaptation of *The Picture of Dorian Gray*.' *Romance Notes* 27, no.1 (Autumn, 1986), 27–35.

Debusscher, Gilbert. 'French Stowaways on an American Milk Train: Williams, Cocteau and Peyrefitte.' *Modern Drama* 25, no. 3 (1982), 399–408.

DeNitto, Dennis. 'Jean Cocteau's *Beauty and the Beast*.' *American Imago* 33, no. 2 (1976), 123–54.

Galef, David. 'A Sense of Magic: Reality and Illusion in Cocteau's *Beauty and the Beast*.' *Literature Film Quarterly* 12, no.2 (1984), 96–106.

Gates, Laura Doyle. 'Jean Cocteau and "la poésie du théâtre."' *Romance Quarterly* 35, no. 4 (Nov. 1988), 435–41.

Gercke, Daniel. 'Ruin, Style and Fetish: The Corpus of Jean Cocteau.' *Nottingham French Studies* 32, no. 1 (Spring, 1993), 10–18.

Grayson, Susan B. 'The Other as Self in Cocteau's *Les Enfants terribles*.' *Perspectives on Contemporary Literature* 12 (1986), 43–50.

Greene, Naomi. 'Deadly Statues: Eros in the Films of Jean Cocteau.' *The French Review* 61, no. 6 (May 1988), 890–98.

Hammond, Robert M. 'The Authenticity of the Filmscript: Cocteau's *Beauty and the Beast*.' *Style* 9 (1975), 514–32.

_____. 'Jensen's Gradiva: A Clue to the Composition of Cocteau's *Orphée*.' *Symposium* 27 (1974), 126–36.

_____. 'The Mysteries of Cocteau's *Orpheus*.' *Cinema Journal* 2 (Spring 1972), 26–33.

Harvey, Stephen. 'The Mask in the Mirror: The Movies of Jean Cocteau.' In Arthur King Peters (ed.), *Jean Cocteau and the French Scene*, New York: Abbeville, 1984, 185–207.

Hatte, Jennifer. '"La Chambre" as Mental Landscape in Jean Cocteau's *Les Enfants terribles.'Australian Journal of French Studies* 28, no. 2 (May–Aug. 1991), 170–78.

_____. 'Jean Cocteau's Snow.' *The Modern Language Review* 89, no. 2 (April 1994), 328–40.

Hoggard, Lynn. 'Writing with the Ink of Light: Jean Cocteau's *Beauty and the Beast.*' In Wendell Aycock and Michael Schoenecke (ed.), *Film and Literature: A Comparative Approach to Adaptation.* Lubbock: Texas Tech University Press, 1988, 123–34.

Kaplan, Jane P. 'Complexity of Character and the Overlapping of a Single Personality in Cocteau's *Les Enfants terribles.'* *Australian Journal of French Studies* 12 (1975), 89–104.

Long, Chester Clayton. 'Cocteau's *Orphée*: From Myth to Drama and Film.' *The Quarterly Journal of Speech* 50 (1965), 311–25.

Maclean, Mary. 'The Artificial Paradise and the Lost Paradise: Baudelairean Themes in Cocteau's *Les Enfants terribles.'* *Australian Journal of French Studies* 12 (1975), 57–88.

McMunn, Meradith T. 'Filming the Tristan Myth: From Text to Icon.' In Kevin J. Harty (ed.), *Cinema Arthuriana: Essays on Arthurian Film*, New York: Garland, 1991, 169–80.

McNab, James P. 'Jean Cocteau and Orpheus: The Assimilation of the Legend.' In Charles Nelson (ed.), *Studies in Language and Literature.* Richmond: Dept. of Foreign Languages, Eastern Kentucky University, 1976, 383–90.

_____. 'Mythical Space in *Les Enfants terribles.'* *The French Review* NC spec. issue 6, 162–70.

Michalczyk, John J. 'The French Academy and the Cinema.' *Stanford French Review* 5, no. 1 (Spring 1981), 129–40.

Pauly, Rebecca M. '*Beauty and the Beast*: From Fable to Film.' *Literature Film Quarterly* 17, no. 2 (1989), 84–90.

Popkin, Michael. 'Cocteau's *Beauty and the Beast*: The Poet as Monster.' *Literature Film Quarterly* 10, no. 2 (1982), 100–09.

Roudiez, Leon S. 'Cocteau's *Les Enfants terribles* as a Blind Text.' *Mosaic* 5, no. 3 (1972), 159–66.

AGMV
MARQUIS
Québec, Canada
1999